A
Collector's
Guide
to
Antiques

A COLLECTOR'S GUIDE TO ANTIQUES

REBO
PRODUCTIONS

CONTENTS

First Published by Rebo International bv, Lisse,
The Netherlands

2000 Rebo International bv
2nd print 2002

Edited and produced by
Book Creation Illustrated Limited,
21 Carnaby Street, London, W1V 1PH

Project editor: Alexa Stace
Editor: Gwen Rigby

Design: Casebourne Rose Design Associates

Picture research: Angela Griggs and
Sophie Mortimer

Photography: Philip de Bay
for Heritage Picture Collection

Typesetting: Casebourne Rose Design Associates and
Book Creation Services

ISBN   1 84053 167 3

4

CONTENTS

5

CONTENTS

CONTENTS

Introduction

FOR MANY PEOPLE, the thought of collectors of antiques may summon up one of two images: either a group of obsessives scouring dimly lit shops and haggling with dealers over the virtues or otherwise of arcane pieces; or an auction room full of rich connoisseurs bidding fantastic sums for precious objets d'art. Needless to say, these views are far from the general reality. Most collectors are perfectly normal people distinguished only by their appreciation of lovely materials, skilled craftsmanship and graceful, functional design.

Buying antiques – generally thought of as objects more than 50 years old – is a very subjective business. Most antique collectors tend to focus on one or two main areas, be it English Regency furniture, glassware from Bohemia, Japanese netsuke, or even dolls. At the same time, they know instinctively that there is no point buying antiques simply because they are widely recognized as 'good taste': after all, one has to live with what one buys. Tastes do change, however. A style that ten years ago might have been rejected as unsympathetic may now be more congenial and possibly even desirable from a collector's point of view. This is where looking at antiques and handling them is valuable, because it is the only way to arrive at an appreciation of their virtues as well as their faults.

INTRODUCTION

Collecting antiques can be enriching in other ways. It can lead to a study of the history, styles, techniques and work of individual craftsmen and workshops. New research and discoveries will ensure that the process of learning is never complete. A collector may also come to understand the wider aspects of apparently unrelated crafts, for it has become increasingly clear that they did not exist in separate worlds, but shared contemporary influences

INTRODUCTION

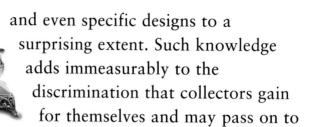

10

and even specific designs to a surprising extent. Such knowledge adds immeasurably to the discrimination that collectors gain for themselves and may pass on to others. Collecting can, therefore, be seen as a form of self-education, as well as a pleasure, for those who achieve even the most modest display.

The other great advantage of collecting is, of course, that it is a form of investment. Investment in antiques is still often misleadingly thought of as a professional business – as the domain of dealers, specialists and experts. But to buy recognized antiques (nothing has an absolute guarantee) in an established market, in which values over recent years have risen steadily, is a perfectly reasonable pursuit for the ordinary collector. The logic is simple: if you buy new, your purchases will have second-hand value; if you buy antiques you will, after a few years, probably see your money back and may also make a profit. This is partly due to rarity value – the number of genuine antiques of a particular period can only decrease. But it is also partly because, as a result of mass-market pressures, both workmanship and the quality of materials have declined drastically. This is not to say that items of the highest quality are no longer made,

INTRODUCTION

but that good craftsmanship and fine materials are now inordinately expensive.

But having decided on the field that one is most interested in, where exactly should one go to find the pieces? The main sources of antiques are specialist dealers, sales rooms, auctions, markets and car boot sales. All approach valuation and selling in different ways, and this needs to be borne in mind during any hunt for antiques.

Antique dealers are hard-headed business people, and they look to make a profit like everyone else. They will seek to sell their stock for whatever the market will bear. What keeps prices down is competition with other dealers and the fact that private buyers can go to sales rooms and bid against dealers. Nevertheless, the best dealers are scholars and considerable experts in their field. For the most part, they respond to intelligent questioning and are able to substantiate their description of a piece from reputable sources. Evident appreciation of their stock may help in the bargaining process – though to bargain properly, you need to know what you are talking about: no dealer is going to sell for less than they think justified. And a discount is much more likely if you offer cash.

Auctions and sales rooms, while more impersonal, are attractive alternative sources for pieces. But you should bear in mind that an auctioneer is only an agent, who is not responsible to

INTRODUCTION

the buyer except in the general terms of auction-room procedure. His function is to raise as much money as he can for the seller, who pays his commission. It is also important to discover the auctioneer's conditions of sale, since they vary from one auction house to another. They are likely to be found in the catalogue of every sale. Here, among other things, you are likely to find a disclaimer which states that the auctioneer is not responsible for the authenticity, attribution, origin, authorship, date or condition of any 'lot'. Imperfections will also not be stated in the description. You should, always therefore examine the pieces in which you are interested during viewing hours, which are usually the day before the sale. The more specialized the sale and the more up-market the auction house, the more likely it will be that there is an expert on hand to answer any questions. It cannot be stressed too often that they rarely give guarantees; the best they can do is offer an opinion.

Finally there are market stalls and car boot sales. Though obviously these are colourful and can be scoured for a good buy (some surprisingly valuable items have been found there in the past), there is always the risk that the item may be overpriced or simply not genuine.

INTRODUCTION

The vendor may not know the real value and provenance of the object and, if he does, may be unwilling to part with the information.

13

There are hundreds of areas of antiques and collectables to choose from, not all of which can be covered by this book – the main emphasis of which inevitably falls on the 18th, 19th and first half of the 20th centuries, when the examples illustrated will be of greatest value for identification. This is in part to do with the scarcity of older and very fine pieces, many of which are housed in museums or form part of permanent collections. Those that can be found in the showrooms of specialist dealers and at auctions are likely to be exorbitantly expensive, and thus beyond the scope of the average collector.

This does not mean that you should ignore them; by establishing what is really good in your chosen field, you will more easily be able to assess the worth of pieces offered for sale. But, in the end, you should buy what you like, even if its condition may not be perfect. Above all, you should enjoy collecting, and for the ordinary collector, a small chip in a cup or plate, for instance, will not greatly detract from its looks and from the pleasure you will get from ownership. It may even whet your appetite for the hunt: after all, you may find another, perfect specimen if you keep on looking!

CERAMICS

CERAMICS

WHAT ARE CERAMICS?

16

THE ABILITY TO harden pieces of shaped clay in fire, and so create earthenware vessels, was one of the earliest human achievements. All pottery and porcelain is made in this way, but pottery and porcelain are quite distinct. Whereas porous earthenware needs to be fired at between 482°C and 816°C, non-porous stoneware and porcelain (also known as china) has to be fired at temperatures up to 1316°C. Porcelain can be distinguished from stoneware by its lightness and translucency.

Early pots were made by winding coils of clay or sticking slabs of clay together. The discovery of the potter's wheel and the 'throwing' of clay revolutionized the craft of ceramics, as did slip casting – the creation of hollow figures by pouring clay into a mould.

The next most important contribution to ceramics was the use of glazes, which were usually made using a tin or lead by-product that sealed and coloured earthenware. Brown, red, yellow and blue monochrome glazes were perfected by the Chinese, who also introduced the practice of painting wares with blue cobalt before glazing – a major advance in decoration.

Most ancient ceramics had a practical rather than a specifically decorative use. Although some of these wares, such as Roman terracotta lamps, may be surprisingly reasonable in price today, in general the average collector can only consider acquiring pieces from the last 200 years or so. But even within this relatively short time span, there is a huge range of shapes, materials and makers to choose from, though it is true to say more table wares are available than anything else.

CERAMICS

Prices may vary wildly, and identifying the object in an antiques market may not be easy. On a fairly modern piece most of what you need to know may be stamped on the back, but older pieces may be blank. In this event, some specialist knowledge about glazes and decoration can be of great use.

FAKES AND FORGERIES

There is no point in collecting ceramics if you are afraid of buying a fake. Indeed, what exactly is a fake? Even in China, porcelain was copied from the earliest times and the copies have become almost indistinguishable from the 'originals'. In this sense, 17th-century Delft pieces are essentially 'fakes' of Chinese porcelain, but this does not diminish their value in our eyes. The problem is further complicated by the fact that some 'fakes' may be worth more than the originals, as is the case with early English copies of Chinese blue-and-white export porcelain. In fact, copies made in the 18th century are no longer regarded with suspicion.

Real fakery in the view of the expert begins around 1820, when Sèvres porcelain began to be extensively copied. This set in train a whole tradition of fakery, in which everything from Meissen to Chinese porcelain of the Qing dynasty was copied – the best modern fakes of Qing porcelain come from China and are so exact that even some experts have been fooled by them.

Considering the size of the collectors' market today, fake porcelain is not a major problem. The chances of being caught out should be small if you buy only from reputable dealers or major auction houses. The guarantee a 'name' offers cannot be stressed too highly. Both major sales rooms and specialist dealers are usually willing to refund customers if they have been sold a fake.

CERAMICS

CHINESE UNDERGLAZE BLUE

18

▲ *The double gourd shape of this vase, with a tea-dust glaze, is traditional, but it was made in 1736–95.*

EARTHENWARE VESSELS WERE PRODUCED in China from at least the 5th millennium BC. By the late 6th century AD, it was beginning to be replaced by stoneware, earthenware fired at high temperatures to make it more durable, and this remained the most common type of ware until at least the 12th century.

Porcelain was first made in the 7th century AD. Possibly it was an accidental discovery, since some Chinese white clays contain both kaolin and feldspar – the two ingredients necessary for porcelain's manufacture. The earliest Tang dynasty (618–906) porcelain is now extremely rare, but it is possible to collect pieces of the Song and Yuan dynasties (960–1368). During this period, cobalt imported from Persia was first used to paint decoration in blue on porcelain, which was then glazed and fired – this is known as underglaze blue.

The Ming dynasty (1368–1643) is synonymous with all that is exquisite in Chinese craftsmanship. Certainly, some Ming vases are sold for huge sums and early blue and whites are too dear for the average collector, but the dynasty lasted 275 years, and many simple pieces are now fairly cheap. After the 15th century Ming wares went into a gradual decline, but some 'kraak' porcelain – named after the Portuguese ships, carracks, that traded through Macao – is extremely fine and often not exorbitantly expensive.

CERAMICS

Ming reached its peak in the 1400s: cobalt blue was used with exquisite control and the designs, with figures, birds and flowers, have a unique delicacy.

◀ The six-character mark on the base of this bowl gives the name of the reigning emperor when it was made. But some potters reused marks from a more respected period, so it is not a foolproof method of dating.

CERAMICS

FAMILLE VERTE & FAMILLE ROSE

GRADUALLY, THE CHINESE DEVELOPED the technique of decorating porcelain in overglaze colours; by the late 1600s they were employing the *wucai*, or five-coloured, palette consisting of yellow, green, iron-red, blue and black, sometimes with manganese-brown. Then, during the reign of Kangxi (1661–1720), this was superseded by the *famille verte* palette of colours, in which fresh greens became important and overglaze, rather than underglaze, blue was used.

20

◀ *In the 1730s, the opaque enamels of famille rose replaced the transparent colours of famille verte. Most designs were traditional, but other designs and shapes, such as the salt cellar and sauce boat shown here, reflected European tastes.*

CERAMICS

This in turn gave way to a line of porcelain known as Imperial *famille rose*, made largely for export and often to fill specific orders from the West, in which a bright rose-pink (introduced from Europe) was the dominant colour. Examples of *famille rose* from the mid-18th century often feature typical Chinese designs of birds, flowers and rocks, but scenes with figures also appear, as do designs imported from Europe. Early pieces can be of exceptional beauty, although those from the 19th century are also well worth looking out for.

▲ Famille-verte *porcelain had a slightly creamy colour. The outline of the design was usually drawn in red or brown, and the painting was done mainly in clean fresh greens, red, brown and purple. The enamels were more translucent and delicate than those of* famille rose.

◀ *Plates in* famille rose *are fairly common and far less expensive than those in* famille verte. *Unusual pieces, such as this small export-ware vase, are very desirable and collectable.*

CERAMICS

JAPANESE KAKIEMON & IMARI

WITH THE END OF THE MING DYNASTY in the mid-17th century, Chinese production of porcelain at Jingdezhen almost ceased, and the Dutch turned to Japan to fill the demand for porcelain in the West. Initially it consisted of blue-and-white wares produced in the town of Arita and exported through the port of Imari. This stimulated the small existing Japanese porcelain industry, which was making a limited amount of wares for home sales. One type was Kakiemon, with a restrained style of decoration and a distinctive palette of sky-blue, turquoise, yellow and iron-red enamel colours; designs were principally floral, although birds, dragons and people featured occasionally.

Japan in the 18th century was an extremely insular country, hostile and virtually closed to foreigners. But the limited trade with Holland allowed impressive Imari dishes – named after the port of export – to reach wealthy European buyers. Imari porcelain, with its rich blue and red glazes and gilding, became much sought-after in Europe as a change from Chinese wares. In the 19th and early 20th centuries, exact copies of Imari pieces were made in vast quantities, and similar designs and colours are still employed in some European porcelain, such as Royal Crown Derby.

22

▼ *The potters at Arita made animals as well as domestic and decorative wares. Generally they had an almost cartoon-like mien, and this Buddhistic lion, despite his rows of large teeth, has a rather comic appearance.*

CERAMICS

◀ *Imari wares were often painted with pictures from Japanese life; this dish shows a scene from classical Japanese Kabuki theatre.*

▾ *Traditional Imari colours of blue and iron-red, enlivened with gilding, and a typically crowded design are used on this large fluted plate.*

▲ *The restrained and spacious decoration of Kakiemon wares, evident on this jar (c.1670), was copied and adaped by many European factories, among them Meissen, Chantilly and Chelsea.*

— CERAMICS —

SATSUMA WARE

THIS DISTINCTIVE TYPE OF POTTERY derives its name from the province in which it was made. It has a long history in Japan, but the pieces generally found in the West were produced for export in the latter part of the 19th century. Satsuma wares were made from a light, porous earthernware with a creamy glaze through which pale brownish tints showed. The finished pieces were exquisitely smooth, with a warm, ivory tone and extremely fine crackling of the glaze, which occurred naturally during the firing process. Early pieces were decorated in a typically restrained Japanese style with landscapes, flowers, and birds, but gradually pieces for export became more and more detailed, with beautifully executed figures, ornate decoration and gilding. By the end of the 19th century and into the 20th century, as well as these fine pieces, much poor, slapdash work was produced to satisfy the market, but it is easy to spot these because the painted decoration lacks the care and precision shown on the best pieces.

24

▼ *The figure of a Japanese woman riding on the elephant's back is, in fact, a* koro, *a type of incense burner.*

▶ *Designs on the best Satsuma vases from the late 1800s are spacious and elegant, with finely painted birds, peonies, chrysanthemums and blossom. The figure represents the goddess of mercy, Kannon.*

▶ *The charming study of a woman breastfeeding her baby is typical of good-quality Satsuma figures. The strongly coloured red and blue flowers on her kimono are a favourite decoration.*

CERAMICS

CERAMICS

▲ *Incense burners were some of the pieces most frequently made by Satsuma potters, and also some of the most beautiful. They were produced in many shapes and sizes, with decoration varying from simple flower sprigs to ornate floral designs enhanced with gilding, exotic dragons and panels painted with scenes of Japanese life.*

Ceramics

Noritake

I N THE EARLY 20TH CENTURY, Japanese porcelain manufacture lost a good deal of its cachet due to overproduction and a progressive coarsening of design. Tea and coffee sets in extremely thin 'eggshell' porcelain from the Noritake factory were exported to almost every corner of the globe. Many pieces are frankly cheap and nasty and have little collection value, but others were beautifully painted and are worth searching for, among them pieces with designs created by the American architect Frank Lloyd Wright.

▼ *Noritake wares show a mixture of near-traditional designs and those strongly influenced by contemporary Western taste, as in the Art Deco-type ashtray.*

CERAMICS

DUTCH DELFT

▾ *Wall tiles are some of the most attractive and affordable Delft pieces.*

28

I N RENAISSANCE EUROPE, the use of 'tin' glaze (a clear lead glaze with added tin ashes) was used to turned ochre- or buff-coloured earthenware white. In the 14th century, tin-glazed ware in the Hispano-Moresque style was popular in Spain; in Italy it was known as maiolica. But growing awareness of Chinese porcelain encouraged alternative traditions, and by the mid-17th century almost every major power in Europe was producing its own distinct tin-glazed ware – Delft in the Low Countries, delftware in England, *faience* in France and *fayencen* in Germany and Scandinavia.

By the late 1600s, demand for imported Oriental pieces was enormous, but their cost put them out of the reach of all but the wealthy. To supply clients of more modest means, Dutch potters made earthenware bowls, plates, vases and jars that were close copies of Oriental styles and decoration, particularly blue-and-white Chinese export wares, and several factories were set up, notably at Delft, where pieces were painted with Chinese landscape scenes and motifs such as chrysanthemums and peonies. Other European makers in France and Germany followed the Dutch lead, adapting and copying Chinese wares.

◂ *A large bowl, very similar to Chinese bowls, was made in 1697 to commemorate the Peace of Ryswyck.*

CERAMICS

▶ *Dutch potters also employed* ▶
Chinese blue-and-white
decoration on peculiarly Dutch
objects – tulip vases. These
were usually in the form of a
brick with several holes in the
top to take the flower stems,
but fantastic shapes such as
this astonishing tower
were also made.

CERAMICS
ENGLISH DELFTWARE

30

EARLY DUTCH DELFT strongly affected the English market after William of Orange, the husband of Queen Mary, became king. A Delft commemorative plate made in Holland for their coronation in 1689 features a rather primitive half-portrait of the two monarchs in blue dye, with floral decoration around the rim. After Mary's death in 1693, an English delftware charger in similar style depicts William standing alone in full regalia.

Tin-glazed earthernware continued to be produced over the next century at several centres in England, notably London, Bristol and Liverpool, and large bowls and chargers, plates, mugs and tiles were made. Subjects ranged from rather humorous depictions of Adam and Eve and events such as hot-air balloon ascents to Chinese-type and floral decoration, including tulips.

▲ *Chinese scenes in blue and white have been used to decorate this delftware punch bowl, which dates from the late 18th century.*

◀ *This large bowl was made c.1740 at either Bristol or Wincanton in the west of England.*

CERAMICS

◄ Typical of delftware is this large plate, or charger, showing a dashing young man on his horse. He bears a resemblance to Charles II, who became king with the restoration of the monarchy in England in 1660. Such pieces, with a border of broad blue brush-strokes, are known as blue-dash chargers. This one was made in London.

▶ Another piece of delftware, made at Bristol, this large circular dish carries Oriental-style floral decoration.

CERAMICS

WEDGWOOD

D UTCH DELFT AND ENGLISH DELFTWARE had one major
defect: they chipped easily. This was a considerable
drawback, since table wares need to be hard-wearing.
The lead-glazed 'creamware' developed by the Englishman Josiah
Wedgwood was more satisfactory for items such as plates and
cups. His later development, 'pearlware', had a fine white colour
and could be easily potted and decorated. It reached a height of
popularity in the 1760s to '80s and was further refined in
'Queen's Ware'. Wedgwood also developed caneware, which
was sometimes moulded to look like bamboo, and in
1767 produced a hard, unglazed stoneware, known
as black basaltes, which could be moulded, carved
and polished.

▼ *Tan-coloured caneware,
made by refining the clay
used for brown wares, was
often decorated with red,
blue or green, as on this
potpourri vase (c.1820).*

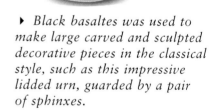

▸ *Black basaltes was used to
make large carved and sculpted
decorative pieces in the classical
style, such as this impressive
lidded urn, guarded by a pair
of sphinxes.*

▲ *Creamware, such as this
dinner plate decorated with
botanical illustrations, was
made from white Devon clay.*

▸ *The more elaborate oval
plate, with a formal design of
blue and gold flowers, dates
from the late 1800s and was
intended as a wall plate or
decorative piece to stand on a
sideboard or dresser.*

CERAMICS

CERAMICS

Wedgwood's best-known contribution to the history of pottery was Jasperware (now often simply called 'Wedgwood'). This was and is a vitrified stoneware usually decorated with white relief figures on a coloured ground, generally blue, although other colours, including a soft green, yellow, lilac and black were used.

The colours were achieved either by staining the body or by adding ground colour to it. Pieces in more than one colour were made by dipping a coloured piece in a second colour, then polishing

CERAMICS

the edge of the design so that the original colour showed through.
Before firing, reliefs were cast in little alabaster moulds and
applied, or 'sprigged', to the piece; they could also be given depth
by cutting and picking out the detail.

   Wedgwood began experimenting with this ware in the 1770s,
and the finest pieces date from the 1780s, when he employed many
well-known English artists, including Flaxman and Stubbs, to
design the classical reliefs.

CERAMICS

STAFFORDSHIRE FIGURES

36

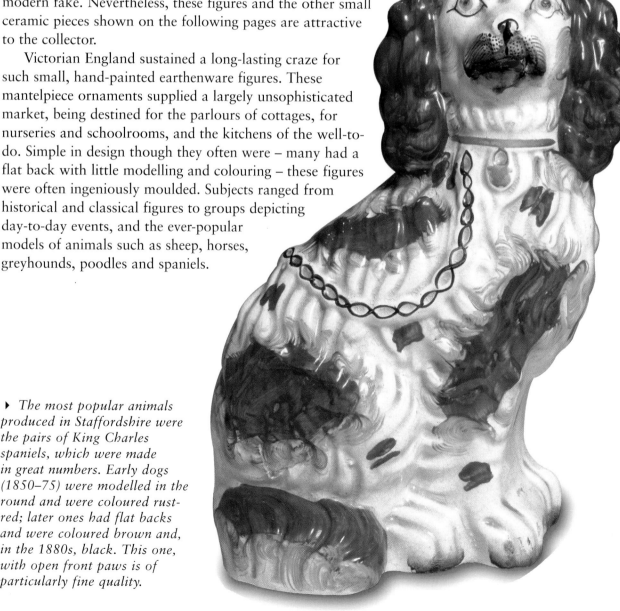

FIGURES WERE FIRST MADE in the English Staffordshire potteries in the late 1700s, in an attempt to emulate the expensive porcelain figures being produced by continental factories such as Meissen, and to provide a cheaper alternative. Fine-quality Cornish china clay became available in 1775, and at the same time improved plaster of Paris moulds meant that a great number of pieces could be produced. Popular designs were copied and adapted and moulds were used time and again, or even taken from existing figures – a practice that is still current – so it is often extremely difficult to tell an early piece from a modern fake. Nevertheless, these figures and the other small ceramic pieces shown on the following pages are attractive to the collector.

Victorian England sustained a long-lasting craze for such small, hand-painted earthenware figures. These mantelpiece ornaments supplied a largely unsophisticated market, being destined for the parlours of cottages, for nurseries and schoolrooms, and the kitchens of the well-to-do. Simple in design though they often were – many had a flat back with little modelling and colouring – these figures were often ingeniously moulded. Subjects ranged from historical and classical figures to groups depicting day-to-day events, and the ever-popular models of animals such as sheep, horses, greyhounds, poodles and spaniels.

▸ *The most popular animals produced in Staffordshire were the pairs of King Charles spaniels, which were made in great numbers. Early dogs (1850–75) were modelled in the round and were coloured rust-red; later ones had flat backs and were coloured brown and, in the 1880s, black. This one, with open front paws is of particularly fine quality.*

CERAMICS

> *These sheep spill holders were given a realistic, woolly texture by adding granules of clay. They are made in bocage style, in which ceramic flowers and foliage are used to support or surround a central subject.*

37

▼ *Stirrup cups, in the shape of a fox's or hound's head, containing a warming drink, were passed around the members of a foxhunt before they set out. The colouring here is typical of wares made by the Pratt family.*

▲ *These two figures, the one a monkey-faced spill holder and the other made to hold a candle, are typical small pieces from the Staffordshire potteries.*

> *Spaniels were not the only dogs made – comforter dogs (a breed no longer in existence), greyhounds, lurchers and, most appealingly, poodles also appeared, in different versions.*

CERAMICS

STAFFORDSHIRE PASTILLE BURNERS

38

IN THE EARLY 1800s, before the advent of proper drains, water-borne sewage and street-cleaning, and facilities for the easy washing of both clothes and people, it was important to counter noxious odours. One of the ways this was done was by burning little tablets of aromatic charcoal, cinnamon and herbs in pastille burners, which had removable pierced lids. The Staffordshire potters rose to the occasion by producing *cottages ornées* – models of cottages and other buildings, such as castles, clock towers and even lighthouses. These were decorated with over-sized flowers and the texture of grass and thatch was often shown naturalistically by adding shavings of clay. The vogue for *cottages ornées* was at its height in 1820–60, when large quantities were produced, and they are highly collectable.

CERAMICS

Cottages ornées *varied in size and style depending on the room they were intended for and the market. Watermills were popular: in the one shown here most of the windows are left unfilled for the incense to escape. Some cottages ornées, such as the church and the cottage shaped like a mushroom, were made in porcelain.*

CERAMICS

COW CREAMERS

MOST COLLECTABLE COW CREAMERS were made between 1750 and 1850, many of them in Staffordshire and Wales, but other potteries in Sunderland, Yorkshire and Scotland also turned them out. Initially intended as a joke, their appeal was such that they became immensely popular and were produced in many different types of ware – salt-glazed stoneware, pearlware, creamware, porcelain and even silver.

The cow stood on a base, with her tail curled over her back to form a handle and her mouth open to serve as a spout. The milk was poured into the cow's belly through a lidded hole in her back. Although the design was universal, the modelling and glazes, and the decoration varied enormously from all-over colour to spots and flowers and, very rarely, naturalistic colouring. The attraction of cow creamers continues today, and there are many avid collectors who search out these entertaining pieces.

CERAMICS

Cow creamers made in Staffordshire usually stand on a green base and the cow's tail curves on to the back. In those from Wales and Sunderland, the cow's tail curves to the side; the eyes of cows from Yorkshire are often outlined in blue. Patterns were often applied with a sponge; attempts to reproduce the Herefordshire breed (below) produced the only naturalistically coloured cows.

41

CERAMICS

FAIRINGS

ALTHOUGH THESE SMALL PIECES – they were generally only about 13cm long – are usually captioned on the base in English, they were chiefly made in Germany, first by the firm of Conta & Boehme of Pössneck in about 1860, and later by three or four other German factories.

From medieval times, and well into the 19th century, as well as having considerable commercial importance, annual fairs all over Europe provided a holiday outing for the entire community. Early 'fairings' were sold or given as prizes at fairs, where farm and domestic workers gathered to buy goods and try their luck at the sideshows, and the subjects and captions on the base of these pieces reflects a robust, cheerful, working-class humour. As the importance of fairs declined, fairings were largely sold in shops, and the subjects and wording changed, becoming more genteel and sentimental, with children, cats and dogs featuring predominantly.

Much as in the music hall, the subjects of fairings are normally stock subjects of fun – flirtatious maids, erring husbands, drunkards and so on, and some of the wording is quite risqué. The figure of the black-clad widow above is unusual and quite touching.

42

Ceramics

CERAMICS
MASON'S IRONSTONE

S TONEWARE IS MADE from a type of clay that can be fired to a higher degree than earthernware, and it is, therefore, harder and non-porous, even when left unglazed. The Rhineland became the centre of the early production of stoneware because suitable clay was available, and through exports the influence of stoneware became widespread in Europe and England. By the 1720s, in Staffordshire, stoneware had been improved by the addition of white clay and ground flint, which gave the greyish body whiteness and made it lighter.

Then, in the early 1800s, Miles Mason developed a particularly strong, hardwearing, slightly transparent stoneware in which the clay was mixed with powdered glassy slag. His son Charles patented it in 1813 under the name of Mason's Patent Ironstone China, and until the mid-1800s the factory turned out a wide range of wares, both domestic and decorative. The factory failed in 1848 and was taken over by Francis Morley; in 1973 it became part of the Wedgwood group of companies.

▼ *The Oriental design and fresh colouring of this ewer and basin, dating from c.1820, are particularly fine. The octagonal shape of the jug and the gilded serpentine handle were popular at this time.*

CERAMICS

▲ *The attraction of Mason's Ironstone lies in its robust nature and its brightly coloured decoration. The vogue for all things Japanese in the mid-19th century inspired the bold Oriental patterns, chiefly in shades of blue, green and red, often with gilding.*

CERAMICS

CERAMICS

◀ *Although Mason's Ironstone is generally thought of in terms of Oriental decoration and colouring, many of the pieces were decorated with very English-looking birds, flowers such as roses, and even landscapes with classical ruins. The patterns were transfer-printed on to the smooth, unglazed white body, and were then painted in bright colours before firing.*

CERAMICS

OTHER STONEWARE

T HE SUCCESS OF MASON'S IRONSTONE encouraged other manufacturers, including Spode and Minton, to produce their own versions of decorative stoneware in the mid-1800s. At the time, 'Japan patterns', based on Kakiemon and Imari porcelain, were popular, and the European imitators tended to follow Oriental designs and colours closely. But other, more traditional designs were also used by some makers.

48

▶ *Both the colouring and style of decoration on this Spode stoneware soup plate from the mid-1800s appear to be based on Imari wares – an interesting variation on the prevailing Japanese theme.*

▶ *Not all stoneware made in the mid-1800s was decorated in Japanese style. More traditional designs were also found, as these attractive blue-and-white soup tureens, with underplates and covers, demonstrate.*

CERAMICS

MINTON

THE MINTON FACTORY was founded in 1793 at Stoke-on-Trent and still flourishes today. Throughout its long history it has produced fine pottery, and has also often led the way in adapting fashions to ceramics. Many of its wares, particularly those produced during the 19th century, such as majolica and Parian ware, were original and innovative.

49

▶ *This stoneware cup and saucer, made by Minton c.1840, is, like Masons' Ironstone, decorated in a floral design in the Japanese Imari style, which was much in favour at the time.*

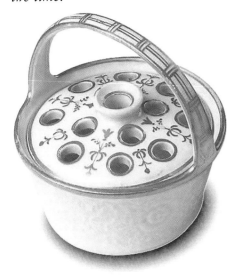

▲ *Dating from c.1820, the little basket-shaped potpourri vase is a good example of early Minton pottery. It is gracefully decorated with gold and may well have been meant for a lady's bedroom.*

▶ *This charming little pottery plate with a child chasing a butterfly, made c.1872, was intended as a wall plate. Such plates often had two holes pierced in the foot rim so that they could be suspended on a wire.*

CERAMICS
MAJOLICA

IN THE MID-19TH CENTURY, Minton developed a lead-glazed pottery, known as majolica because the creamy yellow body was used to offset relief work, strong colours and thick glazes that were reminiscent of the Italian *maiolica* of the 16th century. Other manufacturers in France, Sweden and the USA followed Minton's lead, and between them they produced wares from teapots to vases, cachepots and large pieces for conservatory and garden use, such as jardinières, plant troughs and seats. Styles ranged from japonaiserie to Art Nouveau, both of which enjoyed great popularity towards the end of the century and into the early 20th century.

50

▼ *The plastic qualities, heavy shiny glaze and unusual subject matter common to majolica are well displayed in this large shell resting on a heavy base of branching coral.*

▲ *The Oriental influence prevailing at the turn of the 20th century is evident in this little tea caddy, modelled to look like bamboo.*

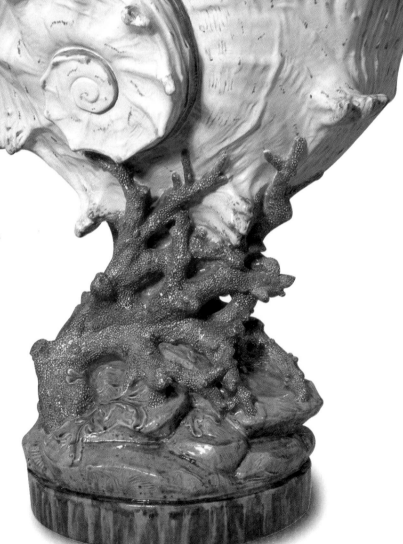

CERAMICS

As this Portuguese-made ape with a tortoise shows, majolica lent itself to lifelike modelling and the creation of texture.

▼ *In the mid- to late 19th century, it became fashionable to fill one's house or conservatory with the exotic species that plant hunters were bringing back from all over the world, and jardinières, such as this large French majolica one, with equally exotic flamingoes, became popular.*

CERAMICS

52

▲ This massive jardinière, made in England c.1896, was given added gravitas by resting the bowl on the shoulders of two Herculean figures and decorating the sides with draped swags and lions' masks in the classical manner.

▶ Majolica was used for many whimsical objects, such as this candle-holder in the form of a clothed and grinning frog produced in Prussia.

CERAMICS

Cachepots for hiding plant pots are among the most attractive objects made in majolica, since their smaller size tended to restrain the potters' exuberance. These two examples with their saucers – the one decorated with moulded spring flowers, the other with latticework and a garland of summer blooms – both date from the end of the 19th century.

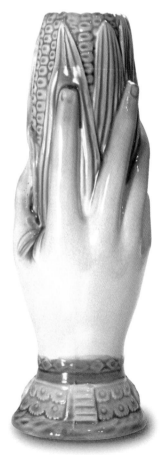

▸ This pair of candle-holders, each with a disembodied hand holding a corn cob, are well modelled, but reflect an unusual, rather macabre attitude of mind on the part of the potter.

CERAMICS

TEAPOTS

A POPULAR FIELD FOR COLLECTORS, teapots can often be bought singly, apart from the cups that they might once have accompanied, for reasonable prices. They can also form a very decorative display. Teapots are quite difficult to make – the spout and handle are made separately and then attached to the body, and the lid, also, is made separately and must fit snugly, so early teapots were a good example of the potter's skill. They were produced in many styles and sizes, with many different glazes and types of decoration, offering the potter scope for imagination and ingenuity. Many followed the classical shapes of contemporary silver, while others, especially towards the end of the 19th century, reflected the current fascination with Japanese style and unusual shapes began to appear; this was especially true of those made in majolica.

During the 1920s and '30s, in the Art Deco period, teapots were moulded, so they often look quite crude, and whimsy was often carried to extremes. 'Novelty' teapots, ranging from nursery-rhyme characters, like Humpty Dumpty, to personalities from cinema cartoons, such as Donald Duck, became the rage.

▲ *The rough texture and spray of applied flowers and leaves on this 'woodland' teapot is typical of the work of followers of the Arts and Crafts Movement.*

▶ *The Oriental-style teapot, with its faux bamboo handle and knop on the lid, was designed by Christopher Dresser (1834–1904), whose designs for ceramics, silver, carpets and textiles were very influential. He believed that design and function should be linked, and that mass production and good design were compatible.*

54

CERAMICS

55

▸ *The potter's ingenious manipulation of his subject is shown in this majolica teapot, where a large fish swallows a small one, whose tail forms the spout.*

▸ *One of the best exponents of majolica, the Staffordshire potter George Jones, made this finely observed teapot in the shape of a cock.*

◂ *The potter's imagination could turn to rather odd subject matter as here, where the teapot is formed from a finely detailed roundel of wood with snails crawling on it.*

CERAMICS

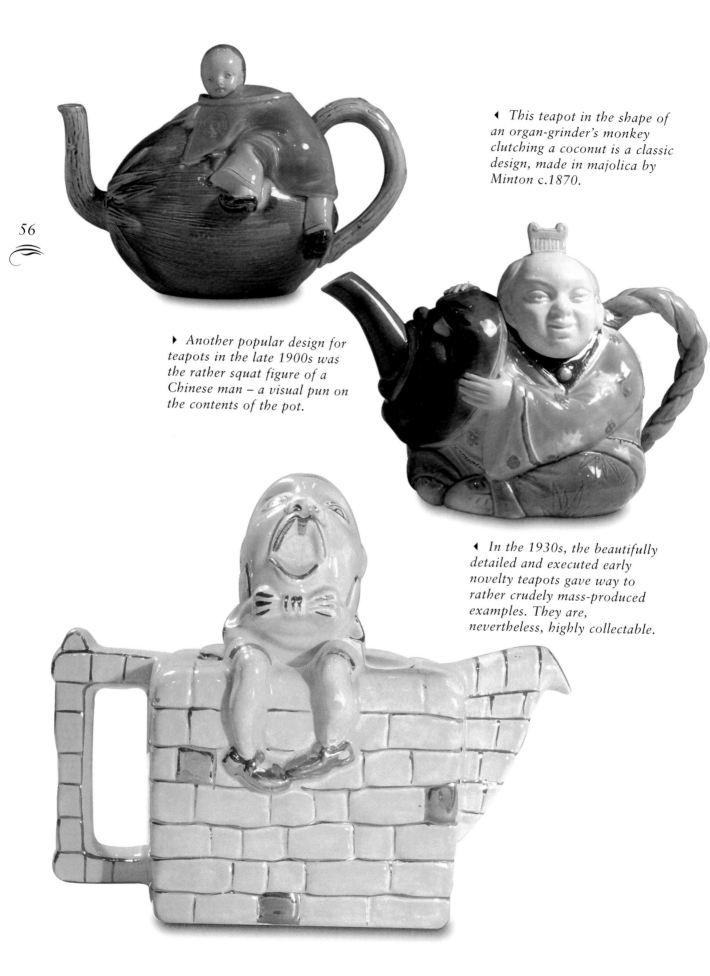

◄ This teapot in the shape of an organ-grinder's monkey clutching a coconut is a classic design, made in majolica by Minton c.1870.

56

▸ Another popular design for teapots in the late 1900s was the rather squat figure of a Chinese man – a visual pun on the contents of the pot.

◄ In the 1930s, the beautifully detailed and executed early novelty teapots gave way to rather crudely mass-produced examples. They are, nevertheless, highly collectable.

CERAMICS

▲ *Sporty little open cars were synonymous with glamour and excitement in the 1930s, and this teapot reflects that sentiment.*

▼ *The tank teapot seems to commemorate a darker passage of history – the days of World War I, when tanks were used for the first time.*

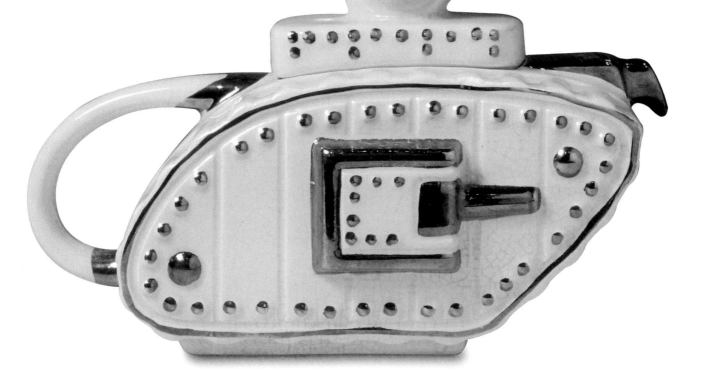

CERAMICS

WEMYSS WARE

ONE OF THE MOST UNMISTAKABLE types of pottery is Wemyss ware, made at the Fife Pottery near Glasgow from the late 19th century to 1930, when it closed; the rights to the ware eventually passed to Royal Doulton. In the 1880s, in an attempt to revive the almost moribund pottery, Robert Heron employed a group of Bohemian artists to decorate the wares by hand, and the style they established, with simple, boldly coloured fruit and flowers, particularly roses, and animals such as cocks, hens and geese, distinguishes the ware. Never produced in any quantity, Wemyss ware was always expensive, and pieces today are not cheap, but there are still many keen collectors. Take care when buying – there are many imitations and only genuine pieces bear the words Wemyss or Wemyss ware, and even then, these words appear on the work of some copyists in the USA.

▲ *Animals, mainly cats and pigs of all sizes, such as this large doorstop, were moulded in two pieces and joined. All were decorated with flowers.*

▶ *The more thinly potted trays, baskets, bowls and candlesticks shown here were also moulded, while thickly potted mugs and jugs were thrown on the wheel.*

Ceramics

CERAMICS

TORQUAY WARE & OTHER SEASIDE SOUVENIRS

WEMYSS WARE WAS MADE FOR, and bought by, the wealthy, but in the late 1800s many small companies, particularly in the West of England, were making cheap, attractive pottery to be sold as souvenirs of the seaside holidays so beloved by Victorians. Often the potteries established shapes, patterns and colours that were as distinctive as the flowers and animals of Wemyss ware. Among the most prolific were several factories around Torquay in Devon, which made pieces bearing the name of seaside resorts all over the country. On so-called motto ware, sayings of a cheerful, lighthearted nature, such as 'Waste not, want not' extolled Victorian virtues – in contrast to the much coarser humour displayed on the comparable fairings. This type of ware was produced well into the 20th century.

60

▲ *Among the more useful souvenirs was this cruet with the pieces in the shape of toadstools.*

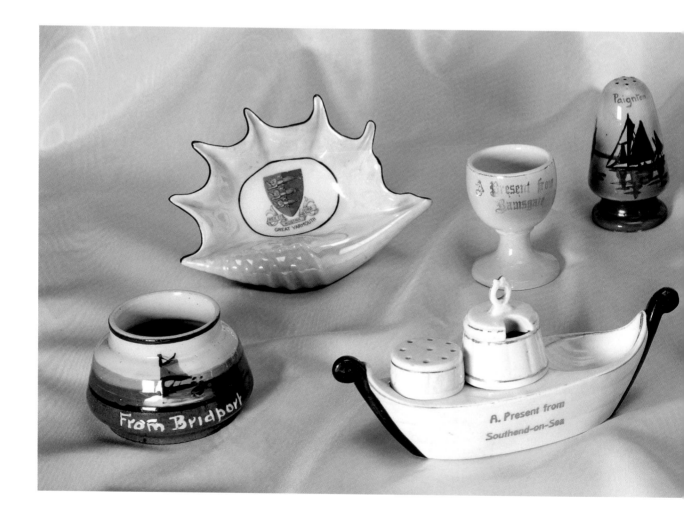

CERAMICS

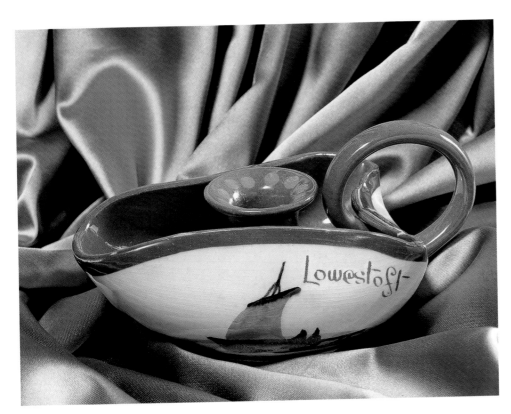

◄ *A typical piece of Torquay pottery, using the local dark red clay, this slip-decorated candle holder was made in 1900–13.*

▼ *Seaside wares were not made only by English factories: the shell, shoe and blue shaving mug, with a picture of the English town of Ramsgate on it, were all made in Germany.*

— CERAMICS —

ENGLISH ART POTTERY

62

A<small>T THE OTHER END OF THE</small> 19<small>TH-CENTURY</small> ceramics market, both in England and on the Continent, was the art pottery made during the last decades as collectors' pieces. In England, a major name for art pottery was Doulton's of Lambeth, London, which originally specialized in the production of drainpipes, but under the leadership of Sir Henry Doulton began, in 1860, to make domestic wares – particularly tea sets and jugs. The success of these lines encouraged the company to branch out into 'art' stoneware and to employ artists from the nearby Lambeth School of Art, notably the Barlow sisters, Hannah and Florence. Pieces produced included terracotta bas-reliefs and plaques with religious subjects for the decoration of churches.

Other well-known and influential art potters were the Martin brothers. Walter and Edwin both worked for Doultons before joining their brothers, Wallace and Charles, and setting up their own pottery in 1873 making domestic wares. Initially their pieces were similar to those they had made at Doultons, but in time their work became more original, and included intricate, carved pieces, fine Japanese-style wares and a selection of unusual creatures, including hedgehogs, toads and lizards. Wallace also made some strange bird-like figures, many with removable heads for use as storage jars; these are much sought after by collectors.

▶ *The small stoneware jug, far left, was made in the early 1870s. Edwin later adapted his talent for intricate incised and relief work to Art Nouveau-style pieces, such as the vase (1903), second left. By 1899 designs had become more abstract and flowing, first right, and geometric design appeared only on the rims and bases of vases, far right.*

Ceramics

CERAMICS

ONE OF THE LATER ENGLISH ART
potters, William Moorcroft
(1872–1946) produced some of
the most attractive pieces at his own
factory, which he set up in Staffordshire
in 1913. He reintroduced the art of slip
trailing (outlining his stylized designs
with a narrow raised band of thin clay)
which had previously been used in the
1600s. His early Florian wares, mainly in
blues, greens and yellows, were Chinese-
inspired; in his later wares, dating from
the 1920s, he used deeper, richer colours.

Pottery from the Della Robbia factory
at Birkenhead, near Liverpool, also
looked to the past – to the potters of
Renaissance Italy. Much of the decoration
used, such as *'sgraffito'* – scratching a
design into the slip before firing to reveal
the colour of the body beneath – was also
a revival of older techniques.

▸ *Moorcroft's Florian ware, left and third
right, was characterized by its slender
shape. The Chinese influence is evident in
the blue and white colouring of some early
work, far right; the small vase, centre
right, is made in the poppy style. Later
work, second left, shows deep, swirling
colours. Yellow and green were popular
Della Robbia colours, third left.
The oddly bulbous vase, centre, was
intended for growing crocuses, which were
planted in holes on top of the gourd shape
and watered by means of the long stem.*

64

CERAMICS

CERAMICS
EUROPEAN ART POTTERY

66

IN THE LATE 19TH CENTURY and into the early 20th century, in Austria-Hungary and Germany much art pottery was also being produced. Some of these pieces were made in a rather heavy, rustic manner, but others were typically Art Nouveau in style and decoration, or had almost Japanese-type designs and glazes.

◄ *This earthernware cachepot, made c.1903 by Eichwald, is appropriately decorated with flowers in a rather heavy variation of Art Nouveau style.*

▲ *The small stoneware pot with a raised design in iridescent glass was produced by the Hungarian firm of Zsolnay and dates from c.1900.*

▲ *Altogether more delicate in style and execution is the pretty little plate decorated with cyclamen, which was made in Austria c.1910.*

CERAMICS

◄ *Probably made by Goldschieder in Vienna, this head of a woman is typical of the work of art potters in the early 20th century. Her Art Nouveau credentials are emphasized by the spray of mistletoe – a device favoured by artists at the time.*

▶ *Around 1900, Zsolnay produced some strangely shaped vases and ornament decorated with iridescent lustre glazes.*

67

▼ *A German-made cachepot from c.1910 has typical Art Nouveau flowers around the rim.*

▼ *In the same style as Eichwald's earlier work, but less heavy, is this cachepot, dating from c.1911.*

▲ *In this Merkelbach tankard with a pewter lid from c.1900, traditional stoneware has been given Art Nouveau styling.*

CERAMICS

EUROPEAN PORCELAIN: MEISSEN

INSPIRED BY THE STEADY FLOW of Chinese porcelain into Europe, European potters strove to make it themselves. Under the patronage of the Medicis in Florence, Italian potters were encouraged to experiment, and by the last quarter of the 16th century had succeeded in producing a creamy, soft-paste type with a glossy surface, by adding powdered glass to the clay.

The search for hard-paste porcelain went on, however, and in 1713 the alchemist Johann Friederich Böttger, who under the patronage of Augustus the Strong, Elector of Saxony, had earlier attempted to make gold, produced the first true hard-paste porcelain. A factory was built at Meissen, 12 miles from Dresden, and by the 1720s, so-called 'Dresden china' had become prized throughout Europe. Augustus encouraged artists to develop their own designs. Chief among them was Johann Höroldt, who in the 1720s to '30s developed a type of chinoiserie that also incorporated more Germanic motifs. In the 1730s, Kakiemon designs were copied and more European flower designs, known as *indianische Blumen* and *deutsche Blumen*, were introduced.

◄ *The Oriental influence was strong in earlier pieces made at Meissen as is shown by this flask in the shape of a Japanese sake bottle, decorated in Imari style and colours.*

CERAMICS

▲ The centrepiece for the Northumberland dinner service, made c.1745, is not only a fine example of Meissen porcelain, but interesting because of its portrayal of a one-horned Indian rhino.

◄ The brilliant whiteness of the porcelain, the delicate painting and basketweave moulding around the top, mark this coffee pot as an example of Meissen's finest work, dating from c.1760.

CERAMICS
MEISSEN & DERIVATIVES

70

EXCELLENT PORCELAIN FIGURES also were made at Meissen, notably by Böttger, Peter Reinecke, and Johann Joachim Kändler, the finest of the modellers. From 1727, he made a series of large white porcelain animals, and figures such as saints and harlequins, drunks and street vendors, which brought a new, sculptural quality to porcelain figure-making.

Eventually, disaffected workers carried the secret of hard-paste porcelain from Meissen, and after the 1750s derivative pieces were made in factories all over Europe. And even before they discovered the secret of hard-paste porcelain, many factories were copying Meissen's wares, with varying degrees of success. Meissen's greatest period ended when production was disrupted by the Seven Years' War (1756–63) and Sèvres became dominant. During the next 100 years or so, although quality remained the same, nothing new came out of the Meissen factory, but towards the end of the 19th century, alongside its regular wares, the factory began to produce fine, innovative pieces in Art Nouveau style.

In the mid-1700s Kändler modelled four splendid groups representing the four continents; Asia, Europe and Africa are shown here. The figures are mounted on contemporary French ormolu plinths.

CERAMICS

◄ These two pots are part of an early Regency garniture made in England in the style of Meissen rococo pieces. Derivative work was not always entirely imitative and was often of very high quality.

◄ Meissen's figure of a hurdy gurdy player, dating from c.1748, was copied in soft-paste porcelain, above, by the English Chelsea factory, but left uncoloured.

▲ The Tartar archer is a copy, made in Moscow at the Popov factory in 1810, of a figure made by Kändler or Reinecke in the mid-1700s.

CERAMICS

BIEDERMEIER

72

I IN THE EARLY 19TH CENTURY, in the Biedermeier period, German porcelain again achieved excellence, with magnificent pieces being produced at the Royal Imperial factory in Vienna and the Royal Porcelain Factory – the Königliche Porzellan Manufaktur (KPM) – in Berlin. The style was Neo-classical, with simple clean lines, and although initially some tableware was produced, most pieces were made for display, rather than use, and decoration became more and more sumptuous. Townscapes and landscapes, as well as country scenes and classical ruins, were painstakingly painted, as were birds, flower sprays and even large bouquets, all accompanied by lavish gilding. Often famous paintings would be copied and reproduced on the porcelain.

▶ *The Vienna factory was famous for exquisite painting of flowers and spectacular gilding, which was often tooled. Sometimes the designs allowed the white porcelain body to show, at other times the entire surface was covered. The two cups on the left date from 1820; the two top right from 1825. The products of the KPM factory, right centre and foreground, were equally splendid, often with all-over gilding interspersed with bands of coloured decoration or else a gilded design painted on a white porcelain background.*

Ceramics

CERAMICS

Although the Königliche Porzellan Manufaktur (KPM) in Berlin tended to follow trends set by the Vienna factory in the Biedermeier period, the standard of workmanship was just as high. It excelled in its decoration of plates, which gave more scope to the artists than the small curved areas provided by cups and saucers. These plates, which were made between 1815 and 1845, exhibit many different styles of decoration, from the classical mask to bird studies, ruins and even, most unusually, an English horse-racing scene – all beautifully painted and gilded, and often set within a broad band of plain colour or on a white background.

Ceramics

CERAMICS
SÈVRES

76

IT WAS THE FRENCH who established the first fully operational European porcelain factories, making soft-paste porcelain at St Cloud in the early 1700s and Chantilly in 1725. Not to be outdone, in 1734 the Duc de Villeroy set up a porcelain factory in Paris (later transferred to Mennecy), and in 1738 a factory was established at Vincennes; in 1756, it transferred to Sèvres under the patronage of King Louis XV.

Although often imitating Meissen, Sèvres porcelain came to epitomise the French Rococo style. Characteristic rich, flat ground colours, including *bleu lapis* (dark blue), applied under the glaze, *bleu céleste* (turquoise), *jaune jonquille* (yellow) and *rose* Pompadour (pink), were enlivened by gilding and framed panels painted with scenes and flowers. The variety and novelty of these colours was one of Sèvres' main claims to fame.

By the 1770s, hard-paste porcelain was increasingly being used, allowing the production of huge bowls and vases, although some simpler pieces were also made. Sèvres dominated the porcelain market in France until the end of the century and was still active and influential into the 1800s, when the early, light Neo-classical designs were superseded by a heavier, Empire style and much of the decoration showed scenes of Napoleon's life, or classical motifs such as garlands, eagles or mythical beasts.

CERAMICS

◀ *Along with other striking gound colours, the brilliant* bleu céleste *(turquoise) glaze was introduced in the 1750s. It was often enriched with gold.*

◀ ▶ *Two early 19th-century cups and saucers with simple shapes have a dark blue background and painted panels depicting scenes from a somewhat idealized contemporary life, as well as a collection of musical instruments.*

CERAMICS

78

▶ *Decorative styles on both Vincennes and, later, Sèvres porcelain, varied from quite simple pieces with floral motifs to severe gilt or coloured grounds enclosing painted scenes.*

▲ *The deep-coloured and gilded borders on early Sèvres pieces enclosed panels of superbly painted figure groups, landscapes, birds and flowers in Rococo style.*

▶ *When the Empire style became fashionable, shapes such as these Neo-classical urns became popular. The bowls are decorated with finely painted pictures of romantic rural scenes.*

CERAMICS

CERAMICS

PARIS PORCELAIN & LIMOGES

THE TERM PARIS PORCELAIN is used to describe the output of several factories set up in Paris towards the end of the 18th century, among them Clignancourt, La Chatille and Fauborg St Denis. All produced fine-quality hard-paste wares, mainly dinner and tea services, which imitated the severe, rigid styles at Sèvres. A important factory was that at Limoges in Limousin, best known for its tea and dessert services, in which the grounds of the design were heightened with raised paste gilding. Decoration consisted mainly of flower designs, many of which were transfer-printed either completely or in outline, when they were hand coloured. The success of the ware relied on its exploitation of the American market, after an American dealer named David Haviland began making his own porcelain in the French town in 1853.

80

▼ *Another cabinet set (made c.1800) was this charming Paris porcelain cup and saucer depicting children playing.*

▶ *These examples of Paris porcelain were made between about 1800 and 1820. The cabinet set, decorated with feathers and meant only for display, was made in Limoges c.1820.*

CERAMICS

CERAMICS

ENGLISH PORCELAIN

EXTENSIVE COPYING of Meissen, Oriental and later Sèvres originals held back the development of the porcelain industry in England in the early 18th century, and although soft-paste porcelain was produced in London at factories at Bow and Chelsea from the mid-1740s, Chinese porcelain was readily available, so discerning customers could afford to pick and choose. The market for specifically English porcelain did not grow until the 1770s, when Worcester began to dominate the scene with elegant tea wares and Derby produced fine ornamental wares as well as a line of porcelain figures. By the 1790s, Staffordshire factories found that they too could sell tea and dessert services with ornate Regency designs, and Minton, Coalport and Spode were soon making splendid porcelain table wares.

82

▼ *The raised design on this ornamental early Worcester plate (c.1768) was modelled separately and applied to the plate; the small sprays of flowers are painted.*

CERAMICS

▶ The Arabic inscription in the border of this plate suggests that it was made to order, possibly as an ornamental plate, since it is so splendid. Although floral decoration was common on porcelain, the plants are generally stylized; this one is a botanically accurate painting of borage.

83

◀ Coalport produced high-quality porcelain dinner services, often with a central floral motif. Here it is set off by a scalloped edge and elaborate gilded scrolls.

▶ This pair of porcelain garniture vases, made by Derby in 1825, are decorated with rural scenes within typical shield-shaped panels. The painting and gilding are beautifully executed.

CERAMICS

WORCESTER

THE NAME THAT STANDS out from all others in the history of English porcelain is Worcester. The factory was established in the town of that name in 1751 and although its name changed several times in the course of its history, it has been making porcelain from that time. In 1862 it became the Worcester Royal Porcelain Factory. During the Regency period the influence of Sèvres began to wane and Worcester produced more simply decorated wares, particularly tea and dinner services and vases. Its great success in the 19th century owed much to its art director, Richard William Binns, who set about expanding the business in 1852. The old 'body' of the porcelain, which contained soap-rock, was replaced by bone china. Binns also formed a collection of Oriental art and displayed it in his own museum to inspire the factory craftsmen. This perhaps explains the Oriental styling of a high proportion of Royal Worcester pieces.

The elegant shapes, simple decoration and restrained gilding of Worcester tea sets and tableware make them very desirable to collectors. The coffee pot dates from c.1806, the dessert plate from c.1815, and the little creamer and cup from c.1810.

CERAMICS

▸ *The blue and gold pattern on the comport – a dish for bonbons or fruit – emphasizes its flowing lines.*

▾ *A strong Oriental influence is evident in the handsome blue and gold plate with a colourful painting of an o-ho bird – a recurrent motif in Chinese art.*

85

▾ *The delicate peach glaze of this cup and saucer, dating from c.1820, is a typical Regency colour.*

CERAMICS

CUPS

A REWARDING FIELD for the collector, especially the beginner, is that of tea cups. Early cups for tea did not have handles but were bowls, like their Chinese and Japanese counter-parts, with saucers. When the price of tea dropped in the late 1600s, the beverage became an everyday necessity for the bourgeoisie and tea wares were produced in quantity. It is still possible today to acquire a single, good-quality porcelain teacup or bowl dating from the 18th century, particularly if you don't mind if it no longer has a saucer, and for a relatively small amount of money 19th-century examples are quite easily found. Coffee cans, with straight sides, are also available, although not in such quantity.

Tea and coffee cups were often made with a single saucer which could be used with either. By studying the shapes and decoration of cups, as well as any maker's or artist's marks, it is possible to build up a basic knowledge of porcelain types and designs throughout the past 150 years or so before going on to larger, more ambitious purchases.

These coffee cans were made between 1790 and 1810 at Worcester, Derby and the Staffordshire factory of Newhall, which produced many attractive designs.

86

CERAMICS

Ceramics

Cream Jugs

88

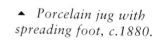

ANOTHER GOOD CHOICE for collectors is jugs. Among the most widely used of all domestic items, jugs measured milk from a churn, collected water from a well and took wine, beer or cider to workers in the fields; they appeared in kitchens and later on tea tables throughout Europe. Early jugs were mostly made from earthenware, though by the late 17th century stoneware began to predominate, and later porcelain took over. Jugs are of particular interest to collectors, since 18th- and 19th-century wares often bear dates, makers' names and registration of design marks. The cream jugs shown here reflect the changes in fashionable design during this period, away from tall, slender shapes to shorter, broader types. Decor-ation, too, changed from elaborate to simpler designs, although there was always a wide range to choose from.

▲ *Porcelain jug with spreading foot, c.1880.*

▸ *Staffordshire jug with a copper lustre band, mid-1800s.*

▸ *Minton majolica jug resembling a cauliflower, 1851–62.*

▲ *Low, boat-shaped Wedgwood jug, 1810.*

CERAMICS

◄ *Jug with high handle, broad spout and feet, c.1840.*

◄ *Small octagonal Mason's Ironstone jug.*

▲ *Mauve transfer-printed jug with lines of lustre, mid-1800s.*

▸ *Chinese-patterned porcelain jug, early 1800s.*

CERAMICS

SPODE

90

THE MAIN CLAIM TO FAME of the Staffordshire factory, founded in 1770 by Josiah Spode, was the invention of bone china in 1794. This is porcelain to which up to 50 per cent of bone ash has been added, to produce a white, translucent and stable body. It is stronger and harder than soft-paste porcelain, but lighter and cheaper to produce than hard-paste, and its introduction was an important step in the development of European ceramics. From the early 1800s it was used by most British and many continental factories and is still being made today.

Spode also produced creamware, pearlware and blue-printed earthernware, and was noted for its excellent use of transfer printing, which was invented in Britain in the middle of the 18th century and is still the most common method of decorating mass-produced ceramics. A design is printed on paper in metallic oxides, which is then wrapped around the piece to be decorated. When the piece is fired, the paper burns away and leaves the design in the glaze.

The factory was taken over by Copelands in 1833 and in 1846 produced Parian ware, a marble-like white porcelain, which was generally left plain and unglazed and used to make busts and dolls' heads. After several changes of name and ownership, the factory today again trades under the name of Spode.

▲ *Two Regency cachepots, the one transfer-printed with rural scenes, the other, with a stand, decorated and gilded in Imari style.*

These potpourri vases, made c.1830, have a 'cracked ice' background. The right-hand vase is decorated in a richly coloured 'Chinese' design. Inner lids helped to preserve the scent when the vase was not in use.

CERAMICS

▲ *A Victorian favourite, the blue-and-white Italian pattern was transfer-printed on earthernware and china and is still used. Older pieces that do not bear the words 'Made in England' are more valuable.*

CERAMICS

POTPOURRI VASES

LTHOUGH THEIR FUNCTION was the same as the pottery pastille burners, the jars, vases or bowls in which to keep potpourri for scenting a room were intended also for display in middle-class homes and so were are generally made in porcelain or bone china. They usually have covers pierced with holes to allow the aroma of the potpourri – a sweet-scented mixture of flower petals, herbs and spices such as cinnamon – to escape, although some had a solid inner lid, whch could be removed, and others had a pierced inner lid and a solid outer cover.

Most of the finest makers produced these containers, and they are an unusual and attractive field for the collector, since the best pieces were hand thrown and they were often decorated with applied flowers or swags, or with richly coloured painting and gilding.

92

▲ *The pretty urn-shaped pot pourri vase in porcelain, with ornate handles and a pattern of blue and pink flowers, was probably meant for a lady's bedroom. Its femininity is emphasized by the flower knop on the lid and delicate gilding.*

◄ *There are only two small holes in the handle of the lid on this bowl, decorated with meadow flowers, so the pot pourri would have retained its scent much longer.*

CERAMICS

▲ This unusual bowl in creamware is shaped like a tureen, and the woven clay resembles caneware.

▲ The ginger-jar shape was popular; this one, with moulded decoration, was made by Spode.

◄ Another ginger-jar shape, with a Chinese design, but on this one, rather unusually, the outer cover is solid and the inner lid is pierced.

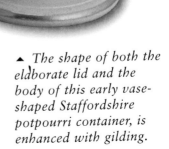

▲ The shape of both the elaborate lid and the body of this early vase-shaped Staffordshire potpourri container, is enhanced with gilding.

CERAMICS

BELLEEK

A

N UNUSUAL TYPE OF PORCELAIN of interest to collectors is
that produced by the factory in County Fermanagh,
Northern Ireland, known as Belleek. It was founded in
1857 and produced fine Parian porcelain, which was fashioned
into splendid ornaments, often in the shape of shells or even sea
urchins, and decorated with other types of marine life. Another
typical use of the delicate porcelain was to weave strips of it into
baskets adorned with flowers and other natural forms; these
can have edges so sharp that they cut the fingers. Pieces were
sometimes left unglazed, or were covered with a pearly, often
iridescent glaze, particularly appropriate on marine subjects.
Bone china was also made and used for tableware.

94

▼ *The large Parian urn is
encrusted with typical Belleek
flowers, while the mythical
figure of the unicorn, the
symbol of purity, is shown in
the grasp of a snake, the symbol
of evil. The jug with floral
garlands – the use of colour is
unusual – is bone china.*

CERAMICS

COPENHAGEN PORCELAIN

SOFT-PASTE PORCELAIN has been used for fine tableware and figures at Denmark's Copenhagen factory since 1759, and hard paste from 1771. In the early 1800s, its products declined, but it was taken over by the Alumina Faience Manufactory in 1882, and a little later Arnold Krog was made artistic director. The most successful of the old patterns were revived and new shapes and patterns introduced. Initially, Copenhagen porcelain was marked with three wavy lines in blue; after 1880 a crown and the word 'Denmark' were added, while the mark 'Royal Copenhagen' was used from the early 20th century.

▲ Among Krog's innovations were a beautiful soft blue colouring and free-hand painting in high-temperature, underglaze colours inspired by Japanese Fukagawa porcelain.

◀ As well as decorative objects, the Copenhagen factory has always produced attractive tableware, as this delicately painted dinner plate with a fluted edge demonstrates.

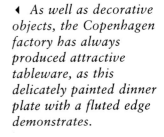

CERAMICS

During the 1890s, new glazes in lustrous colours and finishes appeared that were well suited to Art Nouveau, and in the early 1900s they were used mainly on decorative pieces such as vases, as well as on human figures and, especially, wonderfully lifelike models of animals. Humans and animals were also incorporated into the designs of pieces of practical use, such as bowls and small dishes. Vases were usually decorated with exquisitely painted flowers or plants, sometimes with butterflies.

CERAMICS

Furniture

FURNITURE

COLLECTING
FURNITURE

I
T IS PROBABLY SAFE to say that more people collect
furniture than any other kind of antique. The sheer
range of styles and shapes that have been produced
throughout Europe and America since the 18th century
(a good starting point for the collector of moderate
means) is staggering, and represents a happy hunting
ground for anyone interested in acquiring pieces that
can be both beautiful, functional and valuable.

Every piece of furniture bears mute witness to the
time and place in which it was made, to changing ideas
about was beautiful or functional and the taste and
craftsmanship of its maker or makers. Although
some fashions came and went in a year or two,
as they do today, certain styles were in the
ascendancy for decades.

The solid and heavily embellished baroque
furniture of the late-17th century reflects the
new mercantile wealth of Protestant northern
Europe, while the 18th-century Rococo pieces that
succeeded it – light, ornate, even playful in style – can
be seen as a reaction against this. In the early 18th
century, the Rococo style was expressed in the Low
Countries by such pieces as walnut stools with
quatrefoil (four-leafed) seats and highly-
decorated cabinets on stands. Dutch craftsmen
enjoyed an excellent and growing reputation for
their fine marquetry decoration during the next
30 years or so.

The mathematical proportion and formality of
the Neo-classical style, which emerged later in
the century, was associated with the Age of

FURNITURE

Enlightenment, when philosophy and science, rather than religious belief, were in the ascendancy, and the world's first republics since the fall of those in Greece and Rome were born in the United States and France.

The years following the Napoleonic Wars were a time of industrialization and urbanization in Europe. A new and growing middle class created a new and growing market for furniture with a higher status than the humble, often rough-and-ready joinery of the countryside, but with a lower price-ticket than the individual work of the skilled cabinetmaker. Furniture designers and buyers alike could now afford to pick and choose what they liked from the past, but appeared to have little original vision of their own. As a result, the middle of the 19th century saw new and old forms of furniture offered in an eclectic range of revived styles. Much of it was machine-made, at least in part.

From then until 1940, which is today regarded (perhaps a little arbitrarily) as the cut-off date for what constitutes antique furniture, the evolution of furniture style was dominated by mechanized production. This was expressed either in the enthusiastic exploitation of new techniques and materials characteristic of the 20th-century Modernist and Art Deco movements, or by the reaction against it that was the wellspring of the Arts and Crafts, Orientalist and Art Nouveau styles of the late-19th and early 20th centuries.

Just as there have been fashions in design, so there have been fashions in wood. European

FURNITURE

makers of fine furniture tended to choose oak (and in Germany lime) for their work until the beginning of the 18th century, when walnut – which took carving well – was the main choice. This was supplanted towards the middle of the century by mahogany and other tropical hardwoods.

Only the very best walnut and mahogany furniture was made 'in the solid'. Most furniture had a carcass of oak or pine, or sometimes low-grade mahogany, covered with veneers of more expensive or decorative woods. Rosewood, satinwood, ebony and boxwood, for example, all produced distinctive finishes, but were hardly ever used for the carcass of any furniture

other than an occasional chair. When it became possible to cut veneers by machine in the 19th century, which allowed much thinner layers to be cut, decorative veneering became the norm on most pieces of furniture.

There is an enormous number of furniture forms. The following pages give a general overview of some of the main types – seats, tables, storage and writing furniture and takes a brief look at some more unusual pieces and at the very different traditions of oriental furniture.

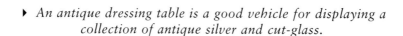

▶ *An antique dressing table is a good vehicle for displaying a collection of antique silver and cut-glass.*

FURNITURE

FURNITURE

SEAT FURNITURE

THE MAIN FORMS OF SEAT FURNITURE in the Middle Ages were stools, benches and settles – basically benches with high backs and maybe sides. Chairs were seen as rather grand objects, reserved for important people and dignitaries, and were often ornately carved, particularly in the 17th century. At this time, most chairs were all wood, although some had cane panels in the back or seat, and padded and upholstered chairs were beginning to be made.

104

The late 17th century saw a golden age of furniture-making in the Low Countries. The Dutch took advantage of the skills of the French Huguenots who fled there to escape religious persecution. One Huguenot craftsman, Daniel Marot, became especially well known for his walnut dining chairs. Typically, these featured exuberant decoration, with pierced leaf-and-scroll cresting above a pierced, curved and carved splat, leaf-carved and scrolled cross-stretchers, velvet seats and scroll-carved cabriole legs ending in hoof feet.

▶ *In the 17th century, chairs were used mainly by the wealthy. This straight-backed example, with a cane seat and rich baroque carving and turning on every element save the seat frame, bears witness to its high status.*

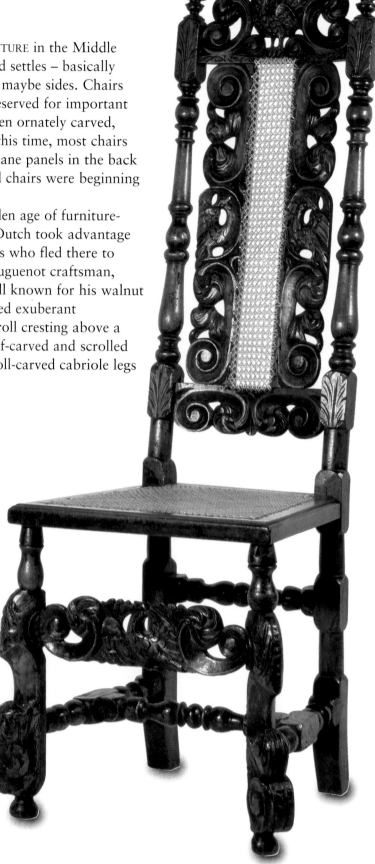

FURNITURE

▶ *The first upholstered chairs were made c.1600, but they were not generally available until the latter half of the 17th century. This low walnut wing chair from the 1690s has the rather delicate legs, braced with H-frame stretchers, that are typical of the period.*

105

FURNITURE
THE 18TH CENTURY

FRANCE WAS A MAJOR EUROPEAN POWER at the start of the 18th century, a country whose colonial conquests had left it bursting at the seams with wealth. As if to reflect this growth in luxury – at least for the more privileged classes – the robust Baroque style in furniture gave way to the more curvaceous, ornate Rococo.

106

The chaise longue – a piece apparently developed to meet the fashion among French society ladies for receiving guests while in a reclining position – emerged early in the 18th century. It took the form of an extended chair or a small bed with an upholstered headpiece. Oeben, Meissonier, Oppenord and Oubry were the great names in furniture in this period.

Some 50 years later the Rococo gave way in turn to the more severe lines of the Neo-classical revival in France. Although not so dominant as in France, the Neo-classical style also flourished in England, where other styles, such as chinoiserie and Gothic (a revival of medieval styles), were also in fashion from the 1760s. One of the most famous English furniture makers and designers, Thomas Chippendale (1718–79), prospered during this period. Although Chippendale published chair designs in several styles, including the Chinese taste, he is best known for bottom-heavy chairs with cabriole legs, which are often carved, ball-and-claw feet and elegant, delicately carved crest rails and back splats.

▸ *Thomas Chippendale's style is exemplified in this mahogany carver, or elbow chair, made c.1770 to his design. The bow-shaped top rail, carved and pierced splat, cabriole legs with decorated knees, down-curving arms and ball-and-claw feet are all typical of his designs.*

FURNITURE

◀ *This 19th-century copy of a Louis XVI sofa shows some hallmarks of the style, such as the use of giltwood, the fluted, tapering legs and the Aubusson tapestry upholstery.*

107

▶ *The shape of this late-19th century copy of a Louis XIV chaise longue is typical of 18th-century French style. It is made of painted and gilded beech and is upholstered in cream damask silk.*

FURNITURE

ENGLISH CHAIRS OF THE 1780s, which were mainly associated with the designs of George Hepplewhite (*d.*1786), tended to be more Neo-classical in inspiration than those of Chippendale. Often they had no splats, and the back supports were a continuation of the back legs. This allowed the seats to be overstuffed (padded and upholstered over the seat frame) at the back as well as at the front, and this became the fashion.

In France, following the Revolution of 1789, furniture styles remained broadly similar in spirit to the classicism of the Louis XVI period, although revolutionary motifs such as caps, arrows and wreaths also made their appearance as decorative features.

108

▸ *The back of this dining chair, with an over-stuffed saddle seat in silk, shows a transitional phase between Chippendale styles and the less exuberant classical formality of Hepplewhite and Sheraton that followed. It was made in 1785.*

Furniture

◄ This French chair is in the Consulate style of around 1800, when Napoleon and two other consuls ruled France. It is signed by the famed maker of Empire furniture, Georges Jacob. The top rail is inlaid with a formal floral design fashioned in mother-of-pearl, pewter and ebony.

▶ The sabre leg, with its gentle, tapering curve, was an introduction of the late 18th century. This sabre-legged Swedish dining chair, with its painted decoration and striped upholstery, dates from the turn of the 19th century, but looks forward to the later styles of the century.

FURNITURE

EMPIRE & REGENCY

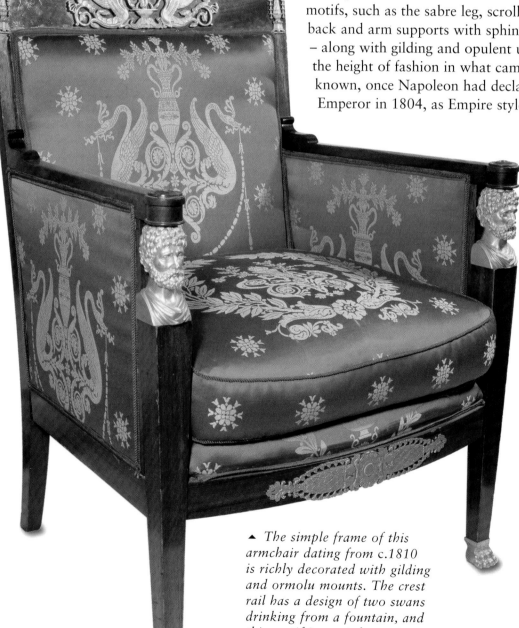

WITH THE RISE OF NAPOLEON in the early 1800s, furniture styles in France became more solid, heavy and rectangular, and almost Spartan in their simplicity. Designers continued to look to the ancient world for inspiration. Greco-Roman and Egyptian motifs, such as the sabre leg, scrolled, padded back and arm supports with sphinx heads, were – along with gilding and opulent upholstery – the height of fashion in what came to be known, once Napoleon had declared himself Emperor in 1804, as Empire style.

▲ *The simple frame of this armchair dating from c.1810 is richly decorated with gilding and ormolu mounts. The crest rail has a design of two swans drinking from a fountain, and this motif is carried over into the silk upholstery, which has recently been specially made to a period design.*

FURNITURE

▸ *The grand formality of the Empire style had already begun to soften by about 1815, when this carved armchair was made.*

◂ *The great Empire style designer Georges Jacob made and signed this dining chair in 1810. The scrolled back is characteristic of French chairs from the Empire period.*

FURNITURE

SHERATON

▼ Sheraton's influence is clearly seen in the shape, the unfussy lines and lightness of touch of this sofa by an English provincial maker working about 1800. The piece was made in beechwood, painted black at a later date, and has eight turned and lightly tapered legs ending in brass castors. The recently renewed padding has a temporary covering of calico prior to reupholstery.

112

IN ENGLAND AT THE SAME TIME, the great designer Thomas Sheraton (1751–1806) was engaged in blending elements of French classicism with often elaborate Egyptian or Greek motifs in his designs. Egypt had become associated with the British Admiral Nelson's victories over the French at the Battle of the Nile and Trafalgar, and various marine motifs, such as dolphins and twists of rope, appeared as decorative motifs alongside the English lion, long a great favourite and always popular in times of war. The so-called Trafalgar chair, with its sabre legs and rope moulding, was a typical example of this sort of patriotic design.

Another furniture shape common in this period was the X-shaped stool, which featured in many Neo-classical paintings and was extremely popular.

FURNITURE

▼ *The characteristic Sheraton style in chair-making featured square backs, tapered legs (turned at the front and swept back for extra stability at the rear), and a crest rail mounted between, rather than above, the back supports.*

113

▲ *The Trafalgar chair, which has a rope-turned cross-piece at the back, was named after Nelson's naval victory over the French fleet in 1805. It was a popular style in England during the time of the Napoleonic Wars.*

▲ *The classical lines, original bolster cushion and deep-buttoned back and sides of this mahogany chaise longue are typical of Regency style, although it was made in Edwardian times.*

FURNITURE

EUROPE

ALTHOUGH THE EMPIRE AND REGENCY STYLES reached their peak in France and England in the first quarter of the 19th century, certain elements of the combined styles – particularly their clean lines, furniture forms, restrained use of decoration and pale veneers – persisted throughout much of the century in Germany, where it evolved into the Biedermeier style, and in Scandinavia.

114

▼ *Only the gently scrolled arms and the slight outward sweep of the legs – for stability rather than style – interrupt the rectangular formality of this sofa. It was made in Denmark in the 1820s and veneered in birch, with satinwood inlays.*

◄ *One of a pair, this elegant upholstered stool with its ebonized finials was made in the 1820s, possibly in Austria.*

FURNITURE

▲ *Later Biedermeier pieces, such as this German* méridienne *(a cross between a sofa and a chaise longue) which dates from the 1830s, developed more flowing lines.*

▲ *This satin birch sofa of the 1830s was made in Germany, and is an excellent example of the way the Empire style influenced Biedermeier furniture.*

FURNITURE

COUNTRY STYLE

NLY A SMALL FRACTION of 18th and 19th-century furniture was the product of highly skilled cabinetmakers in Europe's capital cities. Most people made their furniture themselves or bought simple, joined pieces from local craftsmen. Provincial or 'country' pieces like these either followed the prevailing styles of fine furniture – sometimes with a time lag of up to 30 years – or old, long-standing traditions. Some traditional country chairs were so well made and comfortable that they were bought for the less formal rooms of great houses as well as country kitchens. Walnut and mahogany were too expensive for country pieces and oak was used where it was available. In the USA and Europe, pieces were made in a variety of woods, including elm, beech, yew and various fruitwoods.

Well-worked traditional country pieces are much collected today, especially in their countries of origin, but increasingly across national boundaries. A good example of this is the sturdy, country-made, all-wood British Windsor chair, which seemed immune to the vagaries of fashion, and continued to be popular throughout the century. It came in a number of local versions, but usually had elm seats, back and arms of steamed, bent yew, and legs, spindles and stretchers of turned beech. Such pieces were generally lacking in ornament, apart from a little carving. Some were painted, usually green or black.

116

▶ *Centre splats decorated with fret-cut designs first appeared on Windsor chairs late in the 18th century. This example of a wheelback, one of the most popular motifs, dates from c.1780. It is unusual in that it has all been made entirely from a single wood – yew.*

FURNITURE

▲ *A country piece from northern Europe, this settee was made c.1810 in fruitwood, which has been turned and painted. The seat is rushwork, which was often used on country pieces.*

▼ *The solid elm seat and lack of stretchers indicate that this plain country chair was probably made in Wales. It is similar in construction to chairs that were made all over Europe and in the USA both early in the 19th century and later.*

◄ *The bottom part of this chair, with its bentwood armpieces and curved crest rail, resembles the 'smoker's bow', which developed c.1825; here a high back has been added. The turning on the legs, spindles and stretchers is particularly good.*

FURNITURE

AMERICAN CHAIRS

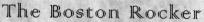

118

IN THE USA IN THE 19TH CENTURY there was already a strong, century-long tradition of vernacular furniture made by local craftsmen who were not concerned with catering for city fashion, which, with an inbuilt time-lag, largely followed styles from across the Atlantic. It was American furniture born and bred, and was often painted rather than veneered.

The most famed American vernacular furniture is the work of members of the 'Shakers', a puritanical and charismatic Christian sect whose insistence on celibacy eventually led to their downfall. Hand-made Shaker pieces are known for the spartan simplicity and elegance of their designs. The typical Shaker chair had four slats and arm posts ending in mushroom-shaped hand finials.

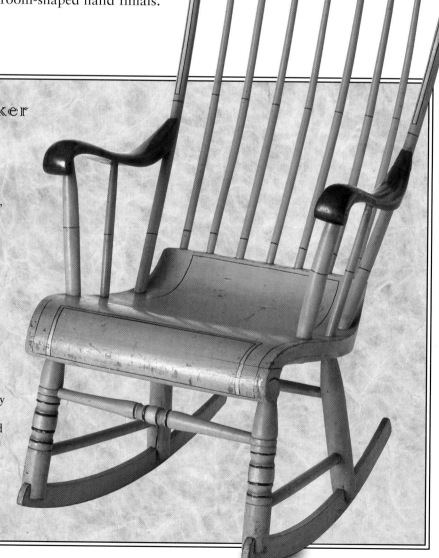

The Boston Rocker

The 'Boston rocker' was produced not only in Massachusetts but throughout the USA from the early 1800s. The style incorporated 'rolling' scrolled-over seats for extra comfort, a vase-shaped central splat to the back and a broad top rail. The runners were extended much farther at the back than they were at the front, which gave the chair greater stability.

Some pieces were painted and decorated all over, while others, as here, had a design only on the crest rail. Painted seats were a particular specialty of the southern states. The decorative designs were applied freehand or, more commonly, with stencils.

FURNITURE

▸ *This tripod chair was made for a child in the USA some time about 1840. The similarities in design with the Welsh chair pictured on page 117 are obvious.*

119

◂ *Although the Shakers themselves have now died out, light but strong furniture is still being made to their classic designs. This chair, in maple with a cotton webbing back and seat, is a reproduction piece. Period Shaker furniture can be very expensive; many pieces are now in museums.*

FURNITURE

MASS PRODUCTION

THE ACCESSION OF VICTORIA to the throne in 1837 heralded a new age in Britain, when the middle classes, who had recently emerged in the wake of the Industrial Revolution, began to reject anything that smacked of the 18th century.

120

Machine production methods were developed rapidly at this time, and factories began to create furniture for the new markets that was intended to be more functional than decorative. There was a proliferation of commercial furniture styles, including mock-Elizabethan or Tudor, Georgian revival and a popular Victorian version of Rococo. By the 1880s, the wheel had came full circle, and 18th-century styles were being revived. Typical of the time are mass-produced 'Chippendale' chairs with square or cabriole legs.

In France, bourgeois fashion opted much less for solid respectability than for an eclectic revival of earlier styles – or for chairs and stools, as was said at the time, 'in the style of all the Louis'. The Gothic 'troubadour' style, for example, gave rise to chairs with cusped arcading to the back and cluster-columned arm supports and legs, while armchairs of a 17th-century or baroque style were heavily embellished.

▲ *The back of this late 19th-century balloon-back English dining chair is vaguely reminiscent of the style of the late 18th-century designer George Hepplewhite, although the turned and carved legs are typically Victorian.*

FURNITURE

◄ *The nursing chair, with its low seat and high back was a 19th-century development. It was intended for use by women nursing infants and was usually regarded as a piece of bedroom furniture. The colourful floral tapestry work of the upholstery here is typical of mid-19th-century taste in Britain and Europe.*

▲ *The balloon-back shape was very popular in the second half of the 19th century. This is a good example in mahogany with curved crest rail, turned and reeded legs and the original leather upholstery.*

▸ *Chippendale's designs never really went out of fashion. This mahogany chair of 1880 is a good pastiche of the style; the main difference is the rather stiff, formalized look given by machine carving rather than the free-flowing look of 18th-century work.*

FURNITURE
CRAFTSMEN-DESIGNERS

122

THE DEVELOPMENT OF CHAIR design in 19th-century North America closely parallels that in Europe. At the beginning of the 19th century, French Empire styles prevailed, and up to about 1850 styles varied in America much as they did in Europe. The revival of Louis XV Rococo gave rise to button-back armchairs with pronounced scrolls, cabriole legs and leaf carving. Georgian styles were also revived in the United States, although in this case it was specifically the resurrection of the country's Georgian colonial past.

In the latter half of the 19th century and on into the 20th, various craftsmen-designers in Britain and the USA reacted against such bland revivalist styles and, influenced by the Arts and Crafts Movement and various new theories of design, began to make simple, elegant chairs that drew on country styles. Today they are among the most collectable and most expensive of all chairs.

▸ *This is an original oak chair by the British Arts and Crafts designer Charles Voysey (1857–1941). It evokes country styles with its rush seat and simple decoration: a heart-shaped piercing in the splat.*

FURNITURE

◀ *The company established by William Morris (1834–96) managed to apply Arts and Crafts principles to something like mass production. This rush-seated, ebonized Sussex chair was introduced in 1865 and produced in large numbers thereafter by teams of craftsmen.*

123

▶ *The main stylistic inspiration of E W Godwin (1833–86) was Japan, a country with no tradition of seat furniture. Godwin interpreted the style, making ebonized chairs that were all straight lines and planes, with delicate, even spindly legs and stretchers. The back and seat on this one are nade from woven cane.*

▲ *The ladderback is another country chair design given an Arts and Crafts overhaul by the designer Ernest Gimson (1864– 1919). The chairs were produced at Gimson's workshop in the depths of rural England.*

FURNITURE

BENTWOOD

▾ *Rocking chairs are naturals for bentwood design techniques; Gebrüder Thonet advertised more than 40 versions of curvaceous rockers in their 1904 catalogue. In this version, each side of the chair is made up of just three pieces of bent wood, making it strong but light – the hallmark of all good bentwood furniture.*

124

IN THE CAFÉS AND BARS of late-19th and early-20th-century Europe, as well as in many homes, simple mass-produced chairs in bentwood held sway. The spread of bentwood furniture was the result of the work of Michael Thonet (1796–1871), the founder of Gebrüder Thonet, an Austrian company whose factories were producing 4000 pieces a day at the turn of the 20th century. Thonet was trained as a cabinetmaker in the Biedermeier style and first experimented with bending and gluing wood in the 1830s. The technique of bending timber using steam was not new, but Thonet found a way of doing so without splitting the wood, and in 1849 established a company of his own in Vienna. It specialized in making bentwood pieces out of birch, which has long, whippy fibres that make it ideal for bending.

Chairs – with seats of cane or, later, pressed wood – were the speciality of Gebrüder Thonet, although other pieces were made. Each was given a special model number to facilitate re-ordering: since its introduction in 1859, more than 50 million copies have been made of chair no.14. Thonet is rarely given the credit he deserves for his innovative designs and methods, which had a great influence on Modernist furniture of the 20th century, particularly that made in tubular steel; indeed, the company began making such chairs in 1923.

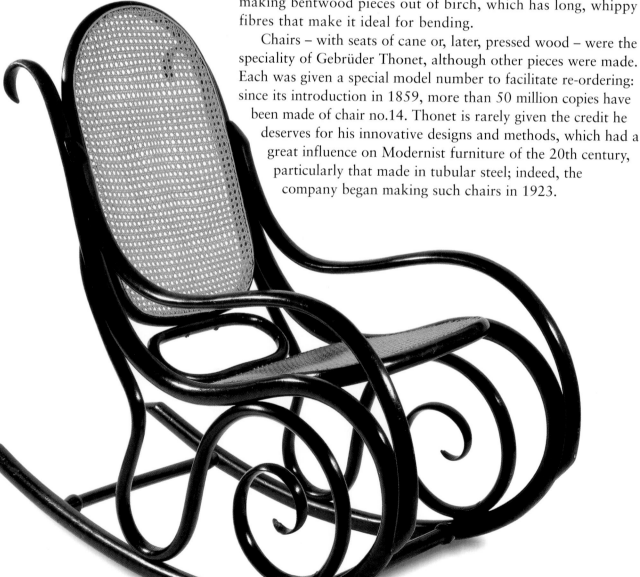

FURNITURE

▼ *A humble magazine rack is transformed in Thonet piece no. 11801 into a brilliant creation with Rococo flourishes.*

125

▲ *All Thonet's designs were numbered. One of his most popular chairs, no. 19, had a solid seat; others were caned, while many chairs were produced on request in upholstered versions.*

▶ *This nest of tables with tapering legs was made around the end of the 19th century by one of Thonet's rivals, the Fischel company.*

FURNITURE
THE TWENTIETH CENTURY

126

THE COMMERCIAL MARKET IN REVIVAL STYLES of furniture continued to be important into the 20th century and throughout the Art Nouveau, then Art Deco periods. These design movements did, however, leave their mark on chair design. During the Art Nouveau period, innovative design was expressed in the high-backed, formally beautiful and often frankly uncomfortable chairs of the Scotsman Charles Rennie Mackintosh, as well as in the increased use of lightweight, previously marginal materials such as wicker, cane, bamboo and even, in the case of the Lloyd Loom process, woven, paper-covered wires.

▸ *The decorative canework of this 1920s chair and its walnut veneers hark back to earlier styles, but the shape looks forward to the bergère styles of the 1930s.*

▲ *Modern copies of old styles were by no means all poorly-produced. This chaise longue, for example, made c.1910, gives a new twist to a 19th-century piece by providing it with a gallery – the extended, padded, straight armrest, which is supported by a serpentine strut carved in a free, Art Nouveau style.*

FURNITURE

▶ Made around 1920, this steamer chair in wicker and bamboo combined a rigid but lightweight construction with an adaptability that allowed the user – who was typically someone on an ocean cruise – to sit up and read or lie back and take in the sun.

▶ The Lloyd Loom process, by which furniture was made from woven wire and paper, was developed in the USA during World War I. Lloyd Loom factories turned out cheap, lightweight furniture in basic styles painted with soft pastel colours. This chair is characteristic of the early ranges.

FURNITURE

IN THE 1920S AND 1930S, seat furniture, on the whole, ranged from the severely functional to opulent, well-padded and extraordinarily comfortable. Art Deco and Modernist designers introduced yet more new materials, including chrome, plywood and bent tubular steel, while during a general proliferation of easy chairs – this was the era of the three-piece suite consisting of a sofa and two easy chairs – there was a revival of the bergère form, a kind of lightweight armchair with a low back and down-curving arms that had originated in 18th-century France.

▼ *This selection of dining chairs from the 1930s includes (clockwise from the left): a leather chair with a solid back in bird's-eye maple; a birchwood design by the Finn, Alvaar Alto; a velvet-seated, curved-back chair in walnut; and one with a leather seat and mahogany veneer.*

FURNITURE

▶ *The chunky, rounded shapes and style of the pattern on the original cut-napped fabric identify this armchair as dating from the 1930s. It was made and sold as part of a three-piece suite, which were all the vogue at the time.*

129

◀ *Art deco tub bergères had deep seats and low curved backs that continued through the arms in a single, sweeping curve. As the sprung and padded seat was deep, such bergères were often made without legs. The ribbed panels of ebonized wood beneath the arms in this example are typical of the style and time.*

FURNITURE
TABLES

130

I N THE MIDDLE AGES, it was rare to find a solid, well-made table. Most people – even the relatively wealthy – ate from, and worked at, boards mounted on trestles. When not in use, these were dismantled and put aside against a wall to save space.

The basic form of the table as we know it today – four legs joined to a frame on which a fixed top rests – first became popular in the 17th century. These early tables were very solid, with their legs and stretchers often heavily embellished with turning and deep-cut carving, and tended to be fashioned from solid oak or walnut. Some 17th-century dining or refectory tables are among the most massive pieces of furniture ever made. These early tables were not veneered.

Around 1640, some simple French walnut tables had a tray top and a drawer supported on octagonal tapering legs, which were joined by a curved 'X' stretcher. In England at this time, gate-leg tables in oak, ash, elm, walnut or yew were much in use. They combined the permanence of the new tables with some of the space-saving convenience of trestles. The gatelegs were frames, hinged like a gate, that could swing out to support hinged, drop-leaf flaps, These tables typically had turned legs, usually simple columns or spirals but sometimes more elaborate work.

In the Low Countries, tables were still very much in the oak country tradition, generally with bulbous legs. By the end of the 17th century, when the Low Countries had became famous for its marquetry, more sophisticated pieces were produced with floral or other designs raised on ebonized, spiral-turned legs.

In the 18th century, the number of types of table proliferated, with the creation of several kinds of small occasional table for use in drawing and living rooms. These included work tables, card tables, and various types of table made to stand against a wall. Among these was the console table, an important item of Italian furniture, while in France during the reign of Louis XV (1723-74), side tables and *bureaux plats* (writing tables) were extremely popular. A typical French side table of the time had curved cabriole legs with bronze-gilt mounts.

FURNITURE

▲ *Small occasional tables such as this were relatively common in Britain around 1750; the cabriole legs and ball-and-claw feet are typical of the period, as is the 'fold-over' top. The top is hinged in the middle and unfolds and swivels through 90 degrees to double its size when needed, while still resting on the same frame.*

FURNITURE

THE 18TH CENTURY

WITH THE INCREASED INFLUENCE of Neo-classicism in the 1770s, French tables became more austere in shape and included various Greco-Roman motifs. Tables made during the 'Directoire' period (1795–99), just after the Revolution, were even more classical in inspiration. The style known as 'Etruscan' was particularly favoured in Paris.

132

Small tripod tables for taking tea were popular in Britain in the 18th century, while other forms were developed for playing cards – at that time, card games were one of the principle recreations of the wealthy – as work-tables, or for use in libraries. Curiosities from the first half of the century include mahogany games tables with baize tops, scoops for counters and cabriole legs carved with acanthus leaves and ball-and-claw feet. Later pieces included tripod tables that had a hinged, galleried top mounted on a four-pillar 'birdcage' mechanism, so the top could be tipped up and the table placed against a wall when not in use, displaying the often decorative top.

▼ *Tilt-top tables often had decorative tops so that they would look well when stored against a wall in the upright position. This one, made at the end of the century, has a well-figured mahogany top edged with cross-banding in rosewood.*

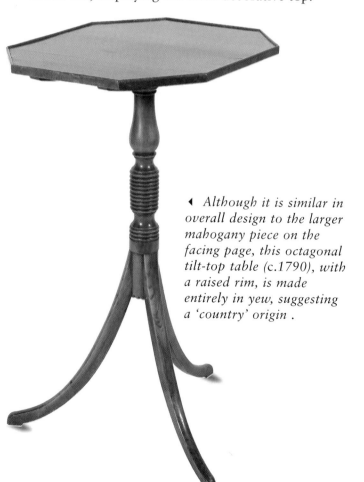

◀ *Although it is similar in overall design to the larger mahogany piece on the facing page, this octagonal tilt-top table (c.1790), with a raised rim, is made entirely in yew, suggesting a 'country' origin .*

FURNITURE

◄ This tilt-top pedestal tea table is typical of English work from about 1760. Although it is relatively simple, with just a little turned decoration, it is well proportioned – when in the 'up' position the edge of the table top should come to rest just above the legs. The table is made of solid mahogany and the top is all one piece of wood; 18th-century tea tables were never veneered.

133

FURNITURE

IN SCANDINAVIA, SIMPLE, sturdy furniture was made in the prevailing European – and more particularly Dutch and German – styles. Some wood was imported, but most furniture, including tables, was made of native pine or deal, decorated with carving and paintwork. A Swedish speciality was to cover the tops of tables not with veneer but with ceramic tiles, some of them specially made for the purpose but others just as likely to be older than the table.

134

Across the Atlantic, tables in the 18th century benefited from a growing mixture of immigrants, including French and Germans as well as English craftsmen, who each brought their native traditions with them and helped to produce a healthy eclecticism of design. Native woods such as American cherry, walnut and pine were used extensively.

▲ *Chinese tiles from the 17th century form the top of this Swedish table dating from the 1790s and determine its colour scheme. Although pine is too soft to take detailed carving it is fine for repetitive pattern work such as the fluting on the tapered legs and the dentil moulding around the apron.*

▲ *This mahogany side table, with its tapering legs and spade feet, is typical of late-19th-century styles. To maintain the plain, even severe lines, there are no handles on the three drawers, which are pulled using a lip that projects down over the frame.*

FURNITURE

Dumbwaiters

Dumbwaiters – two- or three-tiered trays mounted on a central pillar supported by a tripod base – were first made in 18th-century England, but soon spread to France and Germany. They remained popular items until the 1830s.

They were meant for use throughout an informal meal, or at the end of a formal one, when they were laden with sweetmeats. The idea was the same in both cases; servants would load the dumb-waiter, then withdraw, leaving diners to talk without being overheard. Sometimes the trays were fixed; others had a telescopic action, so the piece could be used as an occasional table.

Dumbwaiters continued to be made as period pieces in period styles until around the beginning of World War I. Subsequently, many surviving early examples have been cut down in order to pass them off as more valuable tripod tea tables. The tell-tale mark of this is a filled central hole in the table-top.

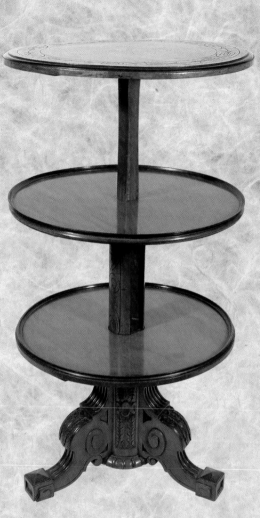

▲ In a telescopic dumbwaiter, pushing down on the top tray also raises the bottom tray so that all three fit together in the middle at the height of an occasional table.

◀ The best way to tell an 18th-century dumbwaiter from a later, machine-made reproduction, such as this, is to check the thickness of the trays. On earlier examples, they are always much thicker.

FURNITURE

SOFA TABLES

136

A POPULAR FORM OF SIDE TABLE that was developed in
England towards the end of the 18th century was the
sofa table. These tall, narrow tables were made to stand
behind a sofa, at that time itself a relatively new form of
furniture. Early sofa tables were typically raised on cheval
supports – a pair of sabre legs joined by a ring-turned stretcher –
with one, two or three drawers in a single flight on one side. The
piece soon became popular all over Europe.

As the sofa table evolved, it began to acquire drop ends,
rather like those seen on a Pembroke table – another table form
developed at the time that could be extended when needed.
Early 19th-century examples of sofa tables were often raised
on a pedestal, rather than a cheval base, and by the mid-19th
century the form had developed into something that was
altogether more substantial.

▲ *This rosewood sofa table from the
1840s, with a heavy pedestal base, has
evolved a long way from the original
concept of a light, portable piece.*

FURNITURE

▲ The stretcher is done away with altogether in this English Regency design in favour of a curved and scrolled support that would allow someone to sit at the table and write or work.

◄ Early sofa tables tended to have a cheval base – single uprights at each end with splayed legs. This elegant mahogany sofa table with a double stretcher was made in the 19th century to an 18th-century design.

◄ Sofa tables acquired drop ends, brass mounts on the feet and cheval supports in the shape of lyres early in the 19th century. Better examples, such as this, had fake drawer fronts on the other side so that the table would still look good when pulled away from the sofa as a free-standing piece.

FURNITURE
THE NINETEENTH CENTURY

138

I N REGENCY ENGLAND (although George IV was regent for his father for just 10 years, 1810–20, the term tends to be used as a shorthand for the first quarter or so of the century), tables were styled with a modified French Empire classicism. There was a vogue for pedestal supports, with a central pillar raised on a solid base with four very short legs. This meant that people could sit around a table without tangling its legs with their own.

The famous craftsman George Bullock, who specialized in marquetry, made some fine dining tables from satinwood. These usually had rounded rectangular tops cross-banded in rosewood, a solid satinwood base and a pedestal support hinged like a tea table so that the top could be tipped up and the table cleared to the side of the room when not in use. This elegant, decorative style soon spread to other nations in Europe.

In France, the Empire style saw the production of common designs for table bases known as guéridons. The tables typically had marble tops and a single central column set on either a flat triangular base, perhaps with metal mounts, or paw feet.

▸ *Made in Denmark in the 1820s, this is a wonderfully opulent tilt-top table. A very simple mahogany tripod base supports a top in which a pictorial roundel is set in mahogany and enclosed in a design marked out in ebonized fruitwood, birch, satinwood and rosewood.*

FURNITURE

◀ The leather top, long legs and drawers (the drawer fronts on the ends of the table are fakes) mark this out as a library table. It is an English Regency piece, with the commonly found tapering legs of the time, enhanced with unusual spiral-turned decoration.

139

▶ Console tables – tall, narrow tables made to stand against a wall and support ornaments or a mirror – became popular in early-19th-century Europe. This example in marble and mahogany with decorative ormolu mounts is characteristic of the French Empire style, but was made in Sweden for an aristocratic client.

◀ The introduction of the central pedestal support was an elegant solution to the design problem of creating large tables with other than a rectangular top. Here, an octagonal example sits on a tapered column and a platform with four feet. It dates from around 1835.

FURNITURE

A DRUM TABLE

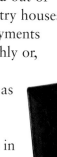RUM TABLES, WHICH HAD A ROUND TOP and a frieze of drawers, first appeared at the end of the 18th century. They evolved out of the so-called rent table, devised for country houses and designed to store rent books and payments from tenants. As this was at best a monthly or, more usually, an annual task, the drum table earned its keep the rest of the time as a hall table or in a library or, perhaps, smoking room.

This example was made in the 1820s in Brazilian rosewood, which yields a deep, lustrous shine and was particularly popular at the time. It is larger than most drum tables at 1.2m in diameter and this, coupled with the fine craftsmanship, suggest the piece was made for a rather large house.

It is set on a pedestal made up of a concave, triform platform with three finely-carved scroll feet and a column that is hexagonal at the top but carved into a lappeted (hanging) lotus flower below.

There are eight steam-curved drawer fronts, alternately real and fake, around the circumference. All are lined with oak and decorated with stringing, beading and simple brass escutcheons.

The top has a reeded edge – echoed in the sides of the pedestal platform – with cross-banding around the outside and a tooled leather insert. The whole top can be made to revolve on its pedestal without too much effort – a sure sign of high-quality workmanship.

FURNITURE

▲ *The drum table lifts off its pedestal to reveal the wooden peg, set into the column, on which the whole top revolves.*

FURNITURE

ROCOCO

LTHOUGH THE FALL of Napoleon effectively signalled the end of the pure Empire style, the design of tables in France continued to bear the stamp of Neo-classicism during the 1820s, but by this time some Rococo elements had been added, hinting at the revival of the style in the middle of the-century. A shortage of mahogany caused by the British blockade of France during the Napoleonic Wars led to the extensive use of native woods, or bois clairs. This continued after the blockade was over. Cherrywood or poplar console tables of around 1825 had white and grey marble tops, with bold, cabriole scrolled legs instead of the Empire-style columns of the early years of the century.

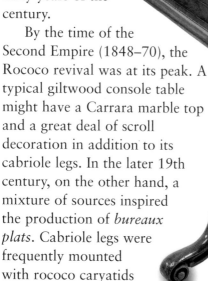

By the time of the Second Empire (1848–70), the Rococo revival was at its peak. A typical giltwood console table might have a Carrara marble top and a great deal of scroll decoration in addition to its cabriole legs. In the later 19th century, on the other hand, a mixture of sources inspired the production of *bureaux plats*. Cabriole legs were frequently mounted with rococo caryatids and masks, as well as Neo–classical panels.

The Victorian period in England saw the creation of solid, heavy tables that personified middle-class respectability and wealth. Extending dining tables were produced in large numbers. The rather aggressively cabriole-legged mahogany version of *c*.1860 had an undulating outline that included carved acanthus leaf, husks and scroll feet ending in gadroons.

▼ *A popular reproduction style was the swivel top card table, which served as a side table when not in use but opened out to make a square card table with a green baize top. The elaborate and mechanically precise carving and turning of the cheval support identify this piece as a 19th-century reproduction.*

142

FURNITURE

Smaller furniture, too, became more substantial than it had been during the 17th century, and the legs on tripod tables tended in some instances almost to disappear into a floor-level plinth. New materials, such as papier mâché, and new influences from around the world also became evident in furniture styles.

With the Gothic revival of the mid-century, tables and other solid furniture emulated stonework rather than wood. Indeed, the central column of a dining table designed by A W N Pugin had the kind of extensive architectural modelling that would not have looked amiss on the spire of a medieval church.

▸ *Papier-mâché was used surprisingly often to make small pieces of furniture, which were usually 'japanned' in imitation of oriental lacquerwork, in the 19th century. Its combination of strength and lightness made it suitable for occasional tables. This piece is based on an 18th-century tea-table.*

▲ *Tripod tables from the 19th century can be identified by their generally sturdier shape, with short, thick legs and a bottom-heavy baluster to aid stability. In addition, the carved decoration present on the stem, was never seen on 18th-century pieces.*

FURNITURE

AT THE SAME TIME, the new urban middle classes had an urgent need to display their ever-growing collections of family knick-knacks and treasures. As a result of this, an increasing number and variety of side and occasional tables was produced in Europe and the USA to accommodate and display them.

In the USA, the mid-century French revival of Neo-classical styles, dubbed 'Neo-grec', introduced firmer, straighter lines to American tables, which were by then being mass produced. The commercial end of the furniture business – serving an ever-increasing market – dominated in the USA and all over Britain and Europe as the 19th century progressed. More and more, mechanized factories produced cheap pieces with pine carcasses and paper-thin machine-cut veneers of mahogany and walnut. Such ornament as there was on tables was generally a pastiche of earlier styles.

Some craftsmen went against the grain of mass production, influenced by a contemporary best-seller, *Hints on Household Taste* by Charles Locke Eastlake (1836–1906), which advocated simple, honest construction and little decoration, and the influence of the Arts and Crafts Movement and Art Nouveau.could be seen in much late 19th-century furniture.

144

▲ *Small but well-made side and occasional tables from the 19th century are greatly in demand today. This simple mahogany side table, with its turned legs and brass fittings and castors, is a good example of the continued influence of elegant Regency style during Victorian times.*

FURNITURE

◀ *The growing influence of Art Nouveau shows in the graceful lines of this nest of four occasional tables, or quartetto. The influence of the Japanese taste can also be seen in its spindly, elongated legs and ebonized finish. The combination dates the quartetto to the late 1880s or early 1890s.*

145

▲ *European furniture began to feel the influence of various other cultures in the second half of the 19th century. This hexagonal table is Islamic in design and has lines in Arabic inlaid as a decoration, but was made in Europe for those who liked a taste of the exotic in their furnishings.*

◀ *This mahogany table of around the turn of the 20th century shows many features redolent of Art Nouveau. The scrolled legs with carved leaves, the free-flowing lines of the pierced stretchers and the wonderfully sinuous version of an octagonal top all reflect the style. The top has a floral marquetry pattern laid on walnut edged with satinwood. The vivid green and red stains of the marquetry flowers have now faded; when first made, the table top would have been brilliantly colourful.*

FURNITURE

EVERYDAY TABLES

Tables in mahogany and rosewood tended to be reserved for special rooms and special occasions, even in the houses of the relatively wealthy. Most people worked and ate at more humble tables. Often meals were taken at the same table at which they were prepared.

146

Kitchen tables had to be sturdy enough to provide a useful work surface yet sufficiently comfortable for the householders – or their servants in middle- and upper-class establishments – to sit and eat their meals. Such furniture was generally made with whatever came to hand – sycamore, elm, or oak were all used extensively – but in 19th-century Europe it was increasingly made of various softwoods imported from Scandinavia that were known generically as pine or deal.

▸ *Sweden was the spiritual home of all pine furniture. This piece c.1780 was never painted, although gilt detailing has been added.*

▲ *The standard design for a kitchen table on both sides of the Atlantic in the 19th century was a rectangular frame with plain or turned legs. There were no stretchers, so people could sit at it and eat, and a single long drawer in the apron was used for storing cutlery, linen and kitchen tools. The top was a board made up of three to six joined planks of pine.*

FURNITURE

By the second half of the 19th century, pine was being used for the carcasses of virtually all cheap, plain furniture in Europe and the USA. Sometimes it was veneered – although this was rare in the case of tables – but more often it would have been painted or left undecorated. Although pine furniture was not always built to last, much of it has survived to the present day.

▸ *An alternative style for the pine kitchen table was for it to have drop sides and a drawer in one or both ends. While the legs and frame were often painted, the tops of kitchen tables were always left as bare boards, suitable for food preparation as well as for eating.*

147

▸ *This pine side table would not have looked out of place in the 1930s, when both the demi-lune shape and three-legged side tables were particularly popular. It was, however, made in the mid-19th century.*

FURNITURE
THE GATELEG TABLE

148

▼ *Gateleg tables traditionally have turned legs and sometimes stretchers as well. This example is from the late 19th century, and is veneered in walnut. It is a relatively large table, with a wider than usual frame.*

SOME TYPES OF TABLE went through the 19th century virtually unchanged. The gate-leg table, which first made its appearance in the 17th century, had continued to evolve through to the latter half of the 18th century. Its design became increasingly sophisticated, with the appearance of variant forms such as the Sutherland table.

After that, it went out of fashion for a while, and continued as a piece of country furniture – often in oak, for strength – until it came back into vogue as part of the general craft-related reaction against factory production late in the 19th century.

Its obvious usefulness as a piece of space-saving furniture in the increasingly cramped apartments and rooms of the 20th century meant that, although its form changed to suit new fashions and materials, it retained its popularity.

FURNITURE

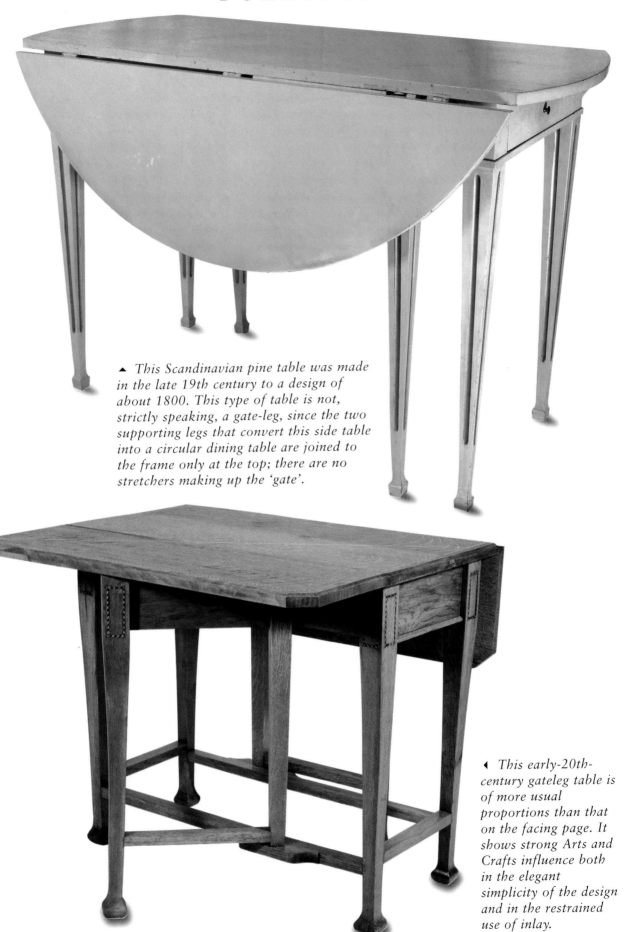

▲ *This Scandinavian pine table was made in the late 19th century to a design of about 1800. This type of table is not, strictly speaking, a gate-leg, since the two supporting legs that convert this side table into a circular dining table are joined to the frame only at the top; there are no stretchers making up the 'gate'.*

149

◄ *This early-20th-century gateleg table is of more usual proportions than that on the facing page. It shows strong Arts and Crafts influence both in the elegant simplicity of the design and in the restrained use of inlay.*

FURNITURE
THE TWENTIETH CENTURY

150

INFLUENCED BY THE THE ARTS AND CRAFTS Movement and Art Nouveau, which both in their different ways advocated a return to plain materials, American designers in the first 20 years of the century sought to use solid wood rather than veneers on tables, and to have exposed joints and few curves.

The first two decades of the 20th century in Europe were dominated by Art Nouveau. The style was not suited to massive dining tables, but centres in Paris, Vienna, Nancy, Munich, Brussels and Milan produced side, tea and occasional tables that were original in design without being divorced from the past.

While many Art Nouveau tables had legs carved to represent stylized plant stems and tops decorated with flowers in marquetry, a *guéridon* by the French master Émile Gallé (1846–1904), for instance, has three legs in the manner of neo-classical monopodia, while tables by Louis Majorelle have cabriole legs mounted with orchids in ormolu that owe much to early Rococo style. In Italy, Bugatti was making coffee tables strongly influenced by Moorish designs.

Large Art Nouveau tables are scarce, and collectors may find small side or occasional tables more easily.

▼ *The French Art Nouveau designer Gallé was responsible for this nest of four tables in walnut. Each has a different inlaid design on the top.*

FURNITURE

▶ This occasional table by Gallé has an extraordinary lightness and portability, emphasised by the inclusion of handles in the tray top. A touch of the exotic is added by the marquetry scene of camels in a desert landscape and the faux-bamboo legs.

◀ This inlaid three-cornered table with a solid stretcher is typical of the flowing work produced by Louis Majorelle, and is signed by him.

▶ The exciting new lines and forms of Art Nouveau – or Jugendstil as it was known in Austria and Germany – were well suited to bentwood. Gebrüder Thonet produced table 9104, with a top and shelf covered in green baize, at the turn of the century.

FURNITURE

WHILE SOME ART NOUVEAU designers, such as Louis Majorelle, continued to work into the 1930s, from 1920 to 1940 furniture styles were dominated by Modernism and Art Deco. Many Modernist tables are severe in design, with glass or plain wood tops on tubular steel frames, while Art Deco designers used a mix of expensive timbers and veneers with new materials such as plywood and decorative mounts in silver and/or ormolu.

Such pieces managed to reconcile traditional comfort and luxury with a modern feeling for abstract shape. Dining and side tables rarely bore any decoration other than their veneers, and were supported either on plain legs or a U-shaped pedestal. The console table was revived as a form by Art Deco designers, and the long, low coffee table, usually placed in front of a sofa, became an established furniture form.

At the same time, with apartment dwelling in cities becoming the rule rather than the exception in the USA, there was a huge demand for space-saving dining tables. One based on early draw-leaf tables was mass-produced from 1920-1940. The top was made in three sections rested on a square-sectioned frame. The two outer 'leaves' were fixed to bearers that slid in and out under the main surface, which dropped into position between them when the table was extended, and completely hid them when it was closed. This practical style was soon adopted in Europe.

152

▼ *This plain round table, veneered in curly birch, and the chair (one of a set of four) were both designed by the Finnish Art Deco master Alvar Aalto.*

FURNITURE

153

▲ The U-shaped pedestal support was a common feature of Art Deco dining tables. It was not always in such a heavy form as in this walnut veneered example from the 1930s.

◀ Console tables in the Art Deco period were often made of metal, with marble tops, but this one is in a satinwood veneer with ebony stringing and distinctive square feet.

FURNITURE
CHESTS & DRESSERS

154

THE LIDDED, BOX-LIKE CHEST is one of the most ancient pieces of furniture. Until at least 1650, it was the principal form of storage for clothes and personal possessions. Thereafter, it was gradually replaced by cupboards and chests of drawers, although in many rural areas it survived as a traditional type. Some chests functioned more as safes than simple storage furniture, being used to hold the family silver and other valuables, and were often fitted with heavy, complex iron locks.

By about 1620, Renaissance styles were gradually being replaced in Europe. As far as chests were concerned, the Italian cassoni of a rectangular, 'sarcophagus' type were superseded by curved carcasses that suited the Baroque style of decoration. The woods used for the manufacture of chests varied enormously – from oak in the Low Countries and Germany to walnut, oak and chestnut in Spain. Some chests – obviously intended as safes – were made of iron.

Early 17th-century Italian cassoni often have one large front panel on which are carved figures, scrolls or coats of arms. In Denmark, chests of boarded construction were carved with love tokens or with patterns simulating the strapping on iron chests.

Most surviving old chests are of a basic 'country' construction, with a frame and panel box topped with a sturdy hinged lid, and perhaps raised off the ground on four simple feet made by extending the framework of the chest. Sometimes these feet may be worn from centuries of sitting on a stone floor, soaked by mopping and battered by brooms. Such aging can actually add to the value of a piece.

In the 18th century, chests tended to take on a more solid, box-like construction without legs. Another popular form, the sea-chest, had a half-cylinder lid instead of a flat one.

▶ *The basic frame and panel construction of this American chest suggests an early date. Chests of this type were rarely made after 1700.*

▶ *After 1700, chests tended to be of the box type that is more familiar to modern eyes. This large dower chest is also American and is painted in the Pennsylvania Dutch style, it includes a date: 1807.*

FURNITURE

TALLBOYS

156

ATE 17TH-CENTURY European chests of drawers and cabinets were often mounted on stands, which usually had drawers of their own. Although they were well supplied with storage-space, these chests on stands were basically show pieces, canvasses for the art of the veneerer.

While cabinets-on-stands continued to be made, after around 1700 chests-on-stands gradually gave way to a very imposing piece of practical furniture, known in the USA as the tallboy. This piece, effectively two chests of drawers one on top of the other, provided plenty of storage for household linen and clothing, although the need to keep the chests in proportion meant the top drawer was often placed more than 2m from the ground.

Tallboys were out of fashion for most of the 19th and much of the 20th century, when 18th-century pieces were often broken down to form two chests of drawers. Their increased rarity, and a new appreciation of their qualities, has meant that their price has gone up, and buyers must now beware of 'marriages', where two old chests have been put together to look like a tallboy.

▶ *Good tallboys reveal their quality in their overall proportion as well as fine detailing. This English example of c.1750 is typical, with bracket feet and a top chest slightly smaller than the bottom one and topped with a cornice. Decorative moulding hides the joint, and the two chests are integrated by the continuous lines of brass fittings and the mahogany veneers.*

FURNITURE

▶ While the tallboy was developed by 'filling in' the stand of the chest on a stand with extra drawers, the so-called lowboy resembled nothing more than the stand of a chest-on-stand with slightly longer legs and a good top. This example in walnut dates from 1715.

▾ A slightly later and more rustic version of the tallboy, this piece has just two drawers below and frame-panelled sides. It was made in the Channel Islands c.1780.

▲ A chest on a stand from c.1720 shows just how imposing and decorative such a piece could be when veneered in fine walnut. The swan-neck drop handles, cabriole legs and pad feet are typical of the time.

FURNITURE

THE CLOTHES PRESS

158

THE CLOTHES PRESS WAS a 17th-century introduction. It was essentially a chest of drawers with a cupboard containing shelves above. In the 18th century, it became an essential item of bedroom or dressing room furniture, and was typically made in oak or mahogany. The clothes press was a major step in the evolution of the basic cupboard, or armoire, of the 16th century into the modern wardrobe, with a shelf or shelves below and a tall cupboard with hanging space above. This first appeared around 1800.

In the 19th century, the choice between using a wardrobe or a clothes press depended on people's attitude to their clothes. Before the invention of the clothes hanger at the end of the century, all clothes had to be hung on hooks, which tended to pull them out of shape if they were left unworn for too long. Anyone who cared about their clothes, but was not planning to wear them for a while, would put them away folded in a clothes press to preserve their shape.

▸ *A top full of open-fronted slider drawers – often made of fragrant woods such as cedar in the belief they repelled moths – is what distinguishes a clothes press from a wardrobe. This is a late 18th-century example.*

FURNITURE

▸ *This large oak press was made c.1800. The drawer arrangement is unusual, as are the shaped panel doors, but the piece has the standard bracket feet and a cornice with dentil moulding.*

▲ *As with tallboys, fine presses are distinguished by their proportions and the quality of the veneers. This piece from the 1830s has a relatively plain shape, but the door panels are veneered with matching sheets of flame mahogany, one of the most highly figured of all veneers.*

▸ *By the 1840s, presses had begun to receive more decoration. The carved cornice, side columns and patterned doors – with a satinwood shell motif laid into a rich, red mahogany veneer – mark this out as a mid-century piece.*

FURNITURE

SIDEBOARDS & CHIFFONIERS

SIDEBOARDS AS WE KNOW THEM TODAY – dining-room furniture with drawers and cupboards for storing cutlery, table glass, linen and so on – first appeared towards the end of the 18th century. They evolved from simple side tables from which food was served. The 18th-century additions of pedestal bases with cupboards for knife cases, plate-warmers and so on, plus a wine cooler below and and urns on top, created a new form of furniture.

Such boards were generally the preserve of grand houses that entertained lavishly. So-called cellaret sideboards, more modest pieces with a row of drawers beneath the board, were popular with the growing middle classes around the turn of the 19th century. They were used to display the family's treasures – ornamental pieces in ceramics, glass and silver – as much as they were as an adjunct to dining.

Later in the 19th century, the chiffonier tended to supplant the cellaret in middle-class homes. This was a more solid piece that sat on a plain plinth rather than stood on legs. The base was a pair of cupboards – with perhaps a central drawer below the board – and a raised back that, as the century went on, tended to become ever more elaborate. Sideboards and chiffoniers dating from the late 19th century tend to be large and ornate, even fussy in style.

160

▼ This British sideboard nods in the direction of the Arts and Crafts Movement in some of its details, but is a machine-made piece from the 1880s or '90s. Sideboard backs had become much more elaborate as the display function of the piece became more important and often included mirrors, as here.

FURNITURE

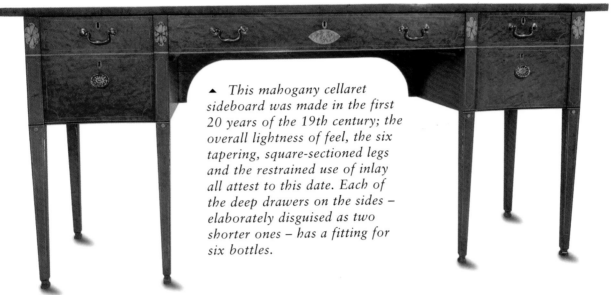

▲ *This mahogany cellaret sideboard was made in the first 20 years of the 19th century; the overall lightness of feel, the six tapering, square-sectioned legs and the restrained use of inlay all attest to this date. Each of the deep drawers on the sides – elaborately disguised as two shorter ones – has a fitting for six bottles.*

▲ *By the end of the 19th century, the distinction between sideboards and display cabinets could sometimes become a little blurred. This piece, with its profusion of glass, open shelving, turned galleries and inlaid panels, is a long way from the simple cellaret sideboards of a century earlier.*

▶ *This chiffonier was made about 10–15 years after the cellaret pictured above and is obviously much heavier and more solid in construction, with carved rather than inlaid decoration. The doors are a lattice of brass over coloured silk.*

FURNITURE
CHESTS OF DRAWERS

▼ *Even in the 18th century, chests of drawers were as likely to be functional pieces of pine rather than* tours de force *of veneering. Many of these chests were originally sold painted – although it is unlikely on this piece – but it is rare to find such an example now, particularly after the fashion for stripping pine to create a country look took hold in the 1970s and 1980s.*

I N 18TH-CENTURY FRANCE the chest of drawers – or commode as it was then known – gradually superseded the low, old-fashioned chest as the main item of storage furniture. Such pieces were often spectacularly formed and decorated. The great French craftsman Boulle, for instance, made a beautiful pair of curved chests of drawers for Louis XIV in 1708-09. Lesser, but still wealthy, patrons of the time were content with three-drawer 'bombé' commodes, with curved fronts and sides. By the 1730s, the full bombé shape with curves from top to bottom and side to side had become popular throughout Europe.

By the mid-18th century, however, the growing fashion for Neo-classical lines meant that some rejected the bombé shape, although it continued to be popular in Germany, the Low Countries and Sweden. Otherwise, chests of drawers tended to have sleeker outlines, with straight sides and serpentine or bow fronts and the use of rich mahogany and rosewood veneers, although lavish marquetry decoration remained popular in France well into the Empire period.

FURNITURE

▶ *Although the fashion for curved and bombé shapes was on the wane, the French were still making fine commodes early in the 19th century. This example from 1810 has a mass of decorative detail in brass and gilt, including the paw feet, key escutcheons and pilasters.*

◀ *This tall chest in the Biedermeier style was made in Germany from birchwood. The only decoration, aside from the handsome veneer, is a little restrained ebonizing on the key escutcheons.*

▲ *New ways of using steam to bend wood allowed 19th-century commercial makers of chests of drawers to emulate the bow and serpentine fronts of the 18th century much more cheaply. This chest from the 1860s has a mild bow and the then-popular soft, glossy mahogany finish.*

FURNITURE

164

BETWEEN 1815 AND ABOUT 1850, chests of drawers became plainer and more functional pieces of furniture: they were by then an essential item of every bourgeois bedroom. In France, there was a growing preference for more 'feminine', lighter coloured fruitwoods, pine and poplar. In Victorian England, huge numbers of chests of drawers of varying quality were produced. They were made of a wide variety of woods, including mahogany, walnut, oak and occasionally satinwood, rosewood, maple and ash.

The great majority of 19th-century chests of drawers were however, made in pine that was either veneered or, in the cheaper examples, painted. After about 1860, chests of drawers often formed part of a bedroom suite with a wash-stand, wardrobe and chair. The typical mid-19th-century chest of drawers was bow-fronted – although not extravagantly so, as in the 18th century – had two short, half-width drawers above three long ones, and stood on turned bun feet.

One piece that was peculiar to England in the 19th century was the Wellington chest. This tall, narrow 'masculine' piece was probably intended for the storage of small valuables and was a feature of many Victorian libraries.

▲ *Although most 19th-century mass-produced chests of drawers had four flights of drawers, small three-flight chests never went out of production. This one, with bleached wood cross-banding outlining the drawers, dates from around mid-century.*

FURNITURE

▲ A rather plain version of the standard shape of three long drawers and two shorter ones is enhanced here by a well-chosen walnut veneer. The machine-cutting of veneers may have led to a lessening of quality, but it allowed far more people to appreciate the beauty of highly polished, well-figured wood.

▲ The revival of old forms included the chest on a stand. This English piece in oak, with four cabriole legs, was made in the 1880s as part of a revival of the Queen Anne (1702–1714) style of furniture.

▸ A steam-bent serpentine front and a well-figured mahogany veneer add value to this 1860s chest of drawers.

ANTIQUES
THE TWENTIETH CENTURY

THE RISE OF THE ART NOUVEAU and Art Deco movements in Europe heralded the fashioning of some extremely exotic cabinets, wardrobes, cupboards and bookcases. In France at the beginning of the century, Carabin, Charpentier and Gallé carved symbolist female nudes and plant forms on their asymmetrical cabinets and bookcases, while other Art Nouveau luminaries such as Guimard, Louis Majorelle and Henri van de Velde designed fine case furniture for clients using rosewood and walnut. Moser of Vienna produced angular cabinets with abstract decoration that anticipated Art Deco.

In the 1920s, the modernist Le Corbusier, working in partnership with Charlotte Perriand, was making wall units that were essentially cubic compartments in a geometrical arrangement. In Paris at the same time the Irish designer Eileen Gray produced richly ornamented and lacquered cabinets of adaptable form.

◄ *The British never quite embraced Art Nouveau in the same way as the rest of northern Europe; in furniture, its influence was felt in the free-flowing lines of the decorative detail, rather than in the form of the piece. This sideboard from the first decade of the century illustrates this perfectly.*

FURNITURE

Most of this furniture was destined for the houses of the better-off. Across the Atlantic, by contrast, a number of gifted American designers, though much impressed by the products of both the English Arts and Crafts Movement and Art Nouveau, were determined to reach a broader public. Both Gustav Stickley – the founder of the Mission style and publisher of the monthly magazine *The Craftsman* – and the architect Frank Lloyd Wright produced a considerable amount of simple, undecorated furniture, including cupboards, that was relatively cheap to buy.

167

▶ *This Italian-designed wardrobe is an example of the unusual hybrid styles that appeared in the 1930s. The general shape and the large oval mirror are very much inspired by Art Deco, while the carved apron and in particular the short, insubstantial-looking cabriole legs hark back to a much earlier age.*

▲ *This flat-fronted wardrobe in bird's eye maple – a favourite veneer of 1930s furniture-makers and buyers – has the sleek lines and unfussy geometric decoration typical of Art Deco furniture.*

FURNITURE

KITCHEN DRESSERS

▼ *This attractive pine dresser was made in Ireland early in the 19th century. Its plain style and a certain rough and ready quality to its craftsmanship only add to its charm.*

I N 19TH CENTURY BRITAIN and northern Europe, dressers were a highly significant piece of furniture. In the country they were considered fine enough for use as a sideboard in the parlours of large farmhouses, while in the towns and cities they formed an integral part of a working kitchen.

Early dressers were often no more than long tables with a single frieze of two or more drawers; a superstructure of shelves or a 'rack' was added in the 18th century. Although this was seldom attached, but merely sat on the top of the 'dresser' proper, this piece of furniture was so popular in the 19th century that few large British houses were without one. They could be very ornate, with machine carving, upturned supports and stretchers made in a Renaissance or Jacobean style, but the majority tended to be plain, sturdy pieces.

English dressers were in general made of sturdy woods such as oak, though mahogany and sometimes walnut veneers were used for decorative cross-banding. Pine was also used in the manufacture of so-called 'Welsh' dressers, which were likely to be used to display the best china in living room, as well as for many more basic kitchen pieces.

FURNITURE

▸ *The rustic simplicity of the dresser, a form that evolved out of basic country furniture, made it an attractive medium to Arts and Crafts furniture makers. This piece, made in a variety of fruitwoods, is one result of this. It is attractive enough for the drawing room but sufficiently practical for the kitchen.*

◀ *Substantial oak dressers such as this mid-19th-century example, with its profusely-carved surfaces, were intended more for drawing-room display than for use in the kitchen.*

Furniture
Writing Furniture

Although only a small minority of the people of any nation were literate before the 19th century, those who could read and write tended to be copious correspondents. Writing letters and so on was part of daily life.

Several kinds of furniture dedicated to writing – the precursors of modern office furniture – were produced. A typical English bureau dating from before 1725, for example, consisted of an upright, rectangular base with two large and two small drawers surmounted by a sloping desk flush with the surrounding woodwork. Generally, it was made of walnut veneer on a pine carcass, although oak was sometimes used for provincial pieces.

After 1740, English bureaux of mahogany and oak were made in one piece, with or without an additional upright cabinet or bookcase, and with bracket feet. This style changed very little over the following 150 years.

French writing furniture before 1760 was typified by the *bureau plat*, a flat-topped writing table. The Louis XV style is an assembly of flowing curves, sometimes without drawers, sometimes with a *cartonnier* – a separate, matching rack of shelves for documents – placed at its end next to the wall. In the Empire period, French writing desks became severely architectural in design, although their stark rectilinearity was sometimes enriched with mounts. Heavy desks with columnar supports and Egyptian or classical mounts were still being made in the 1840s.

▼ *The reading or writing slope was a useful addition to the 18th-century library, since it could be used for propping up heavy volumes as well as making notes. This one, dating from c.1750, folds down into a small mahogany tripod table.*

FURNITURE

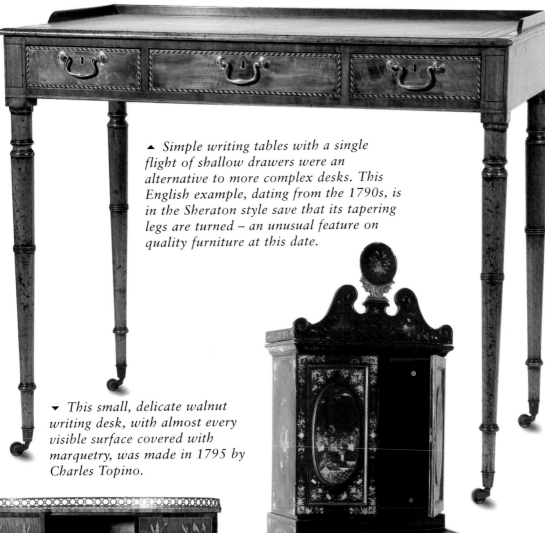

▲ *Simple writing tables with a single flight of shallow drawers were an alternative to more complex desks. This English example, dating from the 1790s, is in the Sheraton style save that its tapering legs are turned – an unusual feature on quality furniture at this date.*

▼ *This small, delicate walnut writing desk, with almost every visible surface covered with marquetry, was made in 1795 by Charles Topino.*

▲ *Extravagantly lacquered and gilded, this writing desk with a fold-down writing slope was made in China for export c.1820 to a pattern that harks back to various styles of the 18th century. The cabriole legs and ball feet are from the first half of the century, while the broken pediment, finial and the cartouches on the door are Neo-classical in inspiration.*

FURNITURE
THE BUREAU BOOKCASE

172

THE BUREAU – a writing table coupled with some storage space for papers and writing materials – developed in the late 17th century. By 1700 it had become a chest of drawers topped either with a writing slope – used standing up – or a drop-front cabinet, with a writing surface inside the drop front.

In the course of the century, craftsmen tried mounting various pieces on bureaux, including mirrors and cabinets. But since most bureaux of the period were intended for the use of gentlemen dealing with their business affairs and personal correspondence, they were often to be found in a library or study; this made a glass-fronted bookcase the most popular choice for combining with a bureau. Bureau-bookcases, veneered, lacquered or decorated in other fashions of the day were popular pieces through into the 19th century, although there was a trend towards much smaller pieces, sometimes with cupboards or bookshelves below the writing surface, rather than the more usual drawers.

The bureau-cabinet combination proved very popular in Germany in the 18th and 19th centuries. Heavy pieces with extensive Rococo decoration exerted a wide influence on the contemporary writing furniture of Scandinavia.

The problem with early pieces, as with breakfront bookcases, clothes presses, tallboys and other 18th-century furniture built on a massive scale, is that they were made for wealthy people who lived in houses with large rooms and high ceilings. This tends to count against them in the antiques market; no matter how fine a piece is, a collector will not buy it if he cannot house it. Good, smaller 19th-century examples may be more valuable than 18th-century ones.

▲ *Bureau-bookcases have always been in demand, and in the 19th and 20th centuries many 'marriages' were made, uniting two extant pieces or one new and one old. Here, a bureau from late in the 18th century has been fitted with a new bookcase some time around 1840. Its hybrid nature is revealed only in the veneers, which are not an exact match. Good marriages from an early date such as this, while not as valuable as an original, are worth far more than later and/or cruder unions.*

FURNITURE

◀ *Bookcases also developed new forms during the 19th century. While almost all 18th-century examples had glazed doors, this French example, reviving the Empire style much later in the century, keeps its contents dust-free by using lattice screens instead.*

173

▲ *This hardwood bureau-bookcase is in the Dutch colonial style and dates from the 1790s.*

◀ *Bureaux continued to develop throughout the 19th century. This example, with ebonized pilasters and a marquetry panel, was made in Sweden c.1820.*

FURNITURE

LADIES' WRITING FURNITURE

I N THE 18TH AND 19TH CENTURIES, the art of letter-writing was
seen as one of the feminine accomplishments. While men
tended to write at bureaux, bureaux-bookcases, or, later,
desks, women were provided with delicate writing-tables with a
drawer or two underneath and a *cartonnier* of small drawers,
pigeonholes and cabinets on the top. The *bonheur du
jour*, originally developed in France in the 1760s,
but revived and often reinterpreted during the
19th century, is a typical form.

174

The *secrétaire-á-capuchin*,
made by the craftsman
Vandercruse and others in
France around the same time,
looked like a small table on
cabriole legs when closed, but
a bank of drawers was
released when the folding top
was extended. Equally elegant
were the *bureau-de-dame* on
cabriole legs and the
secrétaire-á-abattant in Neo-
classical style. Another piece,
the *cheveret*, had a removable
cabinet to make more room
for writing.

The small size, intricate
decoration and elegant
well-worked lines of many
of these ladies' writing
desks, which were made
from the mid-18th century
right up to the early decades
of the 20th, has made them
particularly sought-after
antiques, which can fetch
high prices.

▼ *A hybrid between a*
bonheur du jour *and a drop
front bureau, this unusual piece
was made in the middle of the
19th century.*

FURNITURE

▼ *The most basic form of ladies writing furniture was a scaled-down version of the writing table. This one, made in England in 1810, has a leather top and brass mounts and castors.*

175

▲ *Although French* bonheur du jours *were usually extravagantly decorated, this example from 1790 has an elegant simplicity similar to contemporary English style, particularly in the tapering legs and spade feet. A foldout writing surface allows for much deeper drawers than usual. Other unusual features are the glass-fronted doors and the marble top of the cabinet.*

▶ *In this* bonheur du jour *decoration is paramount, with ebonized wood inlaid with ivory and ormolu mounts on the drawers and a central mirrored cupboard.*

FURNITURE

◄ *This* bonheur du jour, *made in the late 19th century, is larger than most and is prettily decorated with flowing satinwood and fruitwood inlays.*

▼ *The curved X-stretchers, oval shape and elaborately scrolled gallery of this mahogany writing desk identify it as an early 20th-century piece, mildly influenced by Art Nouveau.*

◄ *The small size and elegant proportions of this cylinder roll-top desk mark it out as a ladies' model.*

FURNITURE

DESKS

LADIES' WRITING DESKS were all about letter-writing, while bureau-bookcases had something of leisured study about them. Desks, though, were almost always about work. Surprisingly, the desk developed out of the ladies' kneehole dressing table. The same principle of two flights of drawers separated by a space for the knees and topped with a work surface led to the creation of pedestal desks, albeit on a much larger scale than dressing tables. In the late 19th century, the English pedestal desk was adopted as standard for study and office, while less well-off businessmen tended to favour the American roll-top design.

177

Art Nouveau, Art Deco and Modernist designers all contributed to the development of this type of writing furniture in the early decades of the 20th century. About 1898, the Belgian Art Nouveau designer Henri van de Velde created a desk with a kidney-shaped top mounted on pedestals with drawers and bookshelf extensions.

▼ *The Dickens desk, named after the English novelist Charles Dickens, was a style of pedestal desk with a built-in writing slope that – like the author – was enormously popular in late 19th-century Britain.*

FURNITURE

SEVEN YEARS LATER, LOUIS MAJORELLE designed writing tables with dished tops on semi-cabriole legs. Good Art Nouveau desks have restrained decoration that may include carving, marquetry, inlay in silver and precious stones and/or ormolu mounts. Cheaper Art Nouveau bureaux, on the other hand, have leaded-light glass doors and large, bronzed-metal hinges.

At this time, too, many commercial firms, particularly in the United States, were heavily influenced by Art Nouveau styles. Asymmetrical bureau-cabinets with shelving on one side were all the rage. This lesson was not lost on the Modernist and Art Deco designers of the 1920s and 1930s, but their great emphasis was on functionalism. Modernist pieces formed the prototype of the modern typist's desk, and although they are often unspectacular, most of them are solid and well designed.

178

▼ *Roll-top desks tend to be a little smaller than pedestal desks. This one was made in honey oak around the turn of the century and has a rigid, veneered cylinder top.*

FURNITURE

▶ *A tambour top, made of thin pieces of wood glued to a canvas or linen backing for flexibility, has been fitted to this mid-Victorian mahogany roll-top. The use of a contrasting wood in the interior on the rack of drawers and the top of the pigeonholes at the back is a mark of high quality.*

◀ *The partners' desk is a pedestal desk with a top sufficiently wide for two people to use it at once, sitting opposite each other. This example in light oak, made in the 1890s, has the same arrangement of drawers on the right and roll-front cupboard on the left repeated on the other side.*

▶ *The pedestal desk is a classic furniture form, varying little from its development in the middle of the 19th century to the modern day. This one is in oak, with a gold-embossed leather top.*

FURNITURE
DRESSING TABLES

THE FIRST DRESSING TABLES evolved in the 17th century as a response to the fashion for both men and women for wearing elaborate make-up and wigs. At first, simple tables, usually placed near a window, were used on which to array these grooming accessories and perhaps a hand-held mirror. By the beginning of the 18th century, the piece had evolved into a walnut kneehole table with drawers and a 'toilet glass', a swivelling mirror on a stand.

Later that century, other distinct types evolved. The dressing chest was a chest of drawers with a fitted top drawer and a writing slide. A pedestal version of the dressing table appeared alongside the kneehole variety, while in the 1760s Chippendale introduced a central fixed mirror flanked by small cupboards. This became the model for most later dressing tables, particularly after 1850, when nests of drawers for trinkets and make-up appeared alongside the mirror.

The Art Nouveau and Arts and Crafts movements produced some interestingly detailed dressing tables, which were by now considered a wholly feminine piece of bedroom furniture, but Art Deco ushered in some radical differences in form.

The mirrors tended to get larger. The previously rather rare 'duchess' style, with a full-length mirror flanked by pedestal drawers, experienced a renaissance in subtly altered forms. Asymmetric designs were introduced, while the use of bent plywood covered with veneers made for some very curvaceous pieces.

▼ *This piece epitomises 1930s design. The veneer, bird's eye maple, was in vogue, and the asymmetrical design and the use of curved wood and both clear and mirror glass as part of the design, with nothing but a single knob on the door breaking up the clean lines, was totally up-to-date. Only the slightly squat cabriole legs detract from the effect.*

FURNITURE

◀ *The chunky masculinity of this oak dressing chest, its pewter fittings and the minimalist pierced decoration in the mirror supports all point to a date around the turn of the 20th century.*

▲ *Tasteful and well-veneered kneehole dressing tables such as this were made as parts of suites of bedroom furniture throughout much of the 19th century and well into the 20th.*

◀ *Although basically a commercial piece, this oak dressing table from the late 1920s is, nevertheless, already showing some hallmarks of the Art Deco style, including the skirt of bent and veneered plywood, the geometric carved decoration and a triptych of mirrors. All the drawers but one have been abandoned in the cause of sleekness of line.*

FURNITURE
MIRRORS

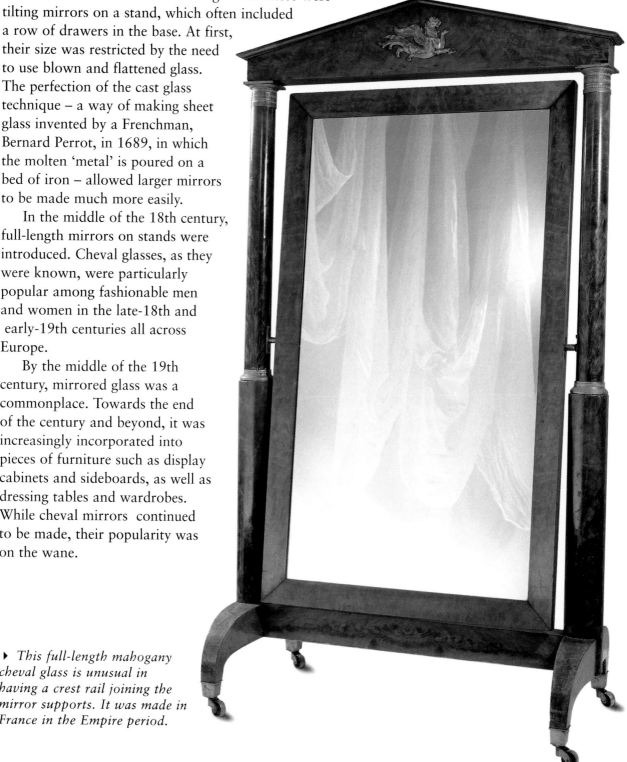

182

MIRRORS WERE FIRST incorporated into pieces of furniture in the 18th century in the form of toilet glasses, made to sit on a dressing table. These were tilting mirrors on a stand, which often included a row of drawers in the base. At first, their size was restricted by the need to use blown and flattened glass. The perfection of the cast glass technique – a way of making sheet glass invented by a Frenchman, Bernard Perrot, in 1689, in which the molten 'metal' is poured on a bed of iron – allowed larger mirrors to be made much more easily.

In the middle of the 18th century, full-length mirrors on stands were introduced. Cheval glasses, as they were known, were particularly popular among fashionable men and women in the late-18th and early-19th centuries all across Europe.

By the middle of the 19th century, mirrored glass was a commonplace. Towards the end of the century and beyond, it was increasingly incorporated into pieces of furniture such as display cabinets and sideboards, as well as dressing tables and wardrobes. While cheval mirrors continued to be made, their popularity was on the wane.

▶ *This full-length mahogany cheval glass is unusual in having a crest rail joining the mirror supports. It was made in France in the Empire period.*

FURNITURE

▼ *Early toilet glasses were made to stand on a table. This example is framed in carved walnut.*

183

▲ *By the middle of the 18th century, toilet glasses had acquired bases with drawers. This is a particularly elegant Chippendale design with a serpentine drawer front, canted corners and blind fret ogee feet.*

▸ *This oak toilet glass with two fitted drawers and oval mirror is representative of the way table-top mirrors developed in the first quarter of the 19th century.*

FURNITURE

WALL MIRRORS

184

WALL-MIRRORS, which had previously been the preserve of the wealthy, also became commonplace in the 19th century, although the highly ornate and gilded wood and plaster frames that were seen as suitable for mirrors in the 18th century and before tended to be replaced by something less showy.

The custom of hanging a mirror above the fireplace in the main sitting room led to the creation of overmantel mirrors. These could be extravagant pieces of furniture, incorporating display stands, decorative carving and finishes, and sometimes open shelves and cupboards, as well as a large mirror and several smaller ones.

These pieces had gone completely out of fashion by the 1930s, when wall mirrors tended to lose their frames altogether, since the glass was bolted directly on to a wooden base. Decorative effects were achieved by moulding, tinting and engraving the glass itself. It was usual for wall mirrors of the period to be made of several shaped and coloured pieces of mirror glass fixed to a shaped base – usually plywood, often cut out with a jigsaw – to make a pattern.

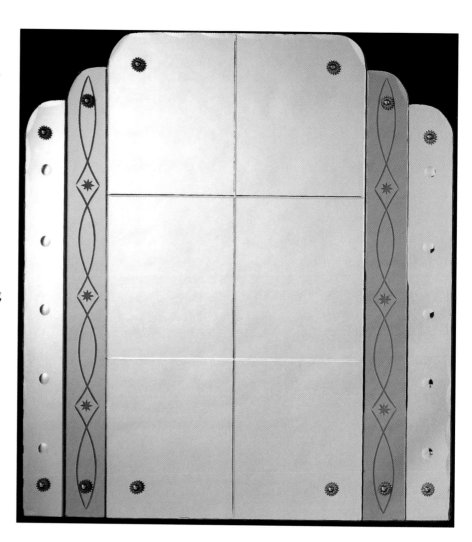

▲ *The 1930s version of the wall mirror featured a great deal of tinted glass – peach was a favourite colour – and engraved decoration.*

FURNITURE

▼ *The carved and gilded style was not all about grandeur. This small wall mirror, with its softly carved frame, was made in Sweden of pine around 1800.*

▶ *At the beginning of the 19th century, wall mirrors were often lavishly framed in the prevailing styles, with highly-carved gilt and ebonized wood.*

185

◀ *Overmantel mirrors became more complex as the 19th century went on. This one, made towards the end of the century in the Japanese taste, is framed in ebonized wood and inset with painted and gilded panels. The small shelves are intended for displaying ornaments.*

FURNITURE
FIRE SCREENS

▾ *This cheval screen dates from the 1840s. The turned and ebonized frame supports two glass panels, between which is sandwiched an arrangement of pressed flowers and ferns.*

186

FIRE SCREENS WERE DESIGNED to protect delicate female faces, (or, more to the point, easily melted make-up) from the heat of an open fire. They were also extremely decorative objects in their own right, offering good opportunities for carving on the stand, while the screen could function as a support for prints, paintings, imported Chinese embroidery or other needlework. The more delicate screens were probably primarily used for hiding the empty hearth in the summer.

Cheval screens, with a panel set between two uprights, were particularly popular in the 18th century and were still being mass produced in the 20th century. In the 19th century, though, they were outstripped in popularity by another type, the pole screen, which usually had a tripod base and a turned pillar, or pole, supporting the screen. Some of these bases were made of papier-mâché. The height and position of the small screen or tapestry banner mounted on the pole could be adjusted to keep the heat from the user's face by loosening and tightening a wooden fixing screw. Pole screens were often made in pairs to stand on either side of the fireplace, and a matching pair is worth much more than two individuals.

FURNITURE

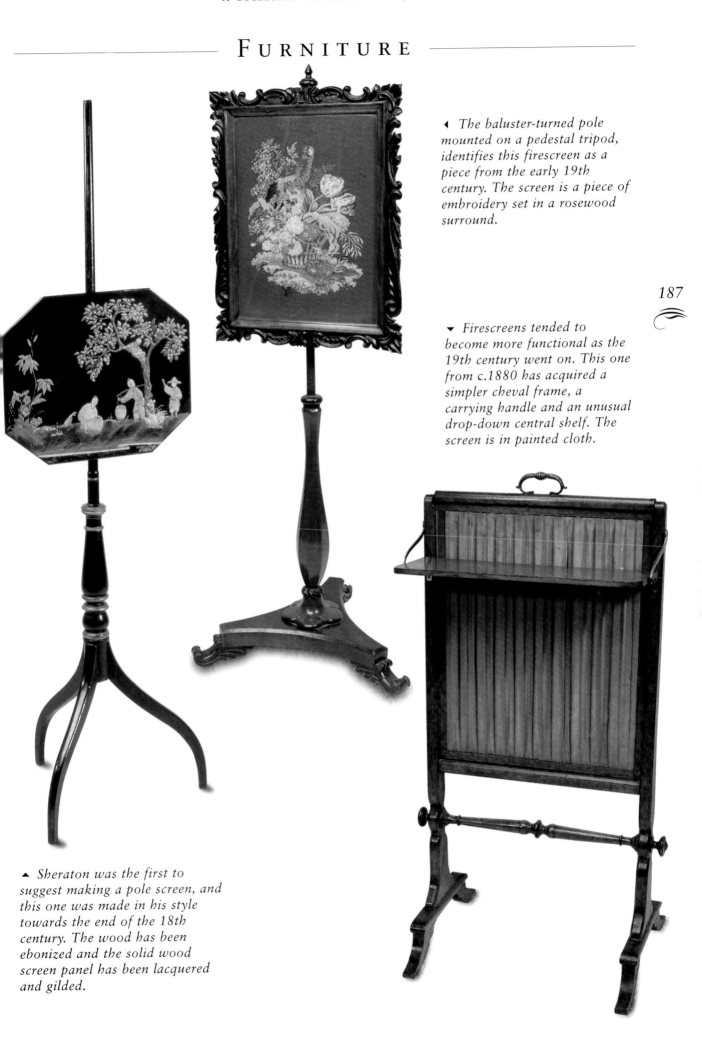

◀ The baluster-turned pole mounted on a pedestal tripod, identifies this firescreen as a piece from the early 19th century. The screen is a piece of embroidery set in a rosewood surround.

187

▼ Firescreens tended to become more functional as the 19th century went on. This one from c.1880 has acquired a simpler cheval frame, a carrying handle and an unusual drop-down central shelf. The screen is in painted cloth.

▲ Sheraton was the first to suggest making a pole screen, and this one was made in his style towards the end of the 18th century. The wood has been ebonized and the solid wood screen panel has been lacquered and gilded.

FURNITURE
FOLDING SCREENS

SCREENS MADE UP OF FOLDING PANELS were a feature of very large houses during the 17th and 18th centuries. Some of them were imported from the Orient, which inspired the style, while others were made in Europe in the styles of the day. They were used to divide up large rooms, keep out draughts and provide private corners.

Folding wicker screens were used in Europe in the Middle Ages, but screens became truly fashionable only under the influence of those imported from China and Japan in the 17th century. Japanese folding screens, or byobu, literally 'protection from the wind', consisted of two to six hinged panels, typically covered in painted paper, although lacquerwork was also used. Screens with lacquer panels – sometimes carved – were a speciality of China. Chinese and Japanese screens of the 18th century and before fetch very high prices today.

By the 18th century, European makers were not only copying oriental styles, but had also woken to other decorative possibilities. The frames might be in carved, gilded walnut, while the panels were covered with painted canvas, leather, needlework or various types of textile. In the later 19th century there was a great vogue for decorating screens at home. Printed scraps were used to build up colourful collages on canvas, and were then protected by several layers of varnish.

▶ *This walnut screen with graduated panels was made in an exuberantly Rococo revival style in the middle of the 19th century.*

FURNITURE

◂ *This French 18th-century screen has oval portraits in gilded and mirrored surrounds at the top of each panel. The rest is filled in with silk.*

▴ *The Egyptian technique of* mashrabiye, *in which small turned spindles are fitted together in a lattice, which may then be filled with a contrasting inlay, provides good material for screens. In Egypt, they are used to divide rooms or are placed in front of windows to filter out harsh light and insects. This one was made c.1890.*

◂ *Large panels of canvas-work or embroidery were a favourite for 19th-century screens. The needlepoint wool embroidery on this mid-century example, with a giltwood frame, benefited from the recent introduction of aniline dyes, which provided a new palette of bright colours.*

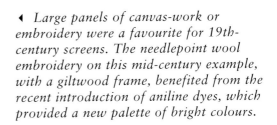

FURNITURE

ORIENTAL FURNITURE

CHINA AND JAPAN have had a great influence on furniture design in Europe and the USA since the 17th century, but both countries have furniture traditions of their own still largely unfamiliar in the West.

190

Traditional Chinese furniture consists largely of pieces in hardwood or lacquer. Some was made for people sitting or working on the floor, and some for those sitting in chairs. Chinese interiors were much more sparse and formal in their arrangement than contemporary European tastes.

The Chinese have been using lacquer on furniture and other pieces since at least the 2nd century BC. Lacquer is made from the prepared sap of the lac tree (*Rhus vernicifera*), which is painted on surfaces, sometimes in literally dozens of coats, to build up a hard, shiny, resistant surface. Dyes, usually black or red, are used to colour the lacquer. This might be painted or inlaid with a design, or the decoration might be cut into it.

When the export market to the West got under way in the 17th century, the Chinese began to produce European forms in Chinese decorative styles, as well as the more traditional screens and cabinets. Such 'chinoiserie' was the height of fashion in Europe in the mid-18th century.

▼ *The flowing design on this eight-leaved, 19th-century screen is carved out of deep layers of lacquer and inlaid with gold and silver in the style now known as Coromandel.*

FURNITURE

◄ *This black and gold cabinet on a stand – which also has lacquer and inlay decoration inside – was made for the European export market around 1840.*

▼ *The wood known as huang hua-li is inset with darker panels of hua-wu in this cupboard. The metal mounts and strong rectangular shapes make the piece similar in feel to Japanese cabinets, although those were never raised on legs.*

◄ *The yoke-back chair, named after its characteristic crest rail, reminiscent of the yoke worn by oxen, is a typical traditional Chinese form. This one, which has a matting seat, was made early in the 19th century from huang hua-li, a wood which is no longer available.*

FURNITURE

JAPANESE LIVES WERE TRADITIONALLY lived at floor level. Long, low tables were used for eating and small stools or rush mats for sitting. Such pieces, and other specifically Japanese furniture such as kimono stands or the household shrine, a tall cabinet containing a statue of the Buddha, were fashioned with great delicacy. The best pieces were made in woods native to Japan, including chestnut and cypress, and were often lacquered in red or black – the technique was learned from the Chinese in the 6th century AD– or decorated with parquetry: veneers laid in geometrical patterns.

192

Larger furniture included screens and storage furniture – *tansu*. The latter were often made of pine, highly polished and figured, and the piece was both protected and decorated with ironwork mounts. Although *tansu* are traditional pieces, by far the largest number of those in existence today date from the 19th and 20th centuries.

In the late 19th century, the English designer E.W. Godwin spearheaded a vogue for furniture that was inspired by Japan without aping Japanese furniture styles. His designs were made around the world. Later, the designer Christopher Dresser and the shop Liberty's of London produced many pieces in a similar style, including some furniture. These 'Anglo-Japanese pieces' resembled traditional Japanese work more in their strong horizontal and vertical lines, asymmetric designs and delicacy of detailing than in their forms and materials. Bamboo was widely used, for example, while chairs – rare in Japan – were produced with spindly legs and rush or cane seating.

▼ *The lovely honey colour of zelkova, a highly prized hard-wood native to Japan, was used c.1850 to make this* funa-dansu, *or sea chest, which is a little smaller than most* tansu.

FURNITURE

◄ *Made of highly polished paulownia wood, this is a fine example of a yaro-dansu, a chest in one piece, dating from c.1850 Mounts in the shape of stylized flowers and foliage have been hand-cut and forged in iron, blackened with paste. Some of the ironwork is functional, such as the carrying handles, lockplates, protective corners and the hinges, but all of it is extremely decorative.*

193

◄ *All 'Japanese' seat furniture is likely to be European in inspiration and origin. This example, made around 1860 in ebonized wood with rushwork seat and back, is one of Godwin's earliest designs.*

► *In the latter part of the 19th century, Anglo-Japanese styles were inspired by pieces such as this shodana, a set of free-standing shelves with minimal decoration and simple design based on strong vertical and horizontal lines.*

GLASS

GLASS

THE FIRST 'MODERN' TEXTBOOK on glass was published in 1612. Its Italian author, Antonio Neri, wrote that 'glass is one of the most noble things which man hath at this day for his use upon the Earth.' This opinion was not new. Indeed, glass had been held in the highest regard by advanced civilizations for at least 2000 years. This continued to be so until the advent of mechanized glass production in the 1850s, when plainer glassware began to be taken for granted.

In chemical terms, glass is not a solid but a super-cooled liquid, formed from the fusion under great heat of silica (usually sand, crushed flint or quartz) with an alkaline 'flux' (usually potash or soda). Lime is added to make the glass more durable. The first glassware is thought to have been made in western Asia, and it is probable that a glass industry was established in Egypt as long ago as the 15th century BC, and later shifted to Alexandria. The Romans learned the techniques of glassmaking from the Egyptians, and in the 1st century AD Imperial Rome became the centre of production.

It was the Romans who made the greatest discovery in glass manufacture – that it could be 'blown'. Before this time, vessels had been made by painstakingly moulding molten glass around a modelled core. Now they were made by blowing air through a tube into a blob of molten glass. With this breakthrough came others, including new ways of shaping molten glass – called 'the metal' at this stage – by blowing it into a preformed mould, and by drawing it out and manipulating it with pincers, tongs and other instruments. This meant that larger vessels and more elaborate pieces could be easily made.

As the centuries went by, the knowledge of glass-

GLASS

making was carried across Europe and different types of glass began to be made that were dependent on locally available ingredients. Soda glass, so called because it contained sodium carbonate obtained from the ash of burnt seaweed, was made in the Mediterranean region. It was light and highly plastic. In forested areas such as Germany and France, potash glass, containing potassium carbonate, was made by adding the ash of trees and plants, giving it a slightly green tinge.

In the 15th century, by exploiting the decolorizing properties of manganese, Venetian glassmakers perfected a glass so much like rock crystal they dubbed it *cristallo*. Over the next 200 years, Venetian techniques spread to England, Bohemia and the Low Countries.

New techniques were developed, such as refiring, colouring, casing (where layers of different coloured glass are applied then cut away to make patterns), cutting and engraving. The development of pressed and moulded glass, along with the discovery of new techniques that expanded the range of colours available and created new iridescent finishes, made glassware a mass-market product in the latter part of the 19th century and the early years of the 20th. Pieces from this era are sought after today.

While craftsmen have fully exploited the unique properties of glass to produce a wonderful variety of functional or ornamental vessels, the inherent fragility of the material – and the fact that it was used to make such everyday objects as drinking vessels – means that relatively little survives from before the mass-production age. The main areas of collection today are glass tableware from the 19th century and before, decorative pieces from virtually any era, and paperweights.

GLASS

18TH-CENTURY TABLE GLASS

CLEAR, COLOURLESS TABLE GLASS had its origins in 15th-century Venice. Over the next 200 years, Venetian techniques spread to Bohemia (now the Czech Republic) and the Low Countries, where a potash flux was used instead of the soda favoured by the Venetians. Then, in the 1670s, in England, George Ravenscroft pioneered the use of lead oxide to create lead 'crystal', which was much clearer than soda glass, less brittle and could be easily cut. This invention allowed English glass-makers to dominate the market during the 18th century. Early in the century, most English table glass had little decoration and was usually in the form of goblets; by the end it was smaller, lighter and finer, with decoration on the stem and sometimes also on the bowl. Subtly different shapes were produced for spirits, wine, ale and cider.

Some of the most commonly found early English drinking glasses are rummers – glasses with short stems and a large bucket or cup-shaped bowl. The name probably derives from the German Römer, which is similar in shape. Larger versions were used for beer or cider, smaller ones for gin or other spirits. The four rummers shown here all date from the late 1700s. Sometimes they were plain and functional pieces, perhaps with a knopped stem; others had added engraved and moulded decoration.

GLASS

▲ A great number of different styles of 18th-century glasses can be found. The goblet (left) has a double opaque-twist stem and honeycomb moulded bowl; the beer mug is engraved with hops and barley; and the plain cordial glass has a knopped stem into which a bubble of air, or 'tear', has been incorporated.

◄ The Irish punch bowl was made later than the glasses above – c.1820 – and has delicately cut decoration within roundels, which are outlined with finely cut vertical lines.

GLASS

GLASS

English Georgian drinking glasses were hand blown, and the variety available is immense, with a great many sizes, shapes and styles of stem. These include stems with facet cuts, knops and spiralled air- and opaque-twists, made by trapping a bubble of air in the molten metal and twisting it, or by introducing rods of opaque or coloured glass. Bowls were often delicately engraved with leaves and flowers or bunches of grapes.

201

--- GLASS ---

19TH-CENTURY
TABLE GLASS

▾ *Etching delicate glass by the use of acid became common in the mid-19th century. It was a fairly cheap means of ornamenting table glass, often with quite elaborate designs.*

INCREASED MECHANIZATION in the 19th century smoothed away the slight irregularities of hand-made glass, and eliminated the small air bubbles that often appeared in 18th-century glass. The types of glass available was vast, and by the end of the century, glass-makers were producing wine services containing up to a dozen glasses of six different types – sherry, hock, claret, port, liqueur and champagne, as well as tumblers, jugs and decanters. Decorative focus switched from the stems to the bowls of drinking glasses, which were increasingly decorated by acid etching, wheel or diamond-point engraving, or cutting on a rotating wheel. Cutting was generally used for large-scale geometric designs, engraving for detailed, often pictorial work.

GLASS

▲ *The sherry glass on the left is decorated with vines, as is the port glass in the centre, which also has a cut and faceted stem. The liqueur glass on the right, in the shape of a thistle– perhaps intended for the Scottish liqueur whisky, drambuie – is engraved at the top and diamond cut on the base of the bowl.*

◀ *These two glasses were meant for drinking burgundy. The larger glass has a thick, faceted, cut-glass stem, while the more delicate glass, with a slim stem, has a broader foot for stability, and geometric designs etched into the bowl.*

GLASS

DECANTERS &
CLARET JUGS

EVEN BEFORE THE END OF the 17th century, it had become customary to pour wine out of the bottle before serving it by gently tilting, or canting, the bottle in order to leave the sediment in the bottom. This process of 'decanting' wine soon led to glass jugs with a hinged lid or stopper – generally known as claret jugs – being made to hold table wine. Special stoppered bottles, known as decanters, were also produced; they were originally intended for port and sherry but were also used by drinkers at the dining table to serve themselves. These decanters often had rings around the neck to make them easier to lift when they were full and to hold while pouring.

In England in the 1700s, in part due to the use of high-quality lead glass, which was strong enough for everyday use, and in part to more sophisticated dining habits, glass-makers began to produce decanters in many different styles, either singly or in matching sets. Among these, in 1740–80, was the mallet-shaped decanter, usually in heavy glass; in 1740–60, the cruciform decanter with projecting sides that from above looked roughly cross-shaped, and c.1780, the ship's decanter, with a wide base.

Stoppers were ground to fit the neck of the decanter. Early shapes were the spire, or pinnacle, c.1750; the upright disc, sometimes with scalloped or notched edges; and the cut-glass globe. Later, mushroom and bull's-eye stoppers became common. In the 19th century, variations in the shape of both decanters and stoppers were introduced, and the use of coloured glass, and surface decoration – cutting, engraving, enamelling and casing – became more widespread.

▶ *Spirit decanters were generally square-based and straight-sided, with a circular stopper. They usually came in pairs or sets of three, often in their own silver stand with a carrying handle and rings to hold the stoppers when the liquor was poured. This was the forerunner of the 19th-century tantalus.*

▶ *Cut glass and silver seem to have a natural affinity, and they often appear together on the same piece, as on this 19th-century claret jug. Since English silver is hallmarked, it provides a rare opportunity to date a glass piece.*

204

GLASS

206

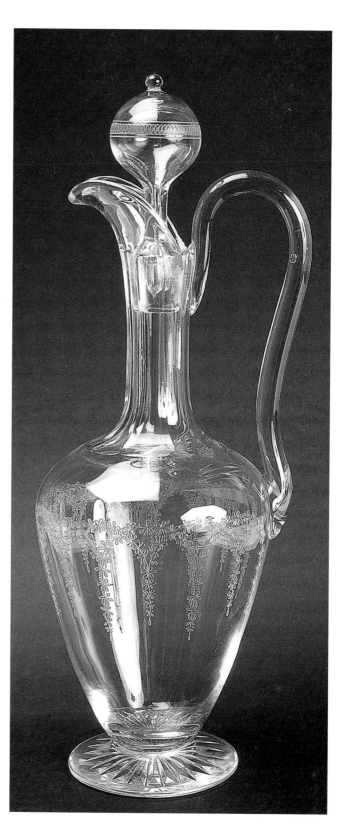

▲ The ancient technique of blowing glass into a mould, so that the inner and outer shapes are the same, has been used to create this clear glass 19th-century decanter with a ground-glass stopper.

▲ Claret jugs are usually much plainer than decanters and are often tall, with long necks. The body has been etched with a delicate flower design, but the stopper is not original. When buying, make sure that the stopper suits the style of the jug.

GLASS

207

▲ The detail shows how removing the top layer of glass to create the design has left a relief pattern in white glass on the surface of the decanter.

◀ Cased glass was used for wine decanters after about 1850. This handsome decanter in the form of a wine bottle with a silver-mounted cork stopper is made in green glass cased in white, which has been cut away to reveal a grape and vine pattern.

▼ Two decanter stoppers illustrate how chips can be repaired. The bottom of the right-hand stopper is badly chipped; the chips on the other one have been ground down to a smooth finish.

GLASS

◄ A freehand countryside scene has been cut through the blue casing on this claret jug to reveal the white glass underneath. The casing on the handle is limited to a single band of colour.

▲ This coloured-glass decanter, with a hooped neck and mushroom-shaped stopper, was made by a technique known as flashing. The clear glass decanter has simply been dipped in red molten glass and the design of grapes and vine leaves then cut through the thin top layer to reveal the clear glass underneath.

▲ As the 19th century progressed, fashions in cut glass became increasingly ornate. This shaft and globe decanter, also known as an onion decanter, made around 1860, is a typical example, with every surface cut. There is scale cutting on the neck, a deeply cut star pattern on the base of the decanter and a cross-cut diamond pattern enclosed in loops with saw-tooth edges repeated on the globe and the hollow stopper.

GLASS

BOHEMIA GLASS

210

▼ *This painted and gilded piece of Bohemian glass carries an angel motif; 19th-century decorators found as good a market for religious subjects as for sentimental and heraldic ones.*

BOHEMIA – NOW PART OF THE Czech Republic – was the world centre of decorative glass-making in the 19th century, famous for lustrous metallic colours and delicate painting and engraving. Bohemian makers found a way to produce red glass using copper rather than gold, and added new shades of blue and green and types of marbled glass.

Early in the 19th century, the Biedermeier period, there were 60 glass-making factories in Bohemia. Many of them made souvenir wares for spa towns such as Baden Baden, Carlsbad and Marienbad, which attracted wealthy and middle-class people from all over Europe. While much of this work was essentially mass-produced, some was made to commission.

A great deal of the added decoration seen on the glass is, however, the work not of the glass-maker but of a separate craftsman, the decorator, whose expertise lies in ornamental techniques such as painting, enamelling and gilding. Nowhere were these techniques better developed than in Bohemia, which had a long tradition in glass-making and a wealth of natural resources close at hand. The work of decorators such as Anton Kothgasser, who specialized in moonlit views, and Samuel and Gottlöb Mohn – pioneers of painting glass in transparent colours, was much in demand.

▶ *Clockwise from the bottom: The simple blue glass beaker was engraved by one of the great masters, Karl Pfohl. Ten different engraved views feature on this piece, in a pale amber colour developed in Bohemia in the 19th century. Lavish gilding and applied ruby glass 'gems' have turned this clear glass wine goblet (c.1850) into one suitable for a medieval king. The wine glass with a stem with many knops is decorated with enamel painting of scrolls and flowers on stem and bowl and with tiny beads of applied white glass. Scrolls and coats of arms were common commissions for Bohemian glass painters.*

GLASS

GLASS

▸ *The goblet and cover in clear and amber glass, with an engraved outdoor scene, was made c.1838.*

▴ *The informal nature of the engraving on this ruby-glass mug indicates that it was more recently made than the other pieces shown here; it dates from c.1890.*

▾ *The brilliant effects and craftsmanship of Bohemian glass were widely copied.*

▴ *Almost all German spa glasses came from Bohemia. This one in clear glass cased in cranberry bears the name of the town of which it is a souvenir, and etched local views.*

▸ *The* Deckelpokal, *a goblet with a cover, was a common form of ornamental Bohemian glass in its great heyday, roughly from 1815 to 1860. These four examples from the middle of the 19th century show a range of decorative techniques. They include, from left to right, a piece in green* Annagrün *glass (made by adding uranium salts to the metal) with an engraved panel; wheel-cut faceting on rose glass with a clear stem; an applied design in yellow – achieved by using silver nitrate – over clear glass; and an engraved hunting scene (a popular theme) on boldly cut and moulded ruby glass.*

GLASS

GLASS

PRESSED GLASS

THE TECHNIQUES OF pressing and moulding have dominated commercial glass production since the late 19th century. Pressed glass was first made in the USA in the 1820s by the New England Glass Company, and the technique was taken up in Britain and the rest of Europe soon after as a much cheaper alternative to cut and engraved glass.

The method involved making a model of a piece in wood and using this to create a cast-iron mould. The inside surface of the mould was then finished with metal tools, ready for use. A blob of white-hot, viscous glass was put into the mould and pressed into place with a 'plunger', which forced it into the mould. Sometimes the plunger was also moulded, to make an impression on the inside of the piece. The pressed piece was then removed to cool, and may have been hand finished, although most pressed glass was entirely machine made.

Early pressed glass usually copied cut-glass vessels in clear glass; tumblers, punchbowls, vases, cruets and comports were all made in this way. Later in the 19th century and into the 20th, makers began to exploit the variety of shapes and patterns allowed by the technique to make a range of practical objects, such as doorknobs, as well as some ornamental pieces.

Ornamental pressed glass made great use of colour and unusual finishes. A British firm, Sowerby's, found a way to make an opaque glass similar to porcelain, and glass also mimicked other decorative materials, including jet and tortoiseshell. Sometimes different colours were swirled together in the same piece.

▸ *The range of pressed glass items to be found at flea markets and on antique stalls is vast. Literally hundreds of thousands of plates, dishes, jugs, baskets, jam pots and ashtrays in dozens of different styles and colours have been produced. The pieces shown here were all made in the late 19th and early 20th centuries.*

▸ *Moulded glass was ideal for making commemorative ware. Once the cast-iron mould had been engraved with portraits, lettering and dates, thousands of items could be easily and quickly produced. The plate in honour of the coronation of King Edward VII of England is now a valuable collector's piece.*

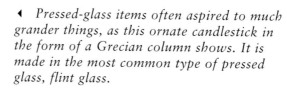

◂ *Pressed-glass items often aspired to much grander things, as this ornate candlestick in the form of a Grecian column shows. It is made in the most common type of pressed glass, flint glass.*

214

GLASS

GLASS

CARNIVAL GLASS

216

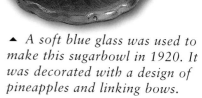

I N 1907, THE FENTON ART GLASS COMPANY of Williamsburg, West Virginia, produced Iridill, an iridescent pressed glass reminiscent of the hand-blown pieces made by Tiffany since the 1880s. Other manufacturers followed suit, notably Northwood of West Virginia, and Imperial and Millersburg from Ohio. The new glass, known as rainbow glass, taffeta glass, 'poor man's Tiffany', and later carnival glass, proved enormously popular in the USA and, after 1918, in Europe. Although they were machine made, the pieces were often given some hand-working as they cooled, giving them a touch of individuality. The rainbow effect was the result of coating the moulded glass as it cooled with metallic salts and refiring it. The iridization was sprayed onto later glass and it was not refired. Decorative motifs were inspired by nature, and great use was made of curves and asymmetric shapes. Frilled edges

▲ *A soft blue glass was used to make this sugarbowl in 1920. It was decorated with a design of pineapples and linking bows.*

▲ *The iridescent colours of cheap Carnival glass are reminiscent of those of the expensive Favrile glass made by Louis Comfort Tiffany.*

GLASS

Clockwise from the top: Mayan patterned radium finished bowl made by Millersburg Glass Co., Ohio; black dish with kingfisher design, made in Australia, c.1920; Nippon-patterned amethyst-coloured fluted bowl with a hand-finished edge; pale green bowl in basket-weave pattern with an open edge, made by Fenton; deep cobalt blue peacock-patterned bowl; large fruit bowl on three legs, in marigold, decorated with a rural design known as Double Dutch; deep purple fluted bowl embossed with scrolls. All except the Australian dish were made c.1910.

217

were popular. Carnival glass is known by its 'base' colour – the colour of the glass before it was iridized. Such pieces tend to be cheaper than other colours. All shades of yellow, from pale gold to a deep orange-red (known as orange-marigold) and purple, which often looks black, were most popular, but green in several shades and cobalt blue were also common. Reds and pastel colours were rarer and are much more collectable.

GLASS

PAPERWEIGHTS

218

GLASS PAPERWEIGHTS WERE first made in Venetian factories in about 1840, but three French manufacturers quickly came to dominate the market; Baccarat and Saint Louis were based in the Vosges, and Clichy in Paris, and all three had access to very pure sand capable of making good clear glass. Paperweights produced by these three firms before 1860 – the Classic period as it is known – are the most sought after by collectors, but American and British pieces from the latter half of the 19th century are also collected.

Most weights were made of domed clear glass with colourful decorative motifs. The most characteristic style is *millefiori*, a technique that involves putting together rods of different coloured glasses, then heating them and drawing them out to make thin, multicoloured canes. Viewed from the end, these canes resemble flowers. By slicing through the canes, many such flowers could be obtained. These were then carefully arranged and covered with a dome of clear glass, which had the effect of magnifying the design. Sometimes a date or initial identifying the factory – B, SL or C – is incorporated in one of the canes. This is usually the only way weights are ever 'signed' – the individual makers remain unknown – or dated.

Other weights contained representations of plants and animals in coloured glass that had been sculpted over heat, or *latticino* decoration, where threads of white or coloured glass are blown into nets. Crown weights have twisted ribbons of coloured glass rising to a central motif, usually a flower, while sulphide weights incorporate a ceramic medallion. Some weights, sulphides in particular, are faceted, to give different views of the decoration.

GLASS

▲ *The paperweights shown here were made by both French and English makers. They include a single flower on a latticino ground by St Louis; a Baccarat butterfly on a muslin ground; and a Clichy pink and white swirl, all c.1850. The English bubble weight and green glass stump date from c.1880.*

SILVER

SILVER

THE GLEAM OF POLISHED SILVER is a welcome sight in a home whether it be from photograph frames on a chest or the sight of a well-laid dining table. Silver has long been regarded as a symbol of prosperity and even today still enjoys a sense of social standing. For the collector it offers a wide variety of scope since he can either concentrate on a particular area such as spoons or boxes or seek to acquire appropriate pieces for the different rooms of his home.

Whichever path you choose to follow it can be a pleasurable and rewarding experience but always make sure that your collection is insured and photographed as a security precaution.

Although in many European countries the guild systems, found in large towns and cities, meant that their silver was marked, in Britain there is a system which has been in existence since 1478, where silver is tested in an assay office and any item over 7.78g will be hallmarked with four marks. One indicates the city, in the case of London a leopard's head, the second indicates the standard and is usually a lion passant which indicates sterling, but some pieces can have a higher silver content than the 92.5% sterling level. The third mark is the date letter and the fourth mark is the maker's mark. Between 1784 and 1890 it was customary for the pieces also to be marked with the Sovereign's head as a sign that tax had been paid. Hallmarks will be found on the separate components of a piece such as a tankard where both the body and lid should be marked

As with many antiques condition plays an important role. Like furniture, silver acquires a patina over the years from cleaning and polishing and it is important never to use an abrasive cleaner since this will scratch

SILVER

the metal and will remove the patina. Silver was, of course, in everyday use and so some pieces will show signs of excessive wear or have holes or splits in their body, such as near the spout on a teapot. These should be avoided, as should pieces which have been repaired using lead solder, which is unsightly, instead of silver solder which, while more acceptable, will still have a detrimental effect on the value. Decoration is also prone to damage, especially pierced decoration which can easily be split or pulled out of shape through careless handling or cleaning. The practice of engraving a piece with initials, crests or armorials has meant that later owners may have had them erased and it is a good idea to feel at the centre of a tray, tankard or whatever to see if the silver feels thinner there than elsewhere.

While hallmarks are generally a reliable guide to the date of a piece, the collector also needs to know a little about the history of silver, since you will come across items that have been made up using elements from earlier pieces, including the hallmarks, but often these will not be in the correct place for the type of object into which they have been incorporated. In the 19th century, particularly, early plain pieces were improved by the addition of chasing and other decoration and some pieces such as tankards were converted into jugs or coffee pots.

If you keep these points in mind and learn to look and handle silver as much as possible, perhaps in the saleroom, or at a specialist dealer, you will grow in confidence and knowledge.

SILVER

DRINKING

THE SERVING OF ALCOHOLIC BEVERAGES at mealtimes is a long-established custom and throughout history silver objects have been made to suit the demands of those imbibing. For the service of wine, goblets were the answer and these were made from the 16th century onwards. Beakers, too, were important vessels and are even older than goblets: examples survive from the the 15th century.

Wine needed to be served cold and in England large wine cisterns were made that could hold numerous bottles, but in the 18th century smaller wine coolers were produced as well as ice pails. The use of smaller wine coolers was widespread on the Continent. Wine labels, small decorative labels that were suspended on chains and were inscribed with the names of various types of wine or spirit, such as port, were hung around the necks of decanters so that their contents could be easily identified. Punch was a popular drink in the 18th century, and punch bowls and ladles were also made in a variety of differing shapes.

224

▾ *Goblets continued to be made into the 18th century and later, even though the use of glass had by then become more usual. The beaker-shaped body of this 19th-century continental silver and silver-gilt goblet has leaf and acanthus decoration and is engraved with the Prince of Wales's feathers. The foot is decorated with gadrooning.*

▸ *The shape of silver beakers was based on that of the drinking horn. Continental examples, such as this 17th-century German beaker with its chasing, were usually more decorative than their English counterparts.*

SILVER

▸ Late 18th century English wine funnels. These were used in the process of decanting wine. The wide top of the funnel has a perforated strainer in which any cork or sediment could be caught. The slightly curved lower part of the funnel ensured that the wine entered the decanter slowly. The funnel can be separated into two pieces to enable it to be cleaned thoroughly after use.

225

◂ Decorative wine coasters such as this Georgian pierced silver pair were used to protect table tops from drips and spillage as the decanters or bottles were passed around during meals. They were also used at the end of a meal, when the gentlemen remained behind to drink their port. (14cm wide)

▸ This pair of late Victorian silver wine coasters is, appropriately, decorated with grapes. You will sometimes find a pair of coasters mounted on wheels rather like a carriage; this is known as a wine trolley. Bottles were placed in it and it was 'pulled' around the table top by gentlemen sitting over their port, since there were no servants present at this stage of the dinner.

SILVER

TANKARDS

THE TANKARD ROSE TO prominence in the 16th century in Northern Europe and England, although relatively few English examples have survived. Tankards produced in Germany and Scandinavia are more heavily decorated than the simpler tapered style found in England. There were some differences in size in European tankards such as the rather squat tankards, on three ball feet, found in 17th century Sweden. Most European tankards have embossed or chased decoration and in some cases the body is inset with coins or medals.

The growing consumption of wine and spirits during the 18th century saw a decline in the consumption of ale and it was only in the 19th century that the production of tankards saw a revival with earlier styles being copied, and even plain, earlier tankards having elaborate decoration added.

Mugs which are basically tankards without lids were made in England and America, from the late 17th century onwards.

226

▲ Late 17th century English tankard - 18cm high. This is a fine plain example of an English tankard with a nice scrolling thumb piece to the lid. Others from this period can be decorated with fluting and foliate motifs and even in some cases chinoiserie decoration can be found.

▲ This late Georgian English tankard dates from 1806. It is decorated with bands and has a dome lid, which is typical of the time, as is its taller, narrower shape. Many tankards are engraved with crests, coats of arms or even inscriptions.

▸ The embossed, or repoussé, decoration of this late 19th-century silver-gilt German tankard is based on that found on 16th- or 17th-century tankards. Many of these were similarly decorated, often with a religious theme such as that seen here.

SILVER

COFFEE POTS

COFFEE WAS INTRODUCED TO the Western world in the 17th century and it soon became a popular drink and coffee houses, where business could be discussed, became meeting places. Because coffee grounds accumulate at the bottom of the pot it was necessary for the spout of the coffee pot to be above them and thus coffee pots are taller than both teapots and chocolate pots. There are two distinctive types of pot found in Europe and England in the 18th century. One pot is the pear-shape found in France which often has spiral fluting and chased decoration and stands on three short feet and with the handle at right-angles to the spout. The other type is where the handle is opposite the spout and this was made in Europe, England and America. Some early English examples have their handles at right angles to the spout but by the 1730s these had disappeared and the tapering, cylindrical form gave way to the baluster and pear shape.

▶ *Georgian coffee pot with wicker handle c.1773 30cm high. The tall, elegant shape of this pot denotes its date. The presence of a lip rather than a spout indicates that this may have been part of a tea and coffee set where it could also double as a hot-water jug. Some coffee pots have discs at the top and bottom of the handle and at the bottom of the spout for reinforcement.*

SILVER

228

▼ *Since coffee pots in the 18th century had spouts, this Irish jug was perhaps used for hot water originally. The pear shape and spreading foot are usual for this period. Irish silver is often more heavily decorated than its English counterpart, and some plain examples have had chased decoration added later.*

▲ *This mid-18th-century coffee pot is an example of the pear-shaped pots found on the Continent. The pouring lip is a typical feature as European coffee of the time tended to be the thick Turkish variety. The spiral chased decoration is also typical of the period.*

SILVER

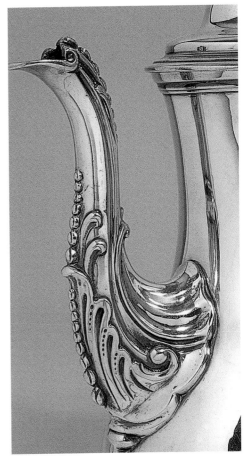

▼ As this detail makes clear, the cast spout of the pot, with its scrolls and anthemion motif, still shows elements of the transition from the Rococo style to Neo-classicism.

▲ The pear-shaped English silver coffee pot, with a wooden handle, was made in London in 1772. Its high, domed lid, taller outline and vase shape are typical of the time and mark the growing influence of Neo-classicism.

SILVER

230

◀ *The style of this tapering, cylindrical English coffee pot by Swift (1733) had started to go out of fashion by about 1730. The flattened domed lid had replaced the earlier, higher domed shape in the mid-1720s. This pot is engraved with a coat of arms, but you should bear in mind that arms and crests will sometimes be later additions.*

▶ *The vogue for Naturalism, which arose in the second half of the 19th century, is evident in this American coffee pot by Kirk & Son. It is richly decorated overall in an ornate scheme of embossed and chased flowers and leaves.*

SILVER

CHOCOLATE POTS

CHOCOLATE, WHICH CAME FROM the West Indies, was another beverage introduced into Europe during the 17th century, and once again special silver pots were made for it. There is, however, one particular difference between coffee and chocolate pots: that is the finial on the cover is either removable or hinged so that a special rod, known as a molinet, could be inserted and used to stir the chocolate before it was poured. Chocolate pots are usually smaller than coffee pots although you will come across examples of conversions of chocolate pots into coffee pots, which will have taken place after the use of chocolate pots declined, with jugs being used instead.

▸ *The domed lid and tapering shape of this chocolate pot by Thomas Terle (1729) is typical of English pots of this date. The fruitwood handle is set at right angles to the spout; this is a feature not found on English pots after 1730.*

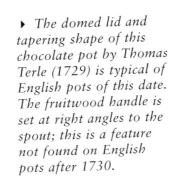

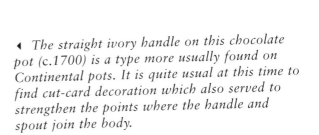

◂ *The straight ivory handle on this chocolate pot (c.1700) is a type more usually found on Continental pots. It is quite usual at this time to find cut-card decoration which also served to strengthen the points where the handle and spout join the body.*

SILVER

TEAPOTS

▼ *The typical attributes of the period – a wooden handle and bird finial – appear on this German teapot made in Augsburg in 1765. The inverted pear shape and branch-shaped spout are also found in contemporary ceramic teapots. Although this shape is found in American examples, it was not so popular in England.*

THE DUTCH EAST INDIA COMPANY first brought tea to Europe in the early 17th century. Since it was a costly and highly-prized drink, early teapots were quite small in size and their form was based on the ceramic wine pots that were also imported from China. The custom of drinking tea – it was normally taken after dinner – grew, and as it did so the size of the teapot became larger, although tea was still expensive. This is why 18th-century tea caddies are fitted with locks aimed at stopping the servants from pilfering the tea. Some teapots still have their original stands. Styles and shape varied throughout the 18th century and a complete tea set, as we know it today, was only really developed in the 19th century, when the idea of afternoon tea became established as habits in eating changed. In addition to teapots, tea kettles, urns and samovars were also used in the serving of tea.

SILVER

▲ The shape of this teapot from 1862 is copied from the shape that was popular in England in the latter part of the 18th century. Many such period teapots have bright-cut decoration, achieved by gouging out the pattern with a tool that burnishes one side as the cut is made. The handle is ebony and the knop ivory.

◀ The pear shape and chased floral decoration of this Victorian teapot from 1885 reflect the interest in nature shown by members of reform movements such as the Aesthetic Style.

SILVER

◂ The lid of the teapot below has a flowerhead finial characteristic of the period. It is important to check hinges, since they may be damaged or worn and any repairs can be expensive.

234

▾ Dating from the 1840s, this lobed, melon-shaped teapot, with its curves and scrolls, is typical of the Rococo Revival of the mid-19th century. It would have been part of a tea service, with hot water jug, creamer and probably sugar bowl.

SILVER

JUGS

SILVER JUGS WERE MADE for a variety of purposes, usually in the prevailing styles of the day. One important and practical point to remember is that jugs with silver handles were meant for cold liquids, since silver is a good conductor of heat.

Jugs served a wide variety of purposes, from serving beer to holding water as part of a ewer and basin set used for the washing of hands or maybe as part of a dressing set. One popular type of jug is that used for wine, and in the 19th century special silver or glass and silver-mounted jugs were made for serving claret and liqueurs. Many examples of these can be found, including some in the shape of an animal such as a walrus, griffin or raven

Such zoomorphic forms were not related just to those jugs containing alcohol, since examples can be found of cream jugs in various shapes of which, perhaps, the most well known is the cow creamer, made in England in Georgian times and copied in silver in Holland in the late 19th and early 20th centuries.

Sauceboats were used to serve sauces and gravy at the table. Continental ones are usually double-lipped, with a lip at each end, while English and American examples usually have a spout for pouring at one end and a handle, often in the form of a scroll, at the other.

235

▲ *Surviving English silver from the late 16th and early 17th centuries is rare, since much was melted down during the Civil Wars to make coins to pay the troops – a custom sadly also seen elsewhere in Europe. The squat shape of this silver-gilt jug, dating from c.1600, is also found in contemporary pottery.*

▸ *Although this elaborately chased and engraved cream jug is a 19th-century copy of an earlier style, the quality of the execution and the hallmarks clearly show the date of its manufacture. Cream jugs were not introduced until the early 18th century.*

Silver
Candlesticks

236

▼ *The overall decoration of these 19th-century English silver candlesticks is heavier than that found in the late 18th century. Foliage and scroll motifs are a common feature in chased decoration, and the nozzle follows the pattern of the base and is similarly decorated.*

IN Britain, most surviving candlesticks were made after the mid-17th century. In the 18th century the process of casting became the method used in the production of candlesticks, with the base, stem and sconce being cast separately and then soldered together. The removable nozzle, which was introduced in the 1740s and whose shape and decoration usually reflected that found on the base, was intended to stop wax running down the stem of the candlestick. In the second half of the 18th century, instead of using large amounts of silver to make a solid candlestick, a central rod with plaster of Paris formed the core, with thinner, rolled silver being used to provide the outer skin. Early candlesticks are usually shorter than their 18th-century counterparts which are normally 23cm high or more.

Various types of candlestick were used in the home, including the chamberstick, which was used in the bedroom and generally had a circular tray and carrying handle; the taperstick, which was used for the lighting of tapers and for sealing wax when closing letters; and the candelabrum for use on a dinner table or in a drawing room, where a candlestick can be fitted with branches to hold more candles and so provide extra light.

SILVER

▲ *These tall, Sheffield silver candlesticks, dating from 1898, are in the form of a Corinthian Column, a shape that enjoyed renewed popularity in the late 19th century. Similar examples are sometimes fitted with cut-glass reservoirs for use as oil lamps. The detail shows the fine workmanship of the column's capital and the gadrooning and anthemion scroll decoration on the base.*

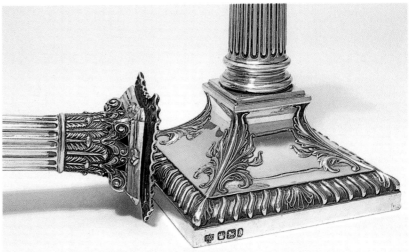

SILVER

This pair of Sheffield plate candlesticks (c.1870) are ornamented with masks, swags, pendants, reeding and beading in the Neoclassical taste. This style had been prevalent in the late 18th century and enjoyed a revival in the second half of the 19th century. Sheffield plate is made by rolling sheet silver on to a copper base and in some instances you can see what is known as 'bleeding', where the plate has worn away to reveal the copper base.

SILVER

These candlesticks are typical of the plated wares produced in the late 19th century. The shape is a pastiche of those found in the Rococo period, as is evident from the detail showing the exuberant die-stamped floral motif on the base, which is repeated elsewhere.

SILVER

240

These rather elegant Austrian chased silver pieces, dating from 1865–70, look back to the 18th century in their design and decoration. The base is ornamented with shell motifs and the stem has a knop in its lower part; the shoulder, towards the top, has reeded decoration.

SILVER

A more decorative interpretation of table candlesticks, this pair of rather delicate, late 19th-century Continental candlabra follows the figurative tradition found in candlesticks from the late 17th century onwards.

241

▼ *Candle snuffers were a convenient way of extinguishing the flame and also trimming the wick to a reasonable length to stop the candle smoking too much. This late 19th-century example is complete with its tray.*

SILVER

PLATES & DISHES

IN THE 18TH AND 19TH CENTURIES meals, especially dinner, were quite elaborate affairs and numerous types of dish were needed to serve the various courses. Among the dishes found on the table would be a soup tureen, which in the 18th century could be massive and highly decorated; a variety of covered dishes for vegetables, and platters of various sizes for meat and other foodstuffs. Plates varied in size, depending on whether they were for a main course or dessert. The style and shape of these plates remained fairly constant over the centuries, but those with a moulded edge are usually older than those with a gadrooned border; and because they were a practical item, decoration was restricted to the rim or edge.

242

▼ *Two early 19-century plates, with gadrooned edges and moulded borders, from a set of 12. In the 18th century a dinner service could consist of several dozen or more dinner plates.*

▲ *Salvers are flat trays with a moulded or gadrooned edge and were used for serving drinks or food as well as for presenting letters or visiting cards. (Late 19th century).*

SILVER

▲ This vegetable tureen, dating from 1888, has a domed lid, decorated with gadrooning, and two handles. Also known as entrée dishes, tureens sometimes had a stand into which hot water was poured to keep the contents warm. The handles on the lids are often detachable, so the lid could be inverted and used to serve cold food.

▼ It was quite common for certain courses to be served in tureens or dishes that represented the animal involved, a feature that is also found in faience and porcelain. This rather fierce example would have been used to serve fish. Fish dishes are more usually found in continental silver than in English.

SILVER

FLATWARE & SERVING IMPLEMENTS

244

FLATWARE DEVELOPED OVER THE centuries and the use of forks for eating was brought to England from the Continent by Charles II. At first spoons and forks were made in matching styles and it was only later in the 17th century that the idea of matching knives was introduced. Early knives do not usually survive in good condition, since their handles were made from rolled silver 'wrapped' around a core of pitch, so it is usual to find that many services have later knives. Many patterns, such as the Trefid pattern, derived from French examples.

The variety of foods forming meals required different implements to serve them, and it was during the 18th century that servers became an integral part of flatware services. They included fish servers, ladles and spoons for serving soup, meat, vegetables and sauces. You will find complete sets of flatware from the early 20th century and some from the 19th century.

Soup spoons and fish knives and forks were introduced in England in the 19th century. For the dessert course there would be a separate set of flatware complete with serving implements, including sugar spoons and grape scissors. One interesting and unusual collectable item is the silver marrow scoop; it was used to scrape marrow, which was considered a delicacy, out of the cooked bones.

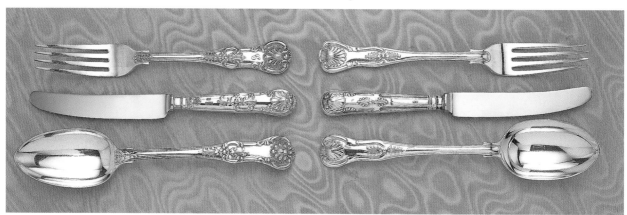

◄ There are many variations of
the King's and Queen's pattern
flatware, whose shapes come
from French flatware. The
King's pattern, on the left, is
usually slightly more elaborate
than the Queen's. Decoration
was done by die-stamping and
where it is found on the front
and back of implements, they
are said to be 'double struck'.

▲ This shows a selection of the
types of flatware patterns in use
at the end of the 19th century.
Some, like the pistol-handled
knife (top row, second from
left) and the Old English
pattern knife and fork (bottom
row, second from right), were
patterns that were first made in
the 18th century.

SILVER

▼ *The diversity of implements used at the table is evident from this group of late 19th- and early 20th-century items. It includes a carving knife and fork, soup ladle, butter knife, pickle fork, asparagus tongs and a cheese scoop. The small lobster pick is decorated with an engraved lobster.*

▲ *Twelve small spoons and a larger serving spoon form this Austrian silver-gilt dessert set, which is still in its original box. The design, with flower-shaped handles, is in Art Nouveau style. Complete sets are always preferable to items bought piecemeal.*

SILVER

▸ *Although fish slices and forks were part of 19th-century canteens, they could also be bought as 'additional items'. This set was made in Sheffield in 1905. The shaped blade was used to part the fish from the bone rather than for cutting.*

SILVER

SPOONS

POONS HAVE BEEN AROUND since Roman times and, as the centuries have passed, have been made for a wide variety of purposes, which has made them a very collectable class of small silver. The Middle Ages saw their use increase, although with the exception of Apostle spoons they were not made in sets until the late 17th century. Until the mid-18th century, most spoons had an upturned handle end because they were laid with the bowl facing downwards on the table. After this date, spoons were laid with the bowl facing upwards and decoration appeared on the front of the handle. Teaspoons were made in sets and also as part of large table services, and in the 19th century decorative and novelty spoons commemorating important events were also made. One attractive 19th-century spoon is the berry spoon, where the bowl is decorated with chased berries, but beware – some of these are earlier spoons which have been decorated later.

▶ *The range of different types of spoon is clearly demonstrated here. From the left they include spoons for salt and mustard, a pierced mote spoon – used to remove floating tea leaves – sugar sifters, bone egg spoons and sugar shovels. The four spoons in the centre were for snuff.*

SILVER

▶ Jam spoons come in a variety of styles and forms, often with decorated bowls. While some are entirely silver, others from the 19th century have bone or ivory handles. Silver-gilt was used as a form of protection against the acidity of some foods, such as fruit.

◀ Caddy spoons are popular with collectors. A wide variety of styles, shapes and materials was used in their production. Shell motifs and shapes were popular, as can be seen here. The spoon appropriately shaped and patterned like a leaf dates from the early 19th century and is particularly collectable.

SILVER
CRUETS & CASTERS

IN THE MIDDLE AGES, salt was regarded as an important commodity for trading and flavouring, and elaborate 'great salts' would be found. The dished trencher salt, which became fashionable in the early 18th century, was superseded by circular salts on small feet, and later they too gave way to the boat shape and the oval form associated with the Neo-classical style.

Casters for sugar and spices originated in France in the mid-17th century and their use soon spread abroad. Sugar casters were to some extent, especially in England, replaced by the use of sugar bowls in the late 18th century. The idea of a stand to hold oil and vinegar bottles, and later casters, came from the wine and water cruets used in churches, and while early ones have silver bottles most have silver-mounted glass bottles. One type of English cruet, known as a Warwick cruet, held casters as well as bottles.

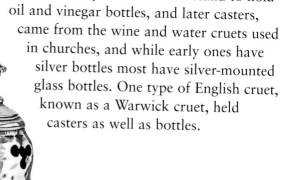

◀ *The detail of the Georgian cruet opposite shows the silver-mounted oil and vinegar bottles and one of the casters. For collectors, it is important that the bottles should be original to the frame and not later replacements and that the stoppers belong to the right bottles.*

SILVER

◄ *This Georgian silver and glass Warwick cruet, with its oval frame and central carrying handle, is a good late 18th-century English example. It holds three bottles and three casters and is larger than earlier cruets. The restrained chased decoration on the silver is typical of the period.*

▼ *These late 18th-century French salts, with their ram's-head corners, hoof feet, garlands and swags, are a fine example of Louis XVI style. The pierced silver frames are beautifully set off by the blue glass liners.*

SILVER

In this 19th- and early 20th-century group are cruets that vary from frames with up to five bottles and condiment sets with pepper, salt and mustard only. As a general rule, simpler glass bottles are of a later date than those with more elaborate cut patterns. Smaller cruets such as these are known as breakfast cruets.

SILVER

▼ *Some of the other items found on the early 20th-century dining table included salt and pepper shakers, a sugar bucket, bottle frames and cruets used to hold boiled eggs. At the centre of the larger egg cruet is a boiler, with a spirit lamp below it, in which the eggs could actually be cooked at the table and then served in the cups with their own spoons. Egg spoons and cups were often lined with gilt to prevent the silver from tarnishing.*

SILVER

256

▲ *A fine set of three octagonal baluster-shaped casters with pierced covers, made by Charles Adams in 1713. The smaller pair would have been used for pepper and spices, while the larger one would have held sugar. The fit and the pierced decoration of the cover are two points to consider when collecting casters.*

◀ *Mustard pots were first used in the second half of the 18th century, when the previous fashion for dry mustard was replaced by the paste form in use today. This pair of mid-19th century continental mustard pots is chased all over with ornate scrolling foliage.*

SILVER

DECORATIVE TABLE PIECES

OWNING SILVER WAS A SYMBOL of prosperity and wealth and so the very rich would have elaborate centrepieces, figures and other table ornaments to relay this message. This display silver could include vases, sometimes in sets or garnitures, for flowers or purely show. Cups and covers were another decorative item that could adorn the table, and in many instances these were sporting trophies for horse races or other such events. Many of these objects continued to be made into the 19th and 20th centuries. One useful type of centrepiece was the epergne, which combined bowls for fruit or flowers with smaller dishes for sweetmeats; some even held cruets. They were normally made in the prevailing taste of the day and in the 19th century many were fitted with glass bowls and dishes.

257

▶ *The centrepiece in the form of a ship was first seen in the Middle Ages in France, where it was a symbol of the host's standing; it was also found in Germany. Some were made to hold wine or salt and would have been used by the highest ranking person present. Ships were extensively copied in the 19th century, and this Spanish silver-plated one dates from the late 1800s.*

◀ *Ornaments such as these late 19th-century fighting cocks were designed as table decorations and were placed along the centre of a dining table with candlesticks, with perhaps a tureen or epergne in the middle.*

DECORATIVE DISHES

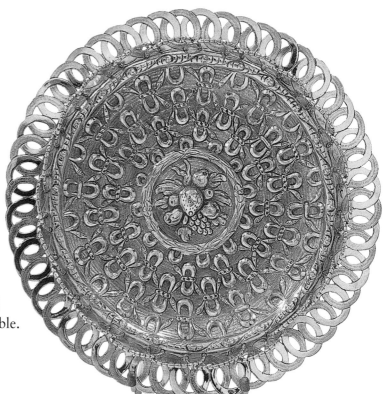

258

ISHES WERE MADE for a variety of useful purposes but there is also a long tradition of decorative dishes made only for display. These are easily identifiable, since the centre, which would have been plain on a useful dish, will have elaborate decoration. Such dishes were displayed on a side table or buffet. However, some items, such as a bread or cake basket, while having a practical function during a meal, could still also be highly decorative on the table.

▲ *A good idea of the type of ornamental dish found in the 16th century can be gained from this German example with embossed decoration and a pierced outer rim, made in silver and silver-gilt c.1660. It may have been used for fruit, but its chief purpose was display.*

◀ *The centre of this Austrian silver dish is embossed with a Neo-classical scene. Decorative dishes were made into the 19th century, when gilding was done by the electrogilding process; the resultant colour is much harder than that on 18th-century pieces on which the noxious mercury-gilding process was used.*

SILVER

▸ *Pierced decoration was common on bread baskets from the 18th century onwards. The central swing handle on this late 19th-century English example is another common feature. Such baskets were used for bread or cake on the dining or tea table.*

◂ *A good example of late 19th-century taste, this German basket is elaborately embossed and has a pedestal foot and pierced handle. Such baskets were used during the dessert course to hold fruit.*

▸ *The Norwegian silver and red glass bonbon dish in the Neo-classical taste was made c.1830. It would have held sweetmeats or bonbons and is decorated with stylized Egyptian masks and trailing vine decoration on its sides and handle. It is always an advantage to have the original glass liner for such pieces.*

SILVER

SMALL SILVER ITEMS

AMONG THE LARGE VARIETY OF BOXES made over the centuries are spice boxes, which held the spices used in the making of punch. Sugar, too, was kept in boxes before the use of sugar bowls became more customary, and you will come across 18th-century German examples. The custom of taking snuff saw the production of silver snuff boxes, and silver tobacco boxes also exist. From the early 20th century, you will find silver cigarette cases.

The range of small silver items is wide and varies from vinaigrettes used to hold spiced vinegar to card cases, posy holders and vases to silver pin cushion holders.

▲ *Although this pair of vases is in the Arts and Crafts Style that developed in England in the second half of the 19th century, they are of South American origin. Their shapes reflect the Gothic influence but the restrained decoration is typical of the style.*

◀ *This collectable novelty candle lamp in the form of a lantern combines silver with Limoges enamel. It is a combination that was used in the mid-19th century for snuff boxes, miniature furniture, clocks and dressing table sets.*

SILVER

◄ *This smaller oval chased box, with a delightful rustic scene of apple picking, may have been used for sweetmeats or trinkets. Some snuff boxes are similarly decorated in high relief.*

▼ *Made in Russia in the late 19th century, this chased Rococo-style silver box may well have been part of a dressing table set, perhaps used to hold jewellery, since it once had a key. Boxes like this, even if once part of a larger set, are still collectable in their own right. Similar boxes were used in the 18th century for sugar.*

▼ *Sets of chairs like these Dutch silver miniatures were made in the 19th century for doll's houses and as display cabinet pieces and are often in an earlier style. In a simple way they recall the silver furniture made for palaces in the 17th and early 18th centuries.*

SILVER

SILVER WAS NOT RESTRICTED to the dining room – it could be found in various other rooms in the house. In grand houses, large dressing-table sets were found in bedrooms, and even middle-class homes would have a silver dressing set of brushes and a hand mirror; there were dressing chests for men as well. Silver inkwells, photograph frames and perhaps even a clock might be found on a desk or writing table in a library or boudoir. Nor were children neglected, since silver mugs and rattles were given as Christening gifts. Silver was even used out of doors for picnics or tea parties in the garden; indeed, some items were specially made for use during outdoor pursuits such as hunting and fishing.

262

▲ *Hip flasks such as this early 20th-century silver-plated one were used by gentlemen taking part in outdoor activities. Many have a curved shape and in some a detachable lower section can be used as a cup. Those with monograms or other signs of ownership are usually cheaper than undecorated ones.*

◀ *It is not unusual to find individual grooming sets. A set such as this in its original fitted case is more valuable than individual pieces. Signs of use are acceptable, but damage is not. Decorated handles are always an appealing factor.*

SILVER

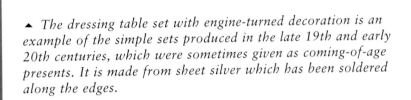

▼ *The shape of the baby's rattle on the right is traditional. It comprises a whistle-type dummy, bells and a teething stick. On earlier examples coral was used for the teething stick, while later ones may be of ivory or mother-of-pearl, as on the left-hand rattle, which has a teddy bear motif.*

263

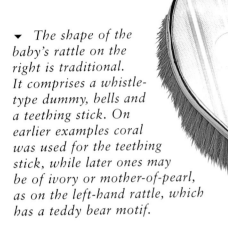

▲ *The dressing table set with engine-turned decoration is an example of the simple sets produced in the late 19th and early 20th centuries, which were sometimes given as coming-of-age presents. It is made from sheet silver which has been soldered along the edges.*

▼ *By the time this inkstand was made in the early 1900s, inkstands were no longer fitted with pouncepots or tapersticks. This silver-plated, machine-stamped example, with ball and claw feet, has two inkwells and a recessed well for the pen. The stand is decorated with gadrooning.*

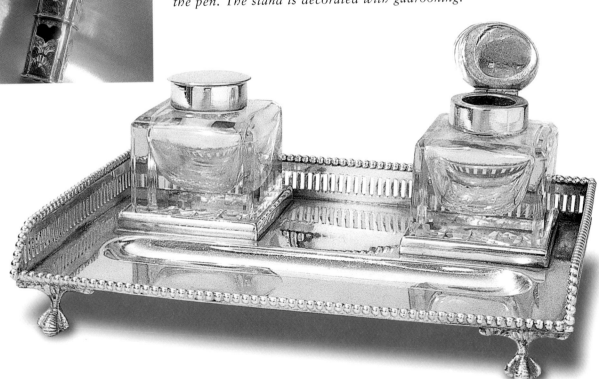

OTHER METALS

PEWTER

264

AN ALLOY OF TIN, PEWTER IS known for its silvery grey colour, which darkens through oxidization as it is used. Local craftsmen made up objects in their workshops, usually by casting, and many pieces have maker's marks. In Britain, a less expensive form of pewter known as Britannia metal was used from the late 18th century onwards.

Pewter was widely used in the 16th to 18th centuries and many of the shapes were taken from those found in silver. In Britain, you will find many examples of pewter plates, dishes and tankards. On the Continent you will find examples of coffee pots, soup tureens, jardinières and even cisterns and basins. In the late 1800s, pewter enjoyed a revival in Britain which started through the Arts and Crafts Movement and went on into the 1930s. But beware, many old pewter forms have been faked and reproduced in the 20th century.

▲ The oval shape of this pewter teapot, dating from the early 19th century, echoes that found in late 18th-century silver. Some shapes in pewter are 'traditional' and dating can be difficult.

▶ The little jug would have been used for milk, the canister for storing tea and the large jug for milk or water. One of the components used to make old pewter was lead and it is worth noting that foodstuffs should not be stored in such items with a high lead content.

PEWTER

▼ This ewer, of Flemish origin, would have been used for cold drinks such as beer. The pouring lip is a typical continental feature that is also found in silver. As with silver, condition is important, although scratches and dents are to be expected and accepted in pewter, more serious damage is not.

▲ The columnar shape of these candlesticks with detachable nozzles is also found in porcelain and silver of the late 1700s and later.

▲ Measures were used for both dry and wet goods to ensure that the customer received the right amount. The piece on the left is a ewer, whose shape denotes its Flemish/Belgian origin.

▶ Pewter pepper pots in the early 18th century were usually of baluster shape, as were sifters, which were taller and often 15cm or more in height. Later in the century the vase shape, reflecting the Neo-classical style, was adopted.

CARPETS
& TEXTILES

RUGS & CARPETS

268

CARPETS WERE FIRST MADE in the Orient at least 1,400 years ago. While in the West carpets have always been viewed as a form of decorative furnishing, and are often partially hidden by other furniture, from early times in the East they had both an aesthetic and practical function: as a pleasing focus for the eye and as protection from the cold or hard ground beneath the tent. With the evolution of Islamic culture, carpets and rugs acquired still greater significance as a kind of sanctuary – a place where a Muslim worshipper could kneel in prayer five times a day. The designs of some prayer rugs actually enabled the worshipper to adjust his position toward the holy city of Mecca.

The primary materials of carpets have been wool, cotton and silk for centuries. On exceptional occasions, silver and gold thread has been added. The basic principal of carpet-making has also remained largely unchanged, involving the alternation of horizontal rows of knots with one or more rows of weft across the entire width of a loom.

The huge variety of carpet decoration is an academic study in itself; details give clues to factors such as place and time of origin and whether the maker came from a nomadic tribe, a city workshop or a large court atelier. In general, though, there were and are two distinct traditions: the geometric style, using straight lines in its patterns, and the floral style, employing curved lines and arabesques.

Before 1870, natural dyes were used for colouring the material, but after that chemical dyes gradually became the norm. Carpets classified as antique usually predate 1920, when they were not yet corrupted by the ornamental requirements of Europe and America.

▸ *The 19th century saw the rise of orientalism, the West's obsession with the exotic East. Nowhere was this obsession more apparent than in the Victorian love of Oriental rugs and carpets.*

CARPETS & TEXTILES

CARPETS & TEXTILES
KILIM RUGS

OME OF THE MOST POPULAR of all rugs are usually referred to as 'Turkish'. Strictly speaking, though, such rugs should be called Anatolian – a region which embraces a much larger area than that covered by Turkey's present-day boundaries. Individual Anatolian rugs are usually named after their place of origin, but rugs in general fall into a number of distinct categories. The largest single category is made up by 'kilims'. Kilims are flat-woven, a method of production that sets them apart from rugs whose piles are made up from closely packed individual strands knotted vertically to the backing. Flat-woven fabrics require far less material and labour to produce than those with a knotted pile and in former times were widely used as draperies, portable floor coverings and day-to-day bags.

Despite the fact that kilims cannot match pile rugs for complexity or subtlety of design, their simple geometric patterns can be highly attractive. Common designs include the tree of life and floral patterns – the latter being often highly stylized. Colour is important, too, and prices tend to reflect whether the rug has been coloured with natural or synthetic dyes. Hand-made examples by 19th-century nomadic tribespeople can fetch the highest prices of all. Much cheaper are the many different kilim bags, such as salt or saddle bags.

Good quality kilims continue to be a fast-appreciating asset and are rarely available at low prices. There are also many fakes on the market. It is therefore safest to buy from a reputable dealer or a major auction house – or wherever the provenance of the rug can be guaranteed.

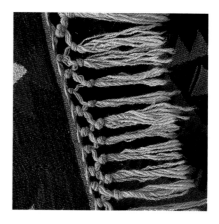

▲ *Knotting the ends on a kilim is a tribal tradition. Like the edges of a rug, the ends are vulnerable to damage and you may find that they have been replaced.*

▼ *The art of carpet making is thought to have begun in Persia more than 2,000 years ago, but it soon spread to Anatolia (Turkey), the Caucasus and Central Asia. This example is Anatolian.*

CARPETS & TEXTILES

▲ *Anatolian rugs tend to be simpler in spirit than their Persian counterparts. This example, made purely for domestic use, has a coarse charm.*

▶ *North-west Anatolian prayer rug. Note the geometric patterning and the pointed mihrab (arch), which the practising Muslim would face towards Mecca during prayers.*

CARPETS & TEXTILES

▸ *Border detail. Small and large bands create a counterpoint.*

▾ *A modern, naturally dyed kilim from Sivrihisar in Western Turkey. The pattern symbolizes fertility.*

CARPETS & TEXTILES

◀ *A popular floral design.*

▼ *A design known as Memling Gül, after a painter noted for including such rugs in his work. 'Gül' is the generic term for decorative medallions of this kind.*

273

◀ *A stylized representation of a plant, common in tribal rugs.*

▶ *This kilim end or 'fringe' has been woven on to the rug.*

CARPETS & TEXTILES

ORIENTAL CARPETS

274

KNOTTED PILE CARPETS are usually made of wool, although some of the finest Persian examples are woven of silk. The carpet foundation is composed of weft (horizontal) and warp (vertical) yarns, traditionally of cotton, linen or hemp. Individual carpet yarns, traditionally dyed with natural substances such as indigo and madder, are then hand-knotted around the warp yarns. The unknotted ends form into a pile which is subsequently sheared to a uniform height. The quality of the carpet is a function of the intricacy and beauty of the design and the density and skill of the knotting. Several different types of knot are found, depending on where the carpet was made – the most important being the Turkish (or 'Ghiordes') and the Persian (or 'Sehna'). There are two main elements to carpet design: a central area called the field, and one or more borders that act as a sort of frame. The field may be decorated with a single design or with a variety of panels or medallions. At its finest, carpet design combines intricacy with harmony and balance.

▶ *Oriental carpets are, in a sense, art you can stand on, although by the 19th century – the heyday of the carpet as collectible – the art was very much to the fore. Nonetheless, it is important to remember that the simplest and the most elaborate designs share, at root, the same functional origins.*

CARPETS & TEXTILES

CARPETS & TEXTILES
20TH-CENTURY RUGS

276

I N THE 20TH CENTURY there was a revival of the 19th-century Arts and Crafts idea of carpets and rugs being designed as part of the total decorative scheme of a house or apartment. The 1920s, in particular, saw an upsurge in the popularity of the art form. Some designers, such as Marion Dorn and Marian Pepler, designed for well-known manufacturers such as Wilton, while others worked with machine-weaving companies which had specialist offshoots. A third option was provided by the cheap labour available in poorer countries. Both Turkey and India produced rugs and carpets to new designs sent out to them from Europe.

Between the wars, rugs were made by a variety of different manufacturing techniques. In general, their designs incorporated the Art Deco styling that was so widespread in the other

▾ This striking Art Deco conception was executed on an imposing scale: it measures 3.5 x 2.7m. The influence of Cubism and the Russian Constructivists is apparent.

CARPETS & TEXTILES

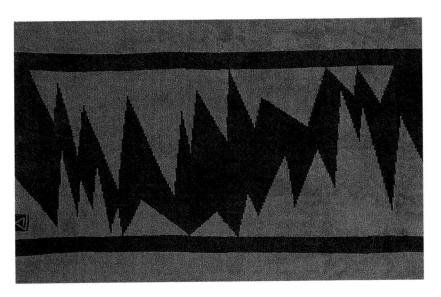

◄ The zigzag design of this rug has a spiky energy suggestive of the jazz music which characterized the age.

decorative arts, as well as the tendency to abstraction that was so influential in painting. Since World War II, however, taste in rugs has become increasingly conservative. The main European manufacturers put most of their energies into traditional patterning, making copies of earlier carpets or approximating earlier styles. Designs by Da Silva Bruhns and Jean Lurcat for the French workshops of the mid-20th century, for example, are based on earlier motifs and forms. Only the manufacturing methods have changed significantly.

Few contemporary artists have worked on rugs. Artists who have created rugs sought to bring out the textural potential of the fabrics and create decorative hangings rather than to make functional articles for the floor.

▼ American textile designer Marion Dorn created this quintessentially modernist design, with its powerful superimposition of curvilinear and rectilinear motifs.

CARPETS & TEXTILES

TEXTILES

278

BEFORE THE 18TH CENTURY, textile-making was literally a cottage industry throughout Europe. Weavers might band together in workshops to reproduce finer materials for the gentry, but most clothes, carpets and coverings were produced by women or lone craftsmen based in a village and using skills and patterns handed down for generations. Indeed the majority of peasant familes would have kept a wheel and a loom to spin and weave their own rough cloth. However, the invention of various powered machines for spinning and weaving in the 18th and early 19th centuries made possible the mass production of cheap textiles, and the tradition of folk weaving soon began to die out across Europe.

Nonetheless, there was a significant reaction against the dominance of machine-made materials in the late 19th century. Under the aegis of the Arts and Crafts Movement, leading designers of the day produced their own fabrics in workshops and studios. Though the anti-machine impetus quickly wore out, the designs of the Arts and Crafts Movement had widespread influence on their Art Nouveau and Art Deco followers – and consequently on the whole of modern design.

In their time, hand-made textiles were rated very highly, if only because of the money and labour involved in their production. They were therefore also looked after very carefully, which explains why so many are still in good condition. It was only during the the second quarter of the 20th century that there was an almost total disregard for the textile arts – though, fortunately, a number of important collectors (particularly in the USA) maintained extensive collections.

Things are very different now. Textile collection – be it of rugs, embroidery, clothes or lace – has boomed over the last decade, and it is now unlikely that anything of historical value will be thrown away or destroyed.

CARPETS & TEXTILES

▲ *Victorians afflicted by gout could suffer in comfort –*
and in harmony with the rest of their surroundings –
with a gout stool such as this one.

CARPETS & TEXTILES
FURNISHING FABRICS

Furnishing fabrics, like many other textiles, began to be machine-made in the early 19th century. Despite this tendency, in Great Britain and the USA members of the Arts and Crafts Movement stressed the importance of individual designs made for particular interiors and settings. For the middle-class home, comfort was achieved with heavy upholstery and a sense of opulence with patterning and draped fabrics – chair coverings being flounced and fringed and their textiles designed with an often confusing exuberance. The designs of fabrics might mix Gothic Revival with oriental motifs. Favourite colours included maroon, purple and mossy green, all of which were translated into thick velvets and lustrous damasks for both upholstery and curtaining.

Of particular importance during the last two decades of the 19th century were the Silver Studios in England. The firm's designs were purveyed to an increasingly discerning public, and their Art Nouveau productions were exported all over Europe and to the USA. Arthur Silver's revival of stencilling for furnishing fabrics was widely imitated, and this had an incalculable effect on the fabric manufacture in the modern era.

▶ *Large box ottoman upholstered in a richly patterned carpeting. The design is Eastern in style, reflecting the ottoman's origins in the Ottoman Empire. The piece is set on a concealed plinth, to protect the edges of the fabric.*

CARPETS & TEXTILES

▲ This ottoman dates from the 1880s. The upholstery is maroon plush, with a patterned needlepoint seat.

▸ Blue plush ottoman with floral patterned needlepoint seat cover. The plinth and feet are of mahogany.

CARPETS & TEXTILES
EASTERN TEXTILES

FOR CENTURIES ISLAMIC TEXTILES, whether the fine tunics of medieval Egypt, the delicate muslins of Syria or the exquisitely soft velvets of Ottoman and Iranian production, delighted customers in the Islamic world and beyond.

282

In the West it is generally held that the golden age of Islamic art was the post-medieval period. But while the textiles of this time represent for many the apogee of design, colouring and technical expertise, the later work is important in reflecting the enormous changes during the 19th century when textile manufacture verged on extinction. The 20th century saw a revival as the public, home and abroad, increasingly associated certain textiles with national and cultural identity.

▲ *Contemporary fabrics in the Turkoman style. The key ingredients are the rich reds, browns and blues typical of Turkoman colour-schemes.*

Eastern textiles available to the collector include a wide array of different articles – embroidery cloths spread under the low tables of the Ottomans to catch crumbs, women's head kerchiefs, Syrian reed screens bearing woven patterns in wool and the embroidered quilts and cushions used to embellish the circumsion-bed of young Turkish boys.

By any standards, the collection of such eastern goods is a specialist field. The best hunting grounds for such items are therefore specialist dealers, textile auctions and the souks and markets of the actual countries of origin.

▶ *Multi-coloured Turkish saddle bags, typical of those brought back from the Crimea as spoils of war. The bag faces are pile-woven, the backings flat-woven. The splits allowed them to be slung over the pommel of a saddle.*

CARPETS & TEXTILES

CUSHIONS

CUSHIONS HAVE BEEN USED from medieval times, but it was in the 16th century, when furniture was generally still hard, that they were most necessary. They were used on chairs, on stools and in window-seats; sheepskin seems to have been the most common lining. Aside from practical considerations, the covers helped to introduce colour and warmth into the home. By 1600, upholstered chairs were more common, so there was less need for cushions. In the late 18th and early 19th centuries the pendulum swung back, and the taste was for greater austerity. By Victorian times, plush upholstery had returned, but the cushions were more luxurious and more plentiful than ever.

▼ *Middle-class Victorian ladies with time on their hands devoted considerable energy to 'fancy work' such as beading, appliqué and silk-thread embroidery – all techniques used in the creation of sumptuous cushions for furniture that was, by and large, already generously upholstered.*

CARPETS & TEXTILES

284

CARPETS & TEXTILES

QUILTS

Q UILTS ARE MADE by stitching flock or poor quality fleeced wool between two layers of fabric. Originally these were fairly rudimentary, functional affairs. In time, though, the stitching became more elaborate and the materials used on the top surface might be formed into dramatic patchwork patterns.

'Plain' quilts made in 19th century Europe had the most elaborate stitching. On the whole they were white or cream and bore rose, heart, wreath or shell designs – depending on the area in which they were made. Much better known and far more collectable are American patchwork quilts. These were made at home by all classes of women using scraps of left-over material from old dresses, shirts, coats, blankets and curtains. Materials ranged from silks, satins and cottons to brocades, velvets and heavy tweeds. Quilts made from printed cotton were most popular, and colours became more vibrant in the 1850s and 1860s as a brighter range of chemical aniline dyes was introduced.

American patchwork quilts might feature a variety of geometrical shapes – squares, triangles, diamonds, hexagons – in contrasting light and dark materials sewn together to form bold designs. Certain communities, such as the Amish Mennonites, were particularly renowned for their striking, very modern-looking designs.

The regular textile sales at auction houses invariably include a few patchwork quilts, but a number of specialist shops in London and elsewhere dealing solely in textiles might also be better options for the collector.

285

◄ *Nobody knows the precise origins of quilting, but it is an ancient practice dating back thousands of years. Victorian and Edwardian ladies spent a great deal of time sewing, and their skills were passed down from generation to generation. The quality of these hand-stitched quilts and coverlets is astonishing.*

CARPETS & TEXTILES

▲ *A variety of American quilts: from right to left, blue, white and red Irish Chain quilt; blocked quilt; and 'Wild Goose Chase', an example of the red on white patterning popular in the late 19th century.*

▶ *More American quilts. The designs are 'Basket of Cherries' and 'Lone Star'.*

CARPETS & TEXTILES

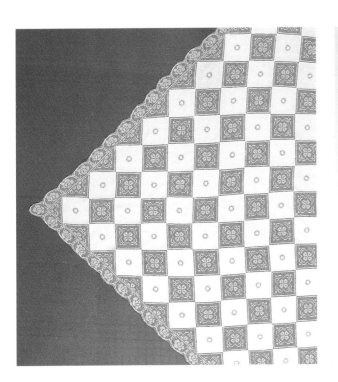

▲ Victorian machine-made tablecloth with lace squares and lace border.

▲ This post-war patchwork from the late 1940s has a fresh, modern look.

▲ Traditional American multi-coloured quilt dating from 1900.

▲ Two-tone Northumberland star quilt. Northumberland was one of three major centres of quilting in the British Isles.

CARPETS & TEXTILES

288

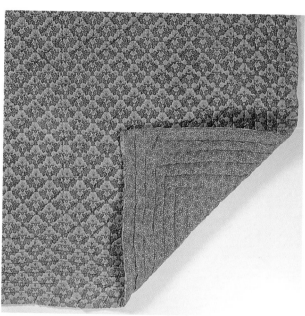

▲ Hand-stitched Durham quilt. A quilt of this degree of precision and complexity would have taken many months of painstaking work.

▲ Many antique quilts have survived from Victorian and Edwardian times, but they may need specialist care to prevent deterioration.

▲ All the elements of this Welsh quilt – colour, pattern, the leisurely spacing of the repeated motif and the sensuously ruched texture – work together to produce a ravishing effect.

CARPETS & TEXTILES

SAMPLERS

THE WORD SAMPLER COMES from the French 'exemplaire', meaning a pattern that could be copied. Samplers were therefore worked as a learning process to try out different embroidery stitches. Dating back at least as far as the 16th century, they were typically made as long narrow strips of linen embroidered with designs – both realistic and fanciful – of animals, flowers and fruit. By the 18th century, square or oblong samplers were often worked with the letters of the alphabet, moral verses and lines from hymns. Finally, by the 19th century, most samplers were being stitched by young girls at school as a part of their education – used not only to teach needlework, but also letters and spelling.

The standard material of samplers was a piece of coarse woollen tammy or glazed fabric, though linen might be used occasionally. The material was usually worked with coloured silks or the less expensive wools using ordinary cross-stitch or marking cross-stitch (ie. the same on both sides of the fabric).

Samplers were never made with a view to sale. Today, however, the extraordinary skill shown in needlework makes them very collectable. This is particularly so in the USA, where samplers are now regarded as part of the American tradition. Decorative examples are highly prized by those wishing to recreate 19th-century styles in their homes, and the demand is often reflected in high prices. Generally speaking, the older the sampler, the higher the price.

Embroidered samplers are usually sold in frames today. Sometimes value is added by the original frame, but generally it make little difference to the price. The best place to look for samplers is at antique fairs and markets.

▾ *School sampler. Many girls went into service after school: a girl with skills such as these could have aspired to become a lady's maid.*

CARPETS & TEXTILES

290

▲ 'Lord watch me with a Father's eye.' Thirteen-year-old Alice Susannah Brown made this attractive prayer sampler in 1873, entirely in cross-stitch.

◄ Weighty sentiments in an elegant hand. Elizabeth Hampshire was sixteen when she made this sampler in 1826.

CARPETS & TEXTILES

◄ *The personal nature of most samplers makes them attractive to collectors. This example, by one Mary Ann Fox, is particularly poignant.*

▲ *The young Victorian seamstress would try out designs and techniques on random samplers. To contemporary eyes, the haphazard effect of this 1897 sampler might seem rather attractive.*

◄ *You can find 19th-century samplers such as this one at most antique fairs and markets, usually on specialist textile stalls.*

CARPETS & TEXTILES

▲ *Alphabet samplers were often used to decorate the nursery.
As the child grew up they became teaching aids.*

◄ *'Waste not, want not' –
good advice now as it was
in 1894. Anne Finlayson's
highly stylized lettering is
particularly attractive.*

▶ *Belgian band sampler,
mainly in cross-stitch.
Band samplers
demonstrated different
types of border pattern
for use on clothes or
household linens.*

CARPETS & TEXTILES

LACE

▲ *Hand-stitched lace table linen in a variety of styles. The drawn threadwork of the rectangular table mat would have been especially labour-intensive. The use of coloured threads was a particular Victorian taste.*

LACE WAS FIRST MADE in Europe during the 16th century in the Low Countries and Italy. Soon the art of lace-making spread across Europe and each manufacturing centre developed its own particular style and the patterns for which it became well-known. Chantilly lace-makers, for example, favoured floral patterns on a hexagonal mesh of fine silk, usually black, while Mechlin lace had a cotton mesh and a flat, heavy outlining thread. But wherever it was made, lace was dedicated to the adornment of well-to-do people and their homes.

The production of lace was a time-consuming, labour-intensive business and usually seen as women's work. There were two main types of lace, bobbin lace and needlepoint lace, and the fabric could be made with linen, cotton or silk threads. Up to the mid-19th century, the wearing of hand-made lace was seen as an indication of status, as well as a symbol of delicacy and femininity. But by this time, demand had outstripped supply.

CARPETS & TEXTILES

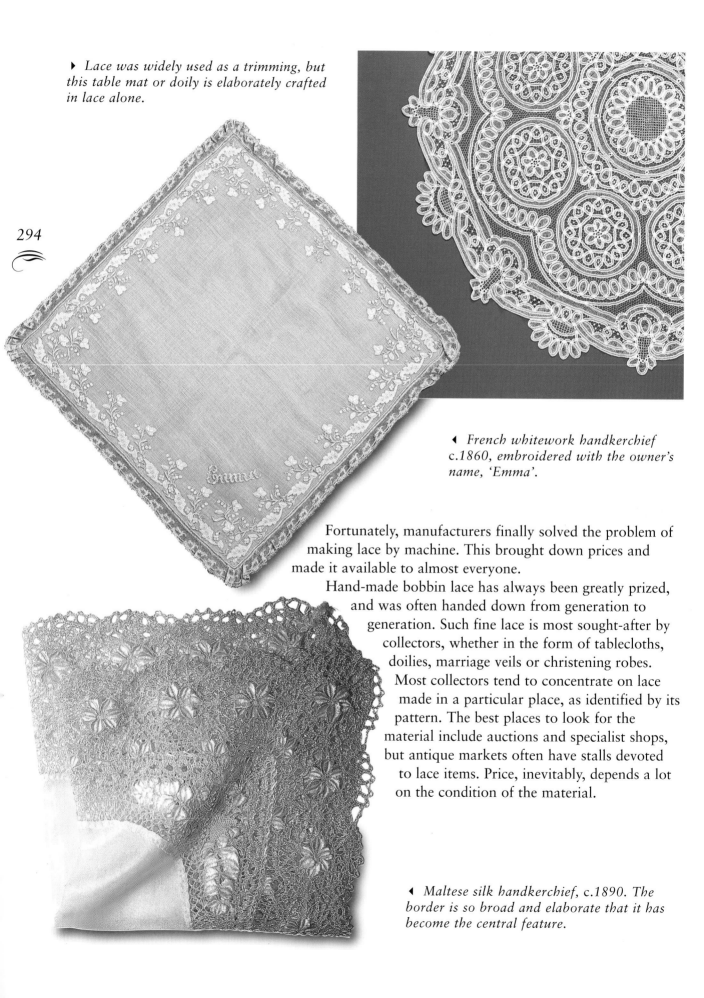

▶ *Lace was widely used as a trimming, but this table mat or doily is elaborately crafted in lace alone.*

294

◀ *French whitework handkerchief c.1860, embroidered with the owner's name, 'Emma'.*

Fortunately, manufacturers finally solved the problem of making lace by machine. This brought down prices and made it available to almost everyone.

Hand-made bobbin lace has always been greatly prized, and was often handed down from generation to generation. Such fine lace is most sought-after by collectors, whether in the form of tablecloths, doilies, marriage veils or christening robes. Most collectors tend to concentrate on lace made in a particular place, as identified by its pattern. The best places to look for the material include auctions and specialist shops, but antique markets often have stalls devoted to lace items. Price, inevitably, depends a lot on the condition of the material.

◀ *Maltese silk handkerchief, c.1890. The border is so broad and elaborate that it has become the central feature.*

CARPETS & TEXTILES

EMBROIDERY

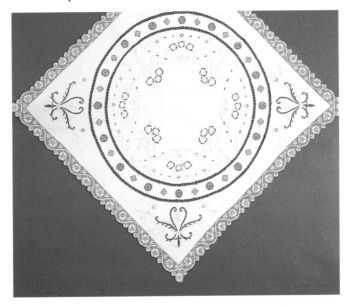

295

THE ART OF EMBROIDERY is hardly less ancient than that of weaving. Embroidery is essentially patterns made by stitching thread with a needle through woven fabric, felt or animal skin. The thread may be of wool, linen, cotton, silk, thin metal wire or – nowadays – synthetic fibre. The four main stitches employed are flat stitches, linked or chain stitches, buttonhole stitches and knot stitches.

In the 17th and 18th centuries the main tendency in design was towards richness of effect in elaborate patterns of flowers and foliage in the style of engravings. Much was produced for upholstery – usually in gros or petit point – and costume. In the 19th century embroidery was a common pastime for women in the home, and traditional techniques continued to be used. But industrialized production became increasingly widespread and from the mid-19th century most embroidery was done by machine. Under the the influence of the Arts and Crafts Movement, however, there was a significant if passing revival of the handicraft and fine work was produced in Great Britain and the USA.

▲ *These beautiful lace cushions and lavender bags would nowadays be considered somewhat impractical pram accessories.*

▶ *This linen place mat uses a technique called 'cutwork', where a pattern is cut out of the fabric and the ragged edges are finished off with fine stitching. Whitework stitching and lace edging complete the design.*

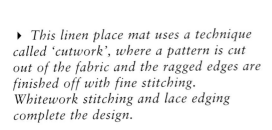

CARPETS & TEXTILES

CLOTHES

IN RECENT YEARS, OLD CLOTHES have become increasingly collectable, inspired perhaps by the popularity of costume drama on TV and at the cinema. Such items as bridal veils from the late 19th century, blazers and dresses from the early 20th century, evening gowns from the 1930s and mini-skirts from the 1960s shed a fascinating light both on contemporary fashions and social mores.

Women's fashions in the late 19th and early 20th centuries tended to be highly elaborate. They relied heavily on decorative touches, such as appliqué, embroidery and other trimmings. Lace was particularly popular, as manufacturers had developed machine-made laces almost as fine as hand-made ones. Fine, delicate fabrics were used to make dresses, skirts and blouses. Chiffon, muslin, crepe-de-chine and gauze were the favoured materials, and pastels, notably pink, mauve and soft blue, were the most fashionable colours.

Men's fashions of the time tended to favour classical lines. Top hats, morning coats and pin-striped trousers were worn for work and dinner jackets in the evening. White shirts with detachable collars were worn both for night and day. Leisure wear, on the other hand, might have included blazers, boater hats and white flannels.

The big problem with clothes of the early 20th century is their scarcity. Much of men's clothing was worn until it fell apart or was moth-eaten, while a good deal of women's clothing was recycled during World War I.

During the 1920s, fashion designers were at great pains to disguise women's more obvious characteristics. Evening dresses tended to be cut along very straight lines and bosoms were flattened out. In the 1930s, however, women's clothes adopted softer lines. Evening dresses and gowns in particular were sumptuously fashioned, being made of satin, crepe or velvet and featuring plunging necklines, gathered waists and flared skirts. Worth, Chanel, Schiaparelli, Adrian, Poiret and Molyneux were the great designers of the day, though items bearing these names are likely to be very expensive now. The best places to look for old clothes are specialist dealers and clothes markets. Before buying, always look for signs of fraying or straining at the seams, and check buttons, clips and other decorative details to see that they are intact and original.

CARPETS & TEXTILES

▲ *19th-century christening robe in cream silk; frills, tucks and flounces were
the order of the day. The christening ceremony was known as the 'shortening'.
Its importance as a family occasion was second only to a wedding.*

CARPETS & TEXTILES

▼ *High-waisted satin wedding dress, c.1900, with embroidered panels of lace and cotton. The styling represents a move away from the stiffness and formality of Victorian wedding gowns towards the softer, more frivolous fashions of the Edwardian era.*

298

▲ *This late Victorian woven silk check waistcoat in navy blue with broad black bands would not look out of place in a modern menswear collection.*

◄ *This flamboyant 18th-century waistcoat is made of heavy silk brocade with embroidered silk floral motifs. Gold braid edging and gilded buttons complete the effect.*

CARPETS & TEXTILES

299

▲ *Collection of Kashmir shawls. Our word shawl derives from the Persian 'shal', which covered a variety of garments made from the finely woven 'pashmina' wool gathered from the soft winter underfleece of Tibetan mountain goats. Of all these garments it was the shawl that appealed most to European taste, but it was an expensive taste: in Victorian times, a top-quality shawl could cost as much as a house.*

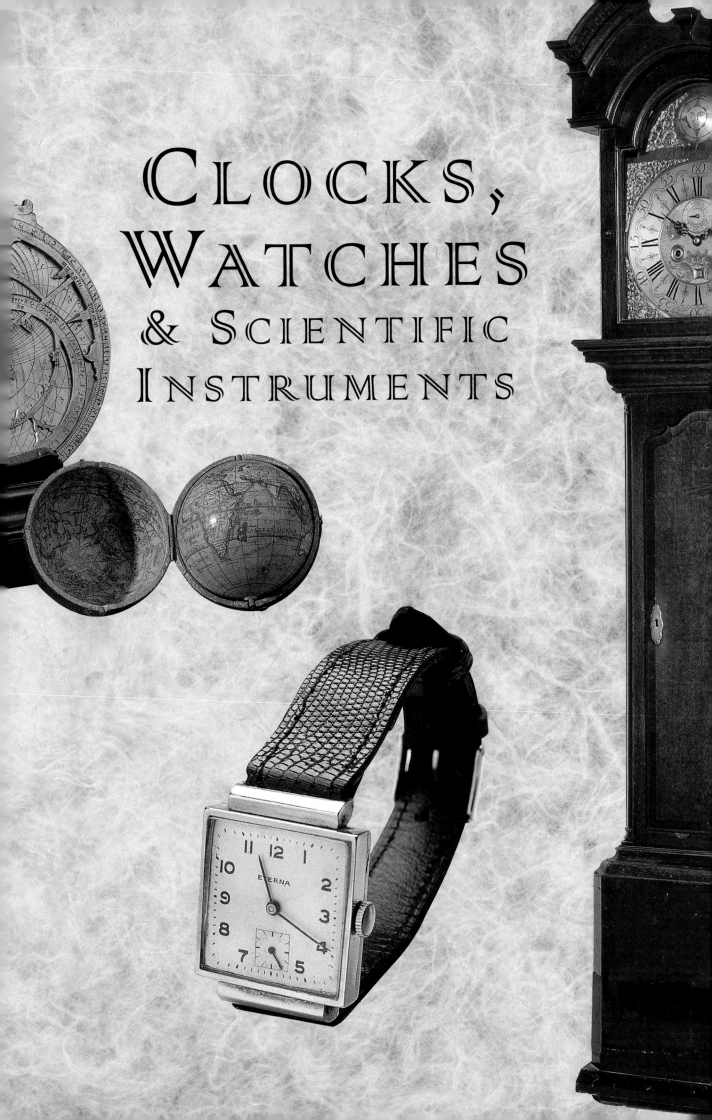

Clocks, Watches
& Scientific
Instruments

CLOCKS & WATCHES

THE INVENTION OF A mechanism that could keep time accurately was a challenge taken up by innumerable craftsmen and men of science down the centuries. The development of timepieces of all kinds bears witness to the slow growth of mechanical ingenuity and scientific knowledge in the West

Before the early 20th century, all clocks were powered by one of three mechanisms – descending weights, pendulums or uncoiling springs. The earliest mechanical clocks, which date from the 13th and 14th centuries, were driven by descending weights. These were large, cumbersome and inaccurate mechanisms, and were to some extent outmoded by clocks containing uncoiled springs (c.1450). But while the uncoiled spring helped clock-makers to make their timepieces more compact, accuracy remained a major problem until the patenting of the pendulum clock 200 years later. The use of the pendulum effectively ushered in a golden age of clock-making, which saw clocks make their way into every bourgeois home and lasted until the invention of the electric clock at the end of the 19th century.

The internal workings of most pendulum-powered clocks varied little over the centuries. The 'escapement' – the mechanism by which the force supplied by the pendulum was released at regular intervals to mark the passing of time – was usually regulated by a transfer balance wheel. This transferred force to the 'movement', a series of geared cogwheels and pinions sandwiched between two plates. Complex refinements were introduced into the movement over time, making it ever more sensitive to the pendulum's force.

CLOCKS & WATCHES

The best guide to the age and origins of a clock is usually the style of the hands and the decorative details of the dial – although sometimes where there is a brass back-plate it may feature an engraved signature and date. The 'chapter ring' marked with the hours may also bear a signature, though this is most likely to be the name of the original retailer or cabinetmaker.

303

The search for highly portable timepieces went on almost contemporaneously with the development of clocks. The first practical watch was invented around 1510, and is credited to the craftsman Peter Henlein of Nuremburg. But though early watches were often beautiful, they were unwieldy and inaccurate. It was not until the 17th and 18th centuries that compact internal workings utilizing balance-coiled springs, cylinder escapements or lever escapements were perfected. Watches, however, continued to be accessories of the well-off. Following the introduction of the true chronograph in 1862 – a watch capable of being stopped, reset and restarted while its hands continued to move – the Swiss began to develop the cheaper end of the market using machine-made parts: watches could now be bought by the man in the street. By World War I, wristwatch manufacture – again dominated by Swiss firms – had come into its own.

LONGCASE CLOCKS

LONGCASE CLOCKS FIRST made their appearance in Europe in the 17th century. From the first, they were designed to be sited in the halls of houses, so that their tick and sounding of the hours could be heard in the other rooms. They became such a feature of the middle-class or merchant home in the 18th century that many regional styles developed. A Dutch clock made of walnut and dating from 1765, for example, was fitted with a fretted hood and a side window through which the movement could be seen, while an English clock of roughly the same period featured a dial in the arch depicting the phases of the moon. But whatever their place of origin, the faces of longcase clocks became more elaborate as the century went on. Painted decorations were a common feature and sometimes the arched section above the dial housed ingenious clockwork figures of characters such as Old Father Time. The numerals around the chapter ring increased in size to compete with such distractions.

There are a number of useful aids to dating longcase clocks. A brass ring bearing Roman numerals usually dates the clock to between c.1680 and 1720, while an arch over a square clock face indicates that the clock was made after c.1715. Early clocks tended to be about 1.85m tall, increasing to about 2.70m in the 1720s. After 1850, the height again decreased to about 2.10m. From a collector's point of view, the smaller the clock, the more desirable it is.

◄ *An oak 'country' longcase clock with heavy hood. The elaborately chased brass dial sets off the chapter ring of silvered brass. The piece dates from around 1800.*

▶ *Late 18th-century painted clock dial featuring a figure of Justice in a cartouche. The maker is one of several London Groves producing clocks in the early Regency period.*

CLOCKS & WATCHES

◄ *Regency longcase clock by William Vale of London. The case is of rich mahogany with brass finishings. The silvered brass dial is elegantly engraved.*

▲ *Perhaps the most striking aspect of this late-Victorian longcase is its elaborately veneered case. The painted arch has a nautical theme.*

CLOCKS & WATCHES

CLOCKS & WATCHES
WALL CLOCKS

▶ *Not all pendulum clocks had standing cases. This pendulum wall clock is only half the height of a contemporary longcase.*

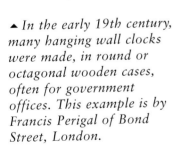

▲ *In the early 19th century, many hanging wall clocks were made, in round or octagonal wooden cases, often for government offices. This example is by Francis Perigal of Bond Street, London.*

◀ *Jas Howden, an Edinburgh maker, produced this elegant longcase clock in the closing years of the 19th century. The reeded columns of the hood provide a stately setting for the sumptuous detailing of dial and arch.*

◀ *The regulator clock was the most important timepiece in a Victorian household. As the name suggests, all other clocks in the house were set to it. As befitted its status, the regulator's case was often intricately embellished.*

CLOCKS & WATCHES
CARRIAGE CLOCKS

CARRIAGE CLOCKS WERE PORTABLE timepieces, invented as chiming equivalents of today's travelling alarm clocks. When they were developed in the 18th century, however, travel was very much a rich man's pursuit, and the clocks were given appropriately ornate and expensive cases. Parisian clock-makers had the largest output of such pieces. English carriage clocks, by contrast, tended to have plainer, heavier cases, although they had a better reputation for time-keeping.

The main focus of collectors' interest today lies in the decorative features of the carriage clock cases. The plinth, pillars and handle were usually made of moulded brass and were often decorated with engraving or machine-turning. The dial on the front panel almost always featured black Roman numerals on a white enamel background. Usually the white enamel filled the whole front panel, but sometimes the dials looked through a mask of brass or coloured enamel. The side panels were often made of bevelled glass, though examples in engraved brass, painted porcelain, cloisonné or other types of enamelling can also be found.

Carriage clocks were usually marked with their maker's names. Dent, Frodsham, Vulliamy and James McCabe were among the main English makers, while the names of Drocourt, Japy, Bourdin, Jacot and Margaine are to be found on many French examples.

308

▶ *A selection of Regency carriage clocks. The classic carriage clock is rectangular in shape; the serpentine or oval (centre) is less common. More sophisticated versions had alarms (top and bottom left).*

▼ *Carriage clocks come in many styles, from simple to highly elaborate. The French were always the main producers, and they maintained a thriving export trade well into the 20th century. The examples here date from the early years of this period.*

CLOCKS & WATCHES

CLOCKS & WATCHES

MANTEL CLOCKS

310

CLOCKS MADE PURELY for the mantelpiece were first developed in France in the 1750s, and by the mid-19th century had become a feature of virtually every bourgeois European household. The principal French makers were Japy, Jean Vincenti and Samuel Marti.

The Japy company, in particular, was the largest producer of watch and clock parts in the country and was highly regarded. But, like their competitors, they had a fairly fixed idea of what a mantel clock should look like. This meant encasing the clock in a dark limestone from the Ardennes (sometimes known as Belgian slate), polishing it to a high gloss and decorating it with incised patterns inlaid with gilding. Brass bas-relief panels were sometimes pinned to the clock case for extra decoration, as were small columns or panels of contrasting stone such as onyx, malachite or different coloured marbles.

▲ *This flamboyant French ornamental mantel clock with enamel inlay dates from the late 19th century.*

Mantel clocks can be found at auctions, antiques fairs and shops, clock fairs and specialist dealers. The more elaborate the clock's casing, the higher the price. Cases vary from simple box-like shapes to ornate spectaculars fashioned in the style of Greek temples, with a triangular pediment and two to six pillars flanking the dial. One drawback from the collector's point of view is that cases are quite often damaged, with hair-line cracks and chips off protruding edges being common. The clocks also tend to be very heavy and, unless lifted carefully from underneath, the casings can come apart where the cement has loosened over the years.

▶ *With mass production of clock movements, the clock became a domestic commonplace of the Edwardian era. Small, decorative clocks were known as 'boudoir clocks', to differentiate them from the grander shelf and bracket clocks that dominated the drawing-room mantelshelf.*

CLOCKS & WATCHES

POCKET WATCHES

312

PERHAPS THE SINGLE MOST IMPORTANT pocket watch innovation was the introduction of hunter and half-hunter watches in the 19th century. Hunters had heavy metal cases that completely enclosed the watch to protect the glass, while half-hunters featured a small central hole through which one could just read the dial. By the end of the 19th century, a wide variety of optional extras was available, including pictorial enamelled faces and a repeater button that enabled the watch to strike at the most recent hour and a quarter, allowing the wearer to tell the time in the dark. Some pocket watches also had separate second hands and dials showing the phases of the moon, the month and date, and sunset and sunrise; others may have had an alarm and even a stop-watch facility.

Although pocket watches made of gold or featuring scenes in enamel are keenly sought after and may command high prices, plain 19th-century gentlemen's watches are still relatively cheap. But be sure to examine such antiques carefully before buying. Check for dents in the metal case, chips in any enamel used and split hinges. The opening buttons on half-hunters and hunters should be in working order. As for the cleaning and repair of the internal works, this is a job for a qualified watchmaker and may be expensive.

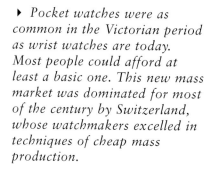

▸ *Pocket watches were as common in the Victorian period as wrist watches are today. Most people could afford at least a basic one. This new mass market was dominated for most of the century by Switzerland, whose watchmakers excelled in techniques of cheap mass production.*

CLOCKS & WATCHES

CLOCKS & WATCHES

WRISTWATCHES

W RISTWATCHES ARE AN ESSENTIALLY 20th-century innovation. By the mid-1920s, they were deemed less pretentious than fob watches and more convenient than pocket watches. By 1935 more than 85 per cent of all watches produced were wristwatches, and the wristwatches most prized are those made up till 1960, the market being dominated by seven great names – Rolex, Vacheron and Constantin, Audemars, Piguet, Omega, A Lange and Jaeger le Coultre. The main factors affecting the value of a wristwatch are the shape of the case, the dial design and material, the style of the numerals and the degree of technical complication. But a word of warning may be in order here: literally thousands of fake wristwatches are on the market today, principally counterfeits of fashionable Rolex, Gucci and Cartier models.

314

▲ *The wearing of wristwatches by men was a military habit that carried over into civilian life after World War I. This elegant fashion statement in a compact steel housing is by Esterna, c.1930.*

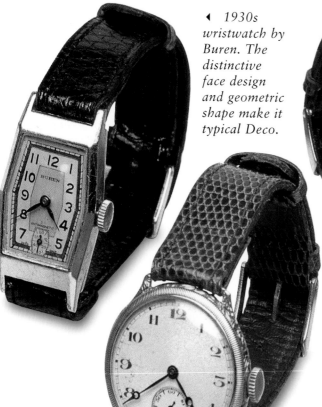

◄ *1930s wristwatch by Buren. The distinctive face design and geometric shape make it typical Deco.*

▼ *Gold wristwatch by Rotary, 1930s. The chunky rectangular design is unmistakably masculine.*

▲ *Man's wristwatch, early 1920s. The case is 14ct gold and the dial is black enamel with gold numerals. The design of the hands is particularly elegant.*

◄ *Late 1930s man's watch in 9ct gold. There is raised decoration on the rim of the case.*

CLOCKS & WATCHES

◀ *Man's wristwatch by Buren, with silver case and dial, c.1930. The lozenge shape is relatively unusual.*

▶ *Longines wristwatch with steel case – an Art Deco classic.*

315

Bedside Clocks

During the Art Deco period of the 1920s and 30s, as well as producing expensive clocks and watches, watchmakers made wristwatches that were available to the masses. The same applied to clocks, and dozens of cheap and cheerful examples were produced. One of the most collectible types is the bedside clock. By their nature these were usually fairly small, often had luminous numbers or hands, and incorporated an alarm mechanism, or some other gadgetry. Among these small clocks are travelling, or carriage, clocks of an earlier age. Many came complete with their own cases, usually made of wood, with leather or cloth stuck to it to provide safe passage for the clock. Such clocks can still be found, but check the condition of the case – many have become rather battered over the years and may not be worth buying.

▲ *1930s bedside clock set in solid, orange-tinted glass with bevelled front edges.*

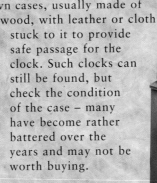

▲ *Travelling alarm clock in painted enamel, made by Bayard in the 1930s. The stepped pediment is typical of Art Deco. The case shown is original.*

▶ *This striking French Art Deco 1930s clock incorporates a cigarette lighter.*

CLOCKS & WATCHES

ANTIQUE SCIENTIFIC
INSTRUMENTS

▼ *In the late 19th and early 20th centuries, barometers became a standard item in middle-class homes. This example is an English combined clock and aneroid barometer set in a brown marble and slate case, c.1900. Aneroid barometers, invented in 1844, needed no mercury or glass tubing, so they were cheaper to produce than the traditional kind.*

316

THE COLLECTING OF ANTIQUE scientific instruments can exercise a considerable fascination for the enthusiast. Not only are instruments such as barometers, sextants, chronometers, microscopes and stethoscopes intriguing objects in their own right, they are often beautifully made and provide a fascinating insight into the search for scientific knowledge.

The great age of scientific enquiry, beginning in the late 18th century and running throughout the 19th century, produced a wide array of instruments to enable both amateur observers (of which there were many) and professional researchers to pursue their studies. Though somewhat insensitive by modern standards, early barometers – instruments that measure air pressure in units called millibars – enabled the first meteorologists to make detailed records of annual weather systems. The development of the microscope had an incalculable effect on medical research, just as the increasingly widespread use of the stethoscope helped doctors to diagnose the illnesses of more patients correctly and saved many lives.

▲ *Another advantage of aneroid barometers was their portability. With no tube, they could be reduced to the size of a pocket watch. This example is English, c.1910. It is made of silver-plated brass.*

CLOCKS & WATCHES

But scientific instruments not only helped to increase knowledge on the domestic front, they also had a vital role to play in the exploration of new lands. The navigation of the great oceans would have been far more haphazard without the use of sextants and chronometers, and it was the successful charting of these waters that paved the way to the mass migrations of peoples and colonization of distant continents.

▲ *This English clock barometer, c.1900, is housed in an oak case somewhat reminiscent of a Gothic folly!*

▲ *Combined aneroid barometer and thermometer in a light oak case, c.1890. The barometer face is porcelain. The case culminates in a broken pediment.*

◄ *An unusual semi-octagonal stick barometer of 1864 by R. Smith of Accrington. The case is boxwood with satinwood inlay. There are thermometers to either side of the barometric scale. Once again, the piece has a Gothic flavour.*

CLOCKS & WATCHES
GLOBES

T HE DISCOVERY AND COLONIZATION of new countries and the exploration of far-flung wildernesses and oceans generated enormous interest in maps, globes and navigational instruments in the late 18th century and throughout the 19th century. Globes, in particular, were symbols of the educated man's desire to follow events in the wider world, and by the 19th century they had, along with brass instruments such as the compass, dividers and telescope, become almost standard features in the studies and libraries of well-to-do households.

Globes were normally sold in pairs – a terrestrial globe representing the Earth and a celestial one showing the heavens. Though made in a large variety of sizes, from small pocket globes of 7cm in diameter to large floor-standing examples of 60cm or more, all were fragile objects, being little more than a spherical core of papier mâché, plaster or wood pasted over with a 'gore', or paper sheet printed with a world map. The whole was then sealed with shellac and a meridian ring, often of brass, connected the globe to its stand.

The most affordable globes date from the early 20th century, and these tend also to be in the best condition.

318

▼ *An astrolabe and a pocket globe in its case. The astrolabe, invented by the Ancient Greeks and perfected by the Arabs, was used to measure the positions of the sun and the stars. On the inner surface of the globe case is a map of the heavens.*

▶ *Celestial globes have a long history; the oldest surviving example dates from around 300 BC. They continued to be made throughout the Middle Ages in Islam but were rare in the West until the 15th century when the manufacture of globes was revolutionized. This example was made around 1860. Celestial globes were often sold together with the conventional terrestrial variety.*

CLOCKS & WATCHES

CLOCKS & WATCHES

NAUTICAL INSTRUMENTS

I N RECENT YEARS, the scientific aspects of early navigation and exploration have become quite a focus of public attention. In an age before computers and satellite views, seafarers employed a number of ingenious instruments to help them find their way around the world's oceans. Sextants, fitted with an arc of a sixth of a circle, were used to measure angular distances relative to the stars or sun. Chronometers kept accurate time at sea and facilitated the calculation of longitude. And increasingly powerful telescopes enabled eagle-eyed vision over great distances.

320

▼ *Sextants were used to find the latitude at sea. The most important sextant makers were Troughton, Ramsden and Berge. This example is of brass, with silver scales and a wooden case, c.1870.*

CLOCKS & WATCHES

▸ *This two-day marine chronometer was made by James Bishop of London, c.1860. Chronometers were cased in rectangular boxes with brass bindings and set on gimbals – a mechanism that kept them horizontal in all conditions.*

These late 18th- and 19th-century instruments had to be well made if they were to function properly at sea. Most were made from high-quality, rust-resistant materials such as brass, and a surprising number have survived in good working order. They are, therefore, much sought after, and prices have risen to match. Chronometers, for example, are extremely expensive today. The centre of production was Great Britain, and the market was dominated by the firms of Arnold, Earnshaw, Mudge, Mercer and Kullberg. Such instruments are at the top of the nautical antiques market, and there are no cheaper alternatives.

Always check the state of an instrument before purchase: replacement parts for most early nautical instruments are virtually impossible to find, and to have precision parts made up is a prohibitively pricey business. On the other hand, a useful rule of thumb is 'the simpler the instrument, the lower the price'. By this logic, simpler instruments such as pairs of compasses and dividers are likely to be the best value for money.

321

▾ *Brass compass made in England, 1918. A well made compass was an essential piece of kit for any officer.*

▾ *Brass-cased barometer, c.1910, manufactured by Negretti and Zambra of London.*

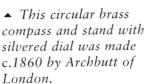

▴ *This circular brass compass and stand with silvered dial was made c.1860 by Archbutt of London.*

CLOCKS & WATCHES

MEDICAL INSTRUMENTS

▲ *Two pottery apothecary's jars dating from 1860 to 1880. Such jars once held the ingredients from which prescriptions were made up.*

THE PARAPHERNALIA of medical history makes interesting, if perhaps somewhat macabre, collectables. The most highly desirable objects tend to come in complete sets. For example, a doctor's Gladstone bag containing all its original instruments – which may include test tubes, lancets, delivery forceps, needles, scalpels, syringes, thermometers, scissors and even bone saws – will command a good price today. Another point to bear in mind is that early examples of a particular item, such as the 19th-century binaural stethoscope, will attract significant interest and prices to match, as will pieces that would have been the top of their range at the time of manufacture. The rarity of certain bottles and jars of dubious or quaint medicines and potions will also have an effect on cost.

The general rule, though, is that the older a medical instrument is, the more desirable. A surgical instrument with a handle made of ivory, mother-of-pearl, or wood, or with a delicate turning, for example, is certain to have been made before 1872, when Lister's principle of sterilization became generally accepted in medical practice. From that time on, instruments tended to be made of steel so that they could easily be boiled before use. The principal centre of manufacture was, of course, Switzerland.

◀ *Brass binocular microscope made by Collins, c.1870; wooden bottle holders and double measuring cup; and doctor's instrument case made by Dakin Bros, c.1850.*

CLOCKS & WATCHES

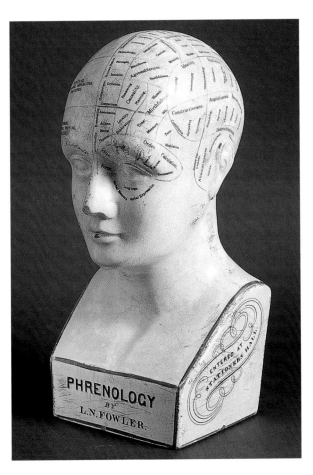

▲ *Phrenology presented an analysis of character and intellect in terms of the external geography of the skull. The Phrenology Head was its foremost map, locating such characteristics as reasoning, mirthfulness and acquisitiveness in specific areas of the skull.*

▼ *Leather Gladstone bag, c.1880 and doctor's case containing test tubes, scissors, scalpels, syringe, thermometer and razor strop.*

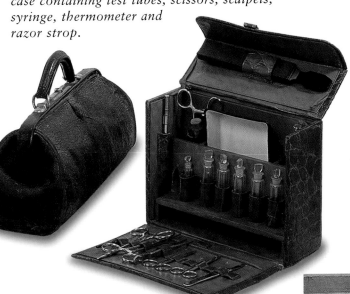

▼ *White's Physiological Manikin, patented in New York in 1886, was an important study aid for medical students. Cardboard flaps open to reveal hidden anatomical details of both male and female. The Manikin folds away into a wooden carrying case.*

323

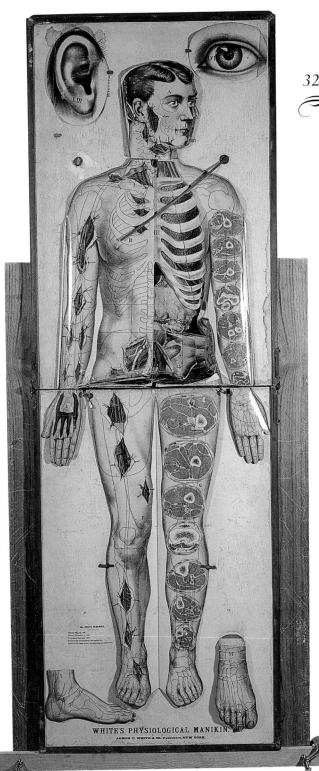

BOUCHERON
PARIS. 26 Place Vendôme
New York, 1 East 57th Street
180, New Bond Street,
LONDON

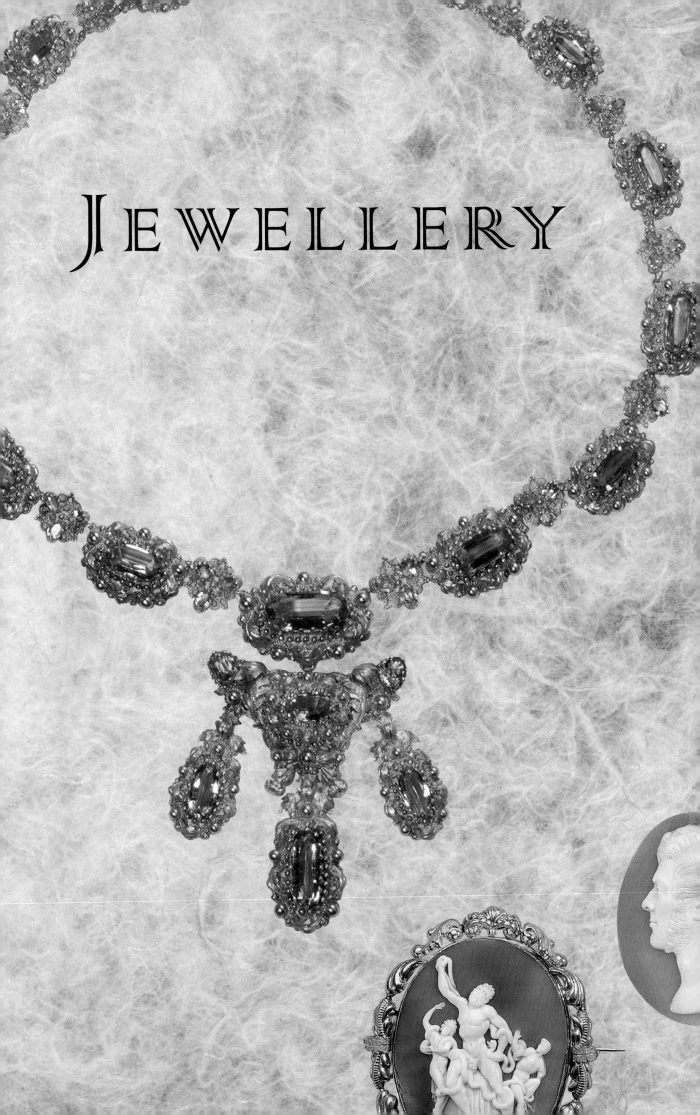

Jewellery

JEWELLERY

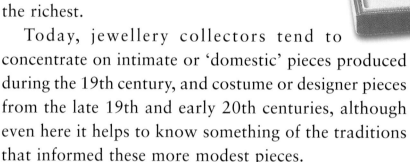

B^{Y THE VERY NATURE OF THE} precious or semiprecious materials used in its manufacture, jewellery tends to be one of the more costly areas of antique collection. Little jewellery prior to the 18th century is likely to come the way of the ordinary collector. Even if it were available – and much is already in the glass cases of museums or major collections – it would be exorbitantly expensive, a target for only the richest.

Today, jewellery collectors tend to concentrate on intimate or 'domestic' pieces produced during the 19th century, and costume or designer pieces from the late 19th and early 20th centuries, although even here it helps to know something of the traditions that informed these more modest pieces.

The period from the beginning of the French First Empire (1804) to the end of the Prince of Wales's regency in England (1820) was a 'golden age' of jewellery design, all the more remarkable since the French Revolution of 1789–99 had led to a significant reversal of fortune for jewellery. The possession of jewels not only indicated aristocratic status, it was a symbol of monarchy: in the Terror, the ownership of a small trinket might be enough to consign someone to the guillotine. Many aristocrats had their jewels confiscated by the fund-starved revolutionaries or took them with them into exile. The sales that inevitably followed flooded the European market and prices fell. In Paris, the only acceptable personal ornaments were iron rings stamped with revolutionary phrases or images of leading revolutionaries.

JEWELLERY

This mood of austerity changed dramatically when Napoleon proclaimed the Empire. He had the jewels of the former French kings reset in Neo-classical style, and the wearing of opulent jewellery at court was again encouraged. Matching sets, or parures – which might include a necklace, bracelets, earrings and hair ornaments all made with the same gems – were common. The Emperor himself was keen on cameos and his second empress, Marie-Louise, had a parure made with 24 ancient cameos from the French royal collection.

Despite the war between their countries, English society women and jewellers avidly followed the fashions of the new French court. However, the English taste that developed from these influences was less for 'heavy', formal pieces such as diamond parures than for strings of pearls and ornaments whose designs featured the so-called 'language of stones' – gems arranged according to their initial letters to spell some deeply held sentiment (for example, lapis lazuli, opal, vermeil and emerald spelt LOVE). Another important accessory for the English woman of society at dinners or balls was the 'Spartan diadem' – a tiara rising to a point and often formed of gems cut into brilliant, multi-faceted 'drops'.

With the fall of Napoleon and the near-bankruptcy of the French state, few people had the money to buy gems. Forced to adapt, the taste grew for semiprecious stones, often in elaborate settings, and for cheaper seed pearls strung on silk or horsehair, and in the early to mid-1800s, fashions in the rest of Europe followed suit.

JEWELLERY

LOCKETS

328

▼ *Several of these lockets are mourning lockets, containing locks of hair, others hold photographs. Most were made to hang on a chain, but some could also be worn as brooches.*

AMONG THE EASIEST PIECES OF jewellery to find – and the most affordable – are 19th-century lockets. These simple ornaments were made in gold, silver, jet and even steel, and were decorated with engraving or enamel, and sometimes set with precious or semiprecious stones. Lockets could be worn as tokens of mourning, or secretly around the neck as tokens of love, and often contained a lock of the beloved's hair or, later, a photograph. By the 1870s, with the advent of mass production, lockets had become so popular that everyone, from the maid to the mistress, owned one. But their very popularity signalled their fall from favour with the elite, who regarded them as fit only for young girls, who were not allowed to wear elaborate jewellery.

JEWELLERY

▲ *This fine locket brooch in gold, set with half pearls, has a curl of hair in the centre.*

▲ *Turquoises are set in an elaborate gold locket in the Etruscan style, which became fashionable towards the end of the 1800s.*

JEWELLERY

PARURES

WHILE SIMPLE LOCKETS WERE common adornment for the bourgeoisie, the wealthy married woman in the 19th century was expected to wear splendid and beautiful jewels as a sign of her husband's status. The most important of these was the *grande parure*, or matching set, containing necklace, pendant, earrings, brooch, rings, bracelets and a tiara. The *demi-parure*, a smaller set, might contain most of these, but not a tiara. Often the pieces could be converted from pendants to brooches, say, or from brooches to hair ornaments, doubling their usefulness. Most of these grand sets of jewellery are beyond the pocket of collectors, but sometimes desirable pieces can be found that are affordable, and if they still have their original case this adds greatly to their value.

◀ *Pink topaz set in gold filigree is used for this impressive set, which contains pins and clips as well as the usual necklace, brooch, earrings, pendant and bracelet.*

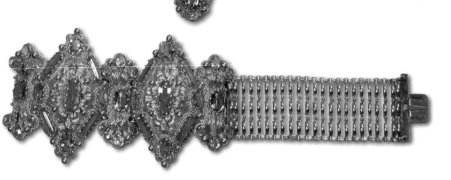

▶ *The sumptuous bracelet in gold with jewels surrounding a large central enamel disc was made in Russia in the late 19th century.*

JEWELLERY

Large green peridots – the mineral olivine chrysolite – effectively combined with diamonds and linked by a gold scrollwork chain form this ornate set of necklace and bracelet.

331

▲ This matching set of necklace and earrings is made from amethysts, set off by pearls, and mounted in gold.

▲ The gems in this three-piece set – still in its original case – are mounted in intricately worked gold filigree.

JEWELLERY

EARLY 20TH-CENTURY JEWELLERY

D IAMONDS WERE THE FAVOURED gemstone of the early 20th century, and any inhibitions that might have existed in the 19th century about wearing such jewels in the daytime disappeared in Britain after Edward VII became king in 1901. The great jewellers – Cartier, Boucheron and Fouquet in Paris and Garrards in London – were the mecca for the wealthy and they dictated the form and style of traditional Edwardian jewellery. In the main, this jewellery was adapted from 19th-century designs, with drop earrings. Pendants and dog-collar necklaces were

▶ *Fashioned in gold, with diamonds and pearls, this pin made by Boucheron shows a woman's head and shoulders. The pin's value is enhanced by having a case that was designed specially for it.*

◀ *Tortoiseshell comb, with cut steel and paste, c.1905; diamond brooch, one of a pair; platinum cuff links set with diamonds and rubies; gold brooch set with an opal and diamonds, c.1900.*

JEWELLERY

popular, but long necklaces with tassels and slave bangles were also introduced. At the same time, 18th-century Neo-classical motifs were employed, such as ribbons, laurel leaves and palmettes; the workmanship was exquisite. For those who could not afford real diamonds, paste gems, made from a hard, shiny glass, offered an often very convincing alternative; paste is well worth buying, especially when it is set in silver.

▼ *Sapphire and diamond earrings in a star shape; platinum and gold pendant with a pearl set in enamel; diamond brooch; openwork brooch with diamonds, sapphires and pearls; enamel and paste pendant; paste drop earrings, set in silver.*

JEWELLERY

▶ *A pale enamel disc, set with a pearl and encircled by a gold, ribbed border, forms the centre of this pendant. The wreath of leaves is composed of diamonds held in place by minute beads of platinum – a technique known as* millegrain.

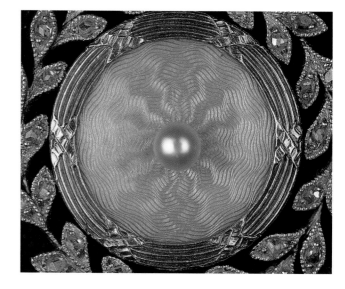

334

▼ *Early 20th-century jewellery was not as heavy as that of the late 1800s. This detail shows delicately carved gold flowers set with diamonds surrounding a fine opal and diamond centrepiece.*

▼ *Edwardian jewellery was much lighter in style than 19th-century jewellery. This bow-shaped brooch has square-cut sapphires and diamonds in an elegant, almost lacy platinum setting in the form of feathers around the central sapphire and square diamond cluster.*

JEWELLERY

GEOLOGICAL JEWELLERY

IN VICTORIAN TIMES, THERE was great interest in the natural world, in making collections of pressed flowers, fossils and shells, so it is not surprising that people made collections of pebbles and semiprecious stones also. As a result, a thriving business grew up cutting and polishing these stones, and making souvenir jewellery from them, particularly at seaside towns and in Scotland – a favourite holiday destination in 19th-century Britain. Clear quartz from Cornwall; amethysts, bloodstones and smoky quartz, or cairngorm, from Scotland, were polished and set in silver, sometimes in gold. Agate, a streaky quartz from Scotland and Germany, and even as far afield as Brazil, was used for brooches and earrings. Amber, fossilized tree resin from the Baltic, and jet, a hard black stone resembling coal formed from fossilized wood, were also popular. Such jewellery is well within the pocket of the average collector today.

335

▼ *Several types of semiprecious stone were used to make these crucifixes: jet, amber, crystal with silver mounts, amethyst and onyx – a form of chalcedony.*

JEWELLERY

In Victorian times, a widow was expected to observe a strict period of mourning. By the 1860s this was stipulated as a year and a day, during which she was to wear only black – a dress code that also extended to jewellery. Black jewellery was usually made of jet, which was light and easily carved and polished. Designs for earrings, bracelets and pendants included the cross, anchor and heart (symbolizing Faith, Hope and Charity) and the Greek letters AEI, meaning 'forever'. Some mourning jewellery, such as lockets and bracelets, was designed to include a lock of the deceased's hair.

▶ This brooch is in the form of a spray of flowers; the pearls enliven what was probably a mourning brooch.

336

▼ Both jet and amber were fairly lightweight, so it was quite comfortable to wear long necklaces with large beads. Sometimes jet was mixed with ivory, as in this bracelet, to provide a pleasing contrast.

JEWELLERY

▼ This set of necklace, bracelet, earrings and brooch, made from pale pink coral cut to resemble flowers, was probably intended as a gift for a young girl.

▲ Scotish agate of different colours, mounted in silver, has been used to make this unusual brooch.

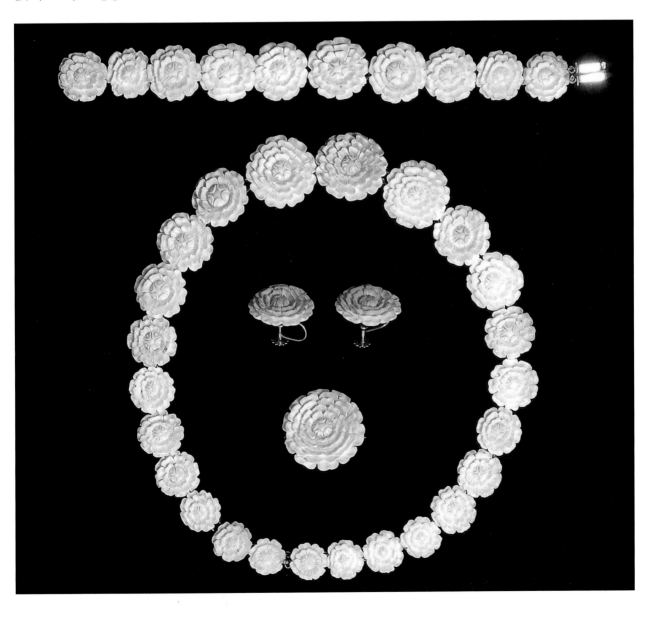

JEWELLERY

CAMEOS

338

▲ *Heads in profile and scenes with classical and mythical figures are the most common subjects for cameos. These shell cameos are particularly fine; the detail in the gold-set brooch is remarkable, considering how small the finished article is – the oval is not more than 4cm in length.*

▼ *Unusual materials were used for cameo-cut articles. This bracelet was made in Italy from volcanic lava carved with heads in Classical style.*

GENERALLY MADE FROM GEM STONES, hard stones or shells with different coloured layers that are cut to create a design in relief, cameos have been known since Roman times. They were fashionable during the Italian Renaissance and again in the late 18th century, when the Neo-classical style was dominant. But the cameos the average collector is likely to be able to find and afford are those produced in the mid- to late 19th century, when people started to travel quite widely, and there was a revival of interest in the craft. Shell cameos, in particular, were carved in Naples and Rome to be sold to tourists, or they were exported to be used for seals and jewellery such as brooches, bracelets and earrings.

JEWELLERY

BIEDERMEIER METAL JEWELLERY

IN THE TURMOIL of the Napoleonic Wars, many of the countries of Europe were in financial crisis, none more so than Prussia. Precious metals were unobtainable – gold and silver jewellery had been surrendered to the State to further the war effort – and the State provided substitutes in iron. The link between iron and patriotism was reinforced by the introduction of the Iron Cross as the highest military honour. Enterprising jewellers and metalworkers set to work and from 1813 to about 1848 produced some remarkable iron and steel jewellery.

The finest jewellery was made at Gleiwitz in Silesia and at Berlin, much of it by casting, and pieces of amazing delicacy were produced – attributable it was claimed to the type of sand used. Other pieces, such as necklaces and brooches, were fashioned by drawing out the iron into fine wire and weaving it to make a delicate mesh. The quality of the workmanship in the finest pieces is astonishing.

339

▲ *The delicacy that could be achieved by weaving metal into a mesh is evident in this flower brooch dating from c.1820.*

▲ *Steel wire has been used to make this cross and chain, which was produced in Gleiwitz c.1820.*

◄ *Loops of black steel wire joined with small daisy-like links make this feather-light necklace.*

JEWELLERY

CHATELAINES

340

AN INTERESTING FIELD for collectors is that of the chatelaine. It originated in Europe and derived from the ornaments worn by the medieval lady of the castle – the *châtelaine*; later it became the badge of the housekeeper in a large establishment. The chatelaine hung from the belt, with all the components – keys to store cupboards, and other useful small objects, perhaps scissors, a thimble and a bodkin – suspended on swivelled chains from the belt plate. Gradually, the chatelaine became a piece of jewellery in its own right, with beautifully fashioned small objects dangling from it. Often the belt plate was highly ornate and set with jewels or enamelled, while the objects hanging from it might be in gold or silver. By the mid-1800s, steel was a favoured metal, but so ornate as to be almost unrecognizable. By the end of the century the fashion for chatelaines as jewellery had waned, and it had become, once more, an object worn for its usefulness by shopworkers, seamstresses and the like.

▶ *This steel chatelaine, dating from 1838, carries more practical items, such as a penknife and tiny corkscrew, as well as decorative ones like the little purse and lucky horseshoe.*

▼ *Among the articles that might have hung from a chatelaine are a miniature scent bottle, with the glass protected by a metal case decorated with silver plate, and the tiny gilded notepad with its accompanying silver pencil.*

▼ *The influence of Art Nouveau is evident in the filigree belt plate and intricate chains of this silver chatelaine, dating from 1892.*

▼ *Made to hold a single gold sovereign as a decorative piece, this silver coin case dates from the mid-19th century.*

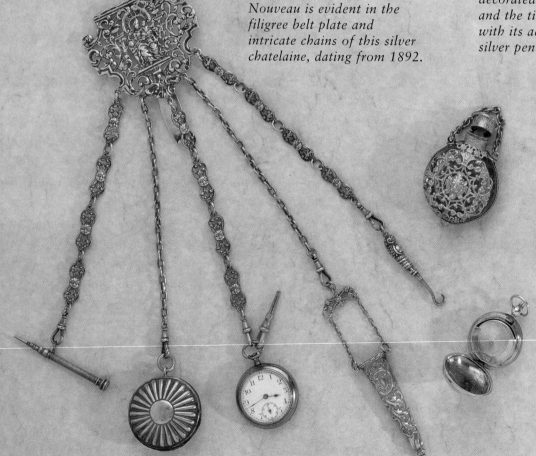

JEWELLERY

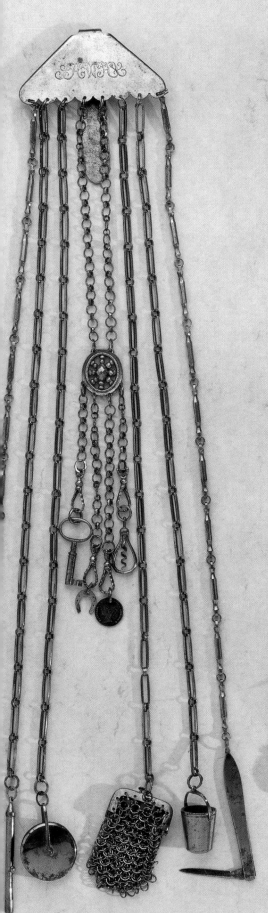

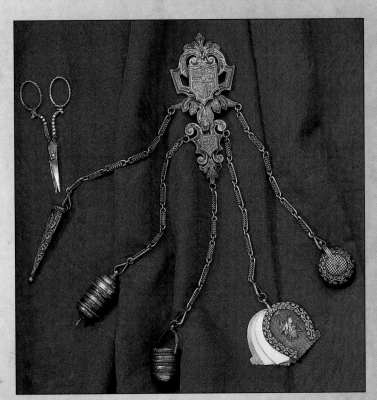

▲ *Nickel, silver, copper and brass have been used for this Continental chatelaine. From the belt plate are suspended the necessities for a seamstress: tape reel, horseshoe-shaped small notebook, bucket thimble, etui for holding needles and a sheath for the scissors shown alongside.*

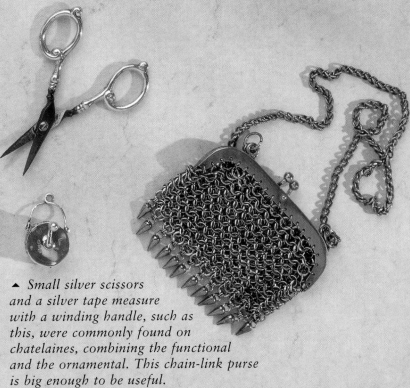

▲ *Small silver scissors and a silver tape measure with a winding handle, such as this, were commonly found on chatelaines, combining the functional and the ornamental. This chain-link purse is big enough to be useful.*

JEWELLERY

INDIAN JEWELLERY

▲ *Clockwise from top right: Hollow gold earrings from Tamil Nadu; gold earrings decorated with applied gold drops; segmented gold choker; large and small head ornaments set with emeralds, white sapphires and rubies; gold hair ornament set with rubies, emeralds and diamonds; gold nose-ring of twisted gold wire, with clusters of seed pearls.*

AN INTERESTING FIELD for the collector is that of Indian jewellery, which first came to the attention of the West in the mid-1800s. In the last decades of the century, when the vogue for all things Oriental gripped Europe, large quantities of jewellery were imported from India, notably by Arthur Lasenby Liberty, the founder of the store of that name in London. In India, jewellery had always been important, not merely for its intrinsic value, but as something of strong religious and, particularly, social significance. On marriage, as part of their dowry, women were given gold and jewels, which became their sole property and were passed on down the family.

Traditionally, both men and women of all castes and of both religions, Hindu and Muslim, wore jewellery of all types: turban

JEWELLERY

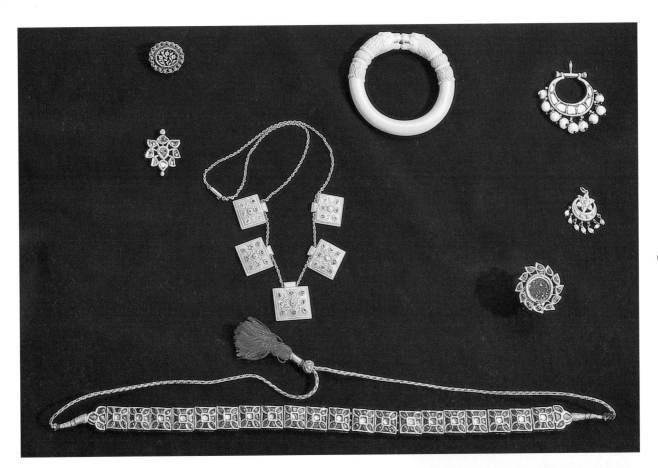

▲ *Clockwise from top right: Forehead ornament set with diamonds; forehead ornament set with turquoises; gold mirror ring that enabled the wearer to check her appearance; choker with stones in kundan setting; white jade necklace set with rubies and emeralds; flower-shaped gold-framed pendant set with diamonds; small gold brooch with enamel panel and flower design; carved ivory bracelet.*

pins, head ornaments, necklaces, bracelets, bangles, anklets, finger and toe rings and rings or studs in their noses. The wealthy would have diamonds, rubies, emeralds, sapphires and pearls in elaborate golden settings; the jewels of the middle classes would be more modest and were probably set in silver.

When the Muslims invaded India, eventually establishing the Mughal Empire in 1526, they adopted many of the forms of Hindu jewellery and styles, such as chasing or *repoussé* work, where the design was beaten out from behind. However, they added their own embellishments, such as enamelling the back of jewellery set with stones. Only in southern India, away from Muslim influence, did the older, less elaborate style survive.

▲ *The back of the mirror ring above. Enamelling the reverse of jewels set with gems prevented soft 24-carat gold wearing away. Enamels were usually red, green and white. This enclosed kundan-technique setting was universal in India until Western claw settings were introduced in the 1800s.*

Style Guide

STYLE GUIDE

NOT EVERYONE IS keen to have a collection of, say, tables or porcelain plates; it can be difficult to find the room for such a collection and a house crammed with only one type of object could soon cease to be a home and become more like a museum. What then is the avid collector to do?

The answer may lie in collecting in style – in deciding on a particular period and the style fashionable at that time, then setting out to acquire pieces of all types in that style, be it furniture, ceramics, glass or even, in more recent times, plastic. In this way it is possible to re-create a room, or an entire house, redolent of a period or a culture.

The traditionalist collector could, perhaps, settle on the 18th-century Georgian and Regency periods, buying Chippendale chairs and elegant silver coffee pots and table silver – but it would be an expensive exercise. It is perhaps more realistic to look at more recent styles, among the most enduring of which is that of Art Nouveau, the dominant style of the late 19th and early 20th centuries. In its extreme forms it is a riot of curves and swirls, with not a straight line in sight, but many of the Art Nouveau designers produced objects that are much easier to live with. The designs of the Scot, Charles Rennie Mackintosh, and Christopher Dresser, for example, owe a great debt to the Arts and Crafts Movement, with its emphasis on handmade objects: simple, honest furniture and artefacts that looked right for the job they were expected to do.

STYLE GUIDE

347

With the Art Deco style of the 1920s and '30s, there would be few problems with having to tailor 21st-century life to fit – it is uncompromisingly modern – perhaps too much so for the taste of many! The strong lines, daring furniture shapes, vibrant colours in ceramics and emphasis on action and speed are not 'comfy', but they are exciting and youthful.

For those yearning for something truly different, Chinese and Japanese style may be alluring in its serenity and simplicity. To achieve this, it is necessary to concentrate on clean lines, pale colours with patches of rich decoration, and to rid your rooms of everything extraneous. This is also the case with Islamic style – where furniture was sparse and almost all easily portable, no figurative design was allowed and colour came from rich carpets and textiles. If you decide to adopt this style, you could bear in mind the belief that a man's wealth lay not in the opulence of the objects in his home, but in the richness of his friendships, and let your life follow a similar pattern.

Style Guide

Eastern Decorative Art

A HUGE ARRAY OF OBJETS D'ART falls under this heading, ranging from Islamic brass lamps through Japanese netsuke and ivory figures to Chinese jade. It is worth keeping in mind, though, that many objects we now consider purely 'decorative' originally had a religious or functional purpose. Examples of this are the bronze incense burners used in Buddhist ritual or the carved jade figures that embodied moral lessons concerning personal conduct.

The pieces shown here are just a tiny fraction of the beautiful and exquisitely crafted objects that have been produced over hundreds of years in the Far and Middle East. It does not touch the wide range of Indian artefacts, although perhaps the most accessible Indian workmanship – jewellery – is discussed in the Jewellery chapter, nor does it cover Chinese and Japanese porcelain, already discussed in Ceramics.

As with ceramics, following the opening up of Japan to Western trade in the 19th century and the inroads the colonial powers made in China, many Oriental craftsmen concentrated on producing objects specifically for export to Europe, and it is largely these items that collectors find for sale. While they were often wonderfully made, and some can be very expensive, as a general rule such export pieces are less highly valued as antiques than earlier work or contemporary work that was intended for the home market.

EASTERN DECORATIVE ART

A travelling writing set, or qalamdan, *consisting of a quill holder and inkwell, was essential for a business man or merchant, since it meant he could write contracts or bills of sale wherever he happened to be. This 19th-century set is in brass, inlaid with copper and white metal.*

The best places to look for Oriental and Middle Eastern antiques are the salerooms of auction houses or specialist dealers. It is rare for anything worthwhile to turn up on stalls at small antique fairs or car boot sales – but then again you may be lucky, since many people have no understanding of such wares and may simply be clearing out the attic.

STYLE GUIDE
LACQUERWORK

▼ *Japanese export furniture, such as this chest on a stand dating from c.1800, followed European furniture styles and was much more elaborate and highly decorated than pieces made for the home market.*

LACQUER IS MADE FROM the sap of *Rhus vernicifera*, a type of sumach tree found in China and later introduced into Japan. The sticky sap is tapped by cutting the bark, then strained and heated to create a free-flowing liquid, sometimes opaque, sometimes clear. This is applied repeatedly in dozens of thin layers to wood, fabric, metal or leather, building up a shiny, durable surface so hard that it can be carved in relief.

By the 4th century BC the Chinese had perfected lacquerwork for the decoration of small objects. A few of these made their way via the trade routes to Europe over the next two millennia, but it was not until the 18th century that large, heavily lacquered items such as work tables and cabinets began to appear there in quantity.

EASTERN DECORATIVE ART

Japan also exported a great many high-quality lacquered items, including *inro* – small, beautifully decorated boxes in interlocking sections. They were originally intended for storing seals and medicines and for carrying on a belt, since traditional Japanese clothing had no pockets.

The secret of making true lacquer – and indeed the lac tree – was unknown in Europe at the time of its greatest popularity in the 18th and early 19th centuries. An appearance of lacquer was created by a process known as 'japanning'. Imitations of lacquer designs were often applied to papier-mâché.

▲ *The stand of this highly decorated Chinese lacquer work cabinet in black and gold, c.1700, contains several compartments. The interior of the cabinet is also decorated in lacquer.*

▶ *This large eight-leaved Chinese screen in black lacquer, with gold and silver inlays, is decorated in the style known as Coromandel.*

STYLE GUIDE

352

◀ *Among the many small articles that the Japanese covered in lacquer were boxes such as this one, made to hold writing paper. Boxes of different types formed the basis of all Japanese storage.*

▶ *Small compartmented containers,* inro, *were carried, almost as a fashion accessory, by Japanese gentlemen, hanging from their belts on a cord. The cord was pulled tight by a small bead, or* ojime, *and ended in a toggle, or* netsuke, *which was caught above the belt. The* inro *were frequently exquisitely decorated in lacquer and silver or gold with scenes from nature – forests, streams and mountains. Flowers and plants, animals and birds were other common themes.*

EASTERN DECORATIVE ART

JAPANESE KIMONOS

◄ *These fine 19th-century kimonos, padded and lined with red silk, were richly decorated in the elegant, sophisticated style of the time. Kimonos with long, hanging sleeves were worn mainly by young girls and geishas, or courtesans.*

UNTIL THE END of the 19th century, Japanese men and women of all social classes normally wore the kimono – a straight-cut, loose coat with very wide sleeves, which was designed to cover up the body rather than to fit. The kimono was wrapped in to the body by a sash, or *obi*; men wore it wrapped to the right, women to the left. The effect was achieved by the fabric and by the decoration and embroidery. Kimonos were made in many different types of fabric, from simple indigo-dyed striped or patterned cotton worn by working people to the sumptuous silks and self-patterned brocades worn by well-to-do people and the elite. On the finest kimonos, exotic designs of scenes, flowers and birds were painted or stencilled, appliquéd or worked in silk and metallic thread to create some of the most beautiful garments ever seen. Kimonos from the 19th century are rare and expensive, but those from the early 20th century can be found fairly easily and make magnificent wall hangings.

▲ *Originally just a narrow cord, the* obi *gradually grew wider and more colourful until it became an article of fashion made from a length of rich fabric. Girls and young married women tied their* obis *in a butterfly bow behind, older women often made a flatter bow at the side.*

STYLE GUIDE
IVORY: JAPANESE
OKIMONO

354

▲ *Many ivory pieces bear the carved signature of the artist.*

VALUED FOR ITS EASE OF CUTTING and the way it polishes to a smooth, lustrous surface, ivory has been carved in China for thousands of years. Religious statuettes, particularly seated Buddhas, have been prominent among the many delicate and intricately carved objects produced over the centuries by Chinese craftsmen for the home market, while large quantities of card cases, pierced concentric balls and fans were made for the export market.

It was, however, in Japan during the Meiji period (1868–1912) that members of the Tokyo School of Art produced the most exquisite ivory pieces, including astonishingly lifelike statuettes of warriors, geishas, peasants and fishermen. Even at the time they were made, these objects – known as *okimono* – were highly regarded and highly priced in both Japan and the West. Today they fetch considerable sums of money.

Although the trade in modern elephant ivory is now illegal virtually everywhere, the antiques market has not been too much affected by the recent international Wildlife Protection Acts. The Japanese did not use elephant ivory on any large scale before the 19th century; earlier small pieces tend to be made of ivory from wild boar, walrus or narwhal.

▶ *This group of figures demonstrates the lifelike, often charming, quality of* okimono, *as well as their variety.*

◀ *Many carvings were entirely naturalistic, conveying a sense of character, and with the detail – here, the woven cane basket and the pattern on the clothing – painstakingly rendered. The piece is signed by the artist Siega.*

EASTERN DECORATIVE ART

STYLE GUIDE

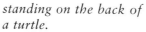
▲ *Geisha musicians and dancers like these used to perform in Japanese tea houses; each figure is made up from small pieces of carved ivory.*

Here an old man is shown gloating over his treasure chest, while alongside him is a poor fisherman with his catch – a favourite subject with Japanese carvers. He is standing on the back of a turtle.

EASTERN DECORATIVE ART

▸ *The charming study of a mother carrying her child is fascinating for the opportunity it gives to study the detail of her dress and the way the baby is strapped on to her back.*

357

▲ *These two figures of geisha girls show different types of finish used on okimono. Small chisel marks are still visible on the figure on the right, while that on the left is smooth and detailed.*

◂ *Sometimes the ivory was stained to help show up the detail of the carving, as in this little group of a peasant, his wife and dog.*

▾ *In the delicately executed figure of a man playing with his child the carver shows penetrating observation and great tenderness.*

EASTERN DECORATIVE ART

359

The deep regard of the Japanese for the natural world is evident in the fine animal and bird carvings that were produced in ivory. The stance of the cranes and their delicately carved feathers are acutely observed, as are those of the hawk. All the birds have inlaid glass eyes and metal legs, an indication that they were made for the Western market, where such realistic features were regarded as desirable. The intertwined dragons are carved from a single piece of ivory and were probably made for the home market, since they do not have inlaid eyes. In the two monkey groups, the carver shows a delightful awareness of the mischievous nature of the animals. The ivory has been stained to imitate the monkeys' fur, and the eyes are made from horn.

STYLE GUIDE
IVORY: NETSUKE

▲ *The most astonishing detail was achieved by the carvers of netsuke; for example in the tiny otter, holding her minute pup in her mouth.*

TINY TOGGLES, or *netsuke*, were used at the top of the cord of an *inro* (see p.352), and also on the cords closing purses and tobacco pouches. Although not regarded as anything special by the Japanese, they were miniature works of art exquisitely carved from bone, horn, nuts and fruit stones, and often, odds and ends of ivory. The skill of the carvers is wonderfully displayed in these small objects, which are easy to show and enjoy, although they are delicate and need to be looked after carefully.

EASTERN DECORATIVE ART

Japanese carvers also made slightly larger ivory ornaments, most often of animals or birds, which are carefully observed or sometimes almost caricatured, like this rotund caparisoned elephant.

▶ *Amongst the subjects in this group a boy holds a split pumpkin on his head, which contains two men seated at a table.*

STYLE GUIDE
IVORY: CHESSMEN

SETS OF CHESSMEN MADE IN China in the workshops of Canton are among the most attractive small ivory pieces to be found. The ivory used comes from Indian elephants and is very white; it is left unstained for the white chess pieces, while the opposing pieces – black in Europe – are stained bright red. You are not likely to come across any chess sets earlier than the late 1700s, and most will date from the 19th and even early 20th century; since designs were repeated time and time again it is very difficult to date them. The chessmen are always delicately carved, showing amazing detail, and they are extremely pleasing to handle. Sometimes they are made to represent opposing armies, with the knights shown as mounted warriors and the pawns as footsoldiers.

362

▼ *Among the many chess sets imported into Europe in the 18th century was this one, in which the white king and queen represent the British King George III and Queen Charlotte (Napoleon and Josephine were also often portrayed). The red pieces are shown as Chinese or Manchu emperors and empresses. All the pawns are Oriental soldiers – the scimitar in the white pawn's hand can be removed – and the castles have become elephants.*

EASTERN DECORATIVE ART
CHINESE JADE

THE TERM JADE IS USED of various hard stones, including nephrite (a silicate of calcium and magnesium) and jadeite (silicate of aluminium and sodium). Nephrite, so hard it has to be painstakingly filed down or ground away rather than carved, has been worked by the Chinese since ancient times.

As well as the green usually associated with jade, there are white and brown types of nephrite. The white variety, known as 'mutton fat', is the most highly prized jade in China. Jadeite tends to be dark green or emerald in colour, and was first carved only in the 18th century. Many of these pieces are within the scope of the ordinary collector.

Do not confuse jade with the similar-looking but soft stone, soapstone or steatite (magnesium silicate), which is vulnerable to scratching. It may be white, red or greenish grey, but it can be distinguished from jade by its 'soapy' feel.

Many of the small jade carvings of animals were regarded as 'pocket pieces', made to be caressed and handled in much the same way as 'worry beads'. The style of the carving changes from period to period – pieces made during the Ming dynasty (1368–1644) are naturalistic, while those of the later Qing dynasty are often finely detailed. Decorative pieces include vases, bowls, statues, and jewellery – all beautifully carved.

▲ *This water-dropper in the form of a duck was carved from white jade in the 17th century. On each wing the carver has portrayed a duck in flight.*

363

◀ *The decorative mountain scene, with two figures, in pale celadon jade dates from the 18th century.*

▲ *A detail of the mountain scene shows the meticulous carving of the face and robes of the old man.*

Style Guide

Islamic Style

B Y WESTERN STANDARDS, living rooms in wealthy homes in the Middle East were sparsely furnished on a day-to-day basis, with perhaps a storage chest, some rugs on the floor and a few cushions scattered on a low divan; low tray tables were used when refreshments were served. More furniture was stored away and brought in when it was required for the comfort of guests, since to show hospitality was the way a man

▲ *Tables were often hexagonal or octagonal. This Syrian example has a top inlaid with a design of arabesques, crescent moons, leaves and lilies in brass, mother-of-pearl and silver. Similar decoration is used on the side panels, which have fret-cut patterns outlined with silver stringing.*

▲ *A western-style sofa such as this would probably have been made for a European living in Cairo or Alexandria c.1890. However, the carved and inlaid work follows the Islamic decorative tradition.*

EASTERN DECORATIVE ART

demonstrated his wealth. Most of the furniture was made of wood, heavily inlaid with brass, silver, tortoiseshell and mother-of-pearl in patterns that echoed those on rugs, wall and floor tiles and the carved wooden *mashrabiye* screens that were used at the windows to filter the sun and preserve privacy in the home.

▼ *Exquisite workmanship, as on this teak bench covered with delicate floral patterns in mother-of-pearl c.1890, is the hallmark of Syrian furniture-makers.*

▲ *Reading the Koran, the Muslim holy book, was a daily activity. It was kept in a box and when taken out was placed on a folding X-framed stand such as this one from Syria, which is about 90cm high.*

STYLE GUIDE

366

◀ This Syrian table top is inlaid with a design of arabesques, crescent moons, leaves and lilies in brass, mother-of-pearl and silver.

▼ The camel statuette, made in Persia (Iran) in the late 19th century, has been ornamented with damascene. This process involves inlaying the base metal, usually steel, with precious metals, generally gold and silver as here. It was a technique frequently employed to decorate the blades of swords.

EASTERN DECORATIVE ART

◄ Small incense burners, such as this brass one, stood around the room. They were used to scent the air with burning spices and herbs in the same way that pastille burners were used in Europe.

► Islamic metalwork was of a very high standard, as this elaborately engraved and pierced mosque lamp shows. Hanging lamps were the main form of lighting, and different types of lamp were made for different locations.

367

▼ Throughout the Middle East, long slender pipes were used for smoking, often when the men gathered to relax or discuss business.

► The workmanship on this Egyptian bronze mosque lamp is extremely fine. The metal has been cut in an intricate design and then patinated to give it a soft, glowing appearance. The small door on the side enables the oil to be replenished easily and the wick tended.

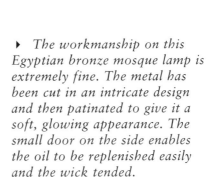

◄ Most buildings were lighted by oil lamps which were hooked up to fittings on the wall. This one is made in bronze and has a removable cover enabling it to be filled.

Style Guide
Art Nouveau

THE ORIGINS OF THE ART NOUVEAU style are still open to debate, but it is generally considered to have grown out of the British Arts and Crafts Movement of the early 1880s. There was little to distinguish the two approaches at first; where the Art Nouveau craftsman differed from his Arts and Crafts colleague was, perhaps, in his growing scepticism about the social function of his work. The emphasis of Art Nouveau was increasingly aesthetic rather than social; craftsmen felt free to draw on a variety of influences, including Gothic and Japanese styles, to create extravagantly shaped, eye-catching pieces that could often stand as artworks in their own right. Later, some of the major figures in the movement broke the great taboo of Arts and Crafts, in adopting some industrial methods of manufacture.

A design made by Arthur Mackmurdo in 1883 for the title page of his book *Wren's City Churches* had a considerable impact on the development of the style. In this image of roosters framing swirling plant forms, Mackmurdo developed the flowing natural motifs seen in textiles made by Arts and Crafts luminaries such as William Morris into a series of stylized sinuous shapes in a way that would be the hallmark of Art Nouveau design.

ART NOUVEAU

The style became known as Art Nouveau in 1895, when a shop, La Maison de l'Art Nouveau, opened in Paris to sell objects made by the new designers and craftsmen. It used natural forms, such as leaves, plants, flowers and peacock feathers, and long swirling shapes and curves. Although Art Nouveau probably originated as a graphic style, it soon influenced the other crafts – furniture, glass-making, jewellery, ceramics, even architecture – with its emphasis on flowing line, elegant asymmetric design and decorative motifs derived from nature.

The style was known as Jugendstil in Germany, where in its heyday (1896–1900) it was typified by rather lifeless flowers and figures; later, under the influence of the Glasgow-born architect and designer Charles Rennie Mackintosh, it became more geometric.

STYLE GUIDE
CERAMICS

▼ *One of a pair, this gilded jug, made by the Amphora factory c.1900, is decorated with flower shapes and inset ceramic 'stones'. In true Jugendstil fashion, a scantily clad nymph forms the handle.*

THE DEVELOPMENT OF THE Art Nouveau style in ceramics centred in France. A new generation of French potters turned their backs on porcelain to concentrate on the production of more coarsely grained stoneware. The elegant shapes and asymmetrical designs of Japanese and Chinese wares were their chief inspiration, while technical innovations and new equipment made possible a variety of new artistic effects.

French ceramicists were responsible for a number of important technical advances. They discovered the secret constituents of the *sang-de-boeuf* (oxblood) glaze used on Chinese stoneware, and also experimented with a wide range of finishes, so that wares might have a polished, pitted, veined or dappled appearance. They also created one of Art Nouveau's most distinctive motifs – a drip glaze poured over the object in a long flowing curve. This method of decoration, derived from the Orient, was used by virtually every major Art Nouveau potter in Europe and the USA. The development of American ceramics essentially ran parallel to that in France, with lustrous glazes applied to simple stoneware

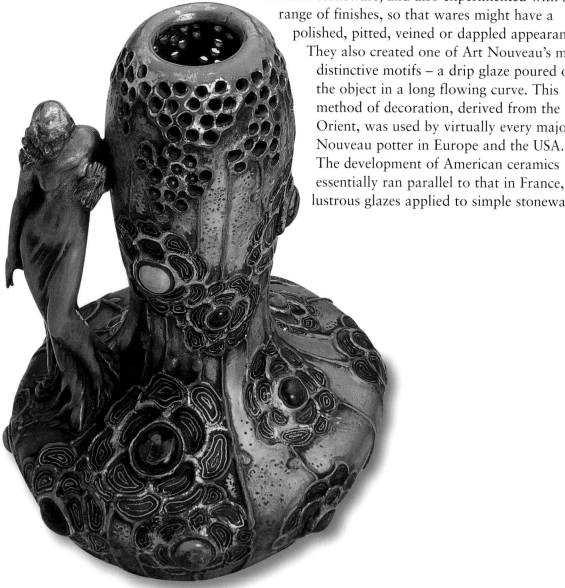

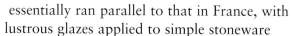

ART NOUVEAU

shapes. The American version of Art Nouveau was evident in the elongated vase forms and sinuous handles and in the use of inlays – lilies, orchids and exotic birds.

In Germany and Austria-Hungary Jugendstil ceramics in both porcelain and pottery were remarkably varied in style and shape, with some pieces decorated in typical Art Nouveau style and others more geometric in concept and decoration.

371

▲ *The motif of a woman's head with flowing hair and surrounded by flowers is typical of Jugendstil designs.*

▲ *A stylized orchid in vibrant colour brings a touch of exoticism to the otherwise simple vase, made in Austria c.1900.*

▶ *The slight wedge shape of this dark blue vase, made by the Hungarian firm of Zsolnay c.1900, is emphasized by the gold geometric pattern incised into the clay.*

STYLE GUIDE

372

◄ Poppies were a favourite flower among Art Nouveau artists. In this piece by Eichwald of Bavaria, the grey-green, sinuous stems and white flowers are set off by the glowing peach body colour and gold band.

▶ Unusually for Art Nouveau ceramics, this pair of amphora vases is made in porcelain. The technique of dripping a glaze over the surface has been carried to its limit here, where even the lips of the vases and the handles appear to have melted on to the body.

ART NOUVEAU

These two late 19th century
Secessionist vases by Minton are
typical in their vibrant colour, and
the use of images from nature.

STYLE GUIDE

FURNITURE

374

IN FURNITURE, the Art Nouveau style was expressed in 'whiplash' forms, asymmetrical curves, broad mouldings and naturalistic carved decoration. The School of Nancy was dominant in France, and tables by Louis Majorelle, the most significant furniture designer there, combine a crossbanded top, leaf frieze and sweeping cabriole legs joined by an undertier. It often seemed as though the craftsmen were trying to defy the limitations of the material.

Furniture that is still stranger in shape – though more austere in terms of materials used – was produced by Belgian designer Henri van der Velde. Some of his pieces, such as the padouk (Burmese sandalwood) armchair he made in 1899 and had covered with cotton batik upholstery, continue to impress with the sheer élan of their conception and skill of their construction.

A chair with a pierced floral design to the back, made by Arthur Heygate Mackmurdo in 1883, is often cited as the starting point for Art Nouveau furniture in Britain, but the most important names are

▶ *Majorelle's walnut cabinet was designed as a multi-storage piece. It is decorated with inlaid butterflies and flowers.*

ART NOUVEAU

those of Charles Rennie Mackintosh and M.H. Baillie-Scott. They did not adopt the sinuous plastic line of Continental designers, but were more influenced by the restrained rectilinear shapes of the Arts and Crafts Movement. They did, however, adopt some Art Nouveau motifs such as pierced and solid heart shapes and flat-capped uprights. Mackintosh is justly celebrated for his break from constructional restraints. His chairs intended for the Argyle Street Tea Rooms in Glasgow, with their pierced headpieces and long rectilinear slats, are fine examples of his style – elongated and with asymmetrical designs. Restrained Celtic decoration was also used, as was opaque enamelled glass on some of his white-painted pieces.

▶ *This cabinet by Gallé is extravagantly decorated with fine open-carved foliage which, together with the curved top, suggests an arbour in a garden.*

STYLE GUIDE

▲ The top and shelf of the table are inlaid in a design of leaves and ferns. The veneers used for the marquetry were chosen for grain and texture as well as for colour to produce a natural effect.

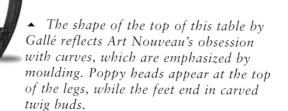

▲ The shape of the top of this table by Gallé reflects Art Nouveau's obsession with curves, which are emphasized by moulding. Poppy heads appear at the top of the legs, while the feet end in carved twig buds.

ART NOUVEAU

A simple stained pine bookcase is embellished with an elaborate carving of peacocks.

STYLE GUIDE
ARTS AND CRAFTS

378

*I*N THE LATE 19TH CENTURY the Arts and Crafts Movement brought a return to plain design and honesty in construction, a revolt against the decorative excess of the Victorian age, and the Rococo and Gothic styles. The inspiration behind the movement was William Morris, who introduced the idea of simple, well-made domestic artefacts. But while the movement favoured modern style, it clung to traditional methods of construction. Their work has therefore a medieval flavour, and the pieces were also extremely expensive to produce.

▲ *The simplicity of design of this brass coal box is typical of the Arts and Crafts Movement.*

▲ *The Arts and Crafts style appealed in the USA also. This oak desk, with little decoration, was made in Grand Rapids, Michigan, which specialized in Arts and Crafts styles.*

ART NOUVEAU

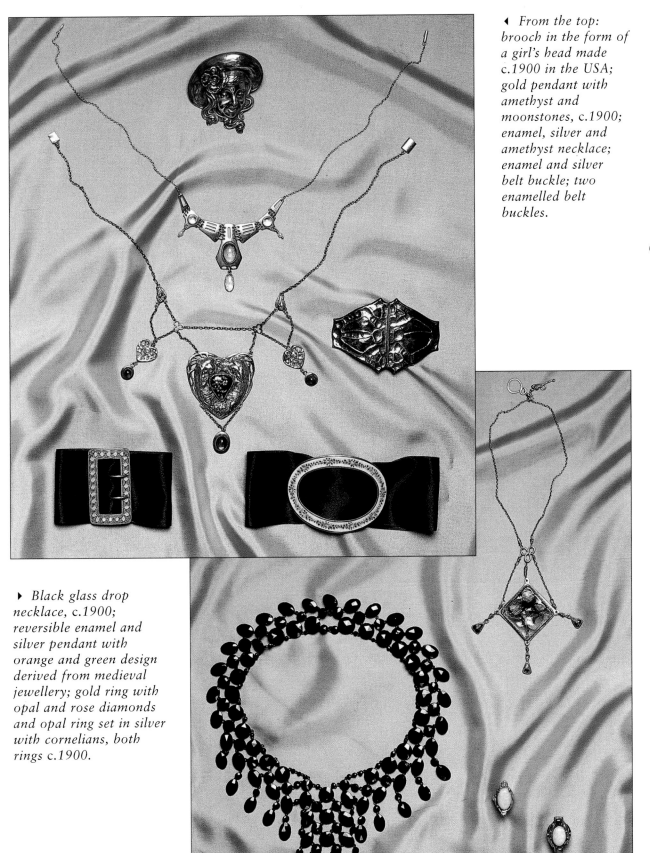

◀ *From the top: brooch in the form of a girl's head made c.1900 in the USA; gold pendant with amethyst and moonstones, c.1900; enamel, silver and amethyst necklace; enamel and silver belt buckle; two enamelled belt buckles.*

▶ *Black glass drop necklace, c.1900; reversible enamel and silver pendant with orange and green design derived from medieval jewellery; gold ring with opal and rose diamonds and opal ring set in silver with cornelians, both rings c.1900.*

STYLE GUIDE
GLASS

▲ *The glass from Gallé's workshop was all signed. with his name. The star indicates that the piece was made after his death in 1904. In the years up to World War I, as mass-production techniques were introduced, quality declined.*

▼ *The detail from one of Gallé's vases demonstrates his close observation of nature.*

GLASS WAS A MALLEABLE MEDIUM of great potential for the Art Nouveau craftsman, in which he could express the fluid contours and arabesques of the style. But it was its translucency that most appealed to designers concerned with lightness and delicacy.

Many of the great innovators of Art Nouveau glassware, among them Emile Gallé, were working around the town of Nancy. The inspirations for Gallé's work were his large knowledge of botany and natural history, and his study of Oriental glass and china in London. He was increasingly interested in the possibilities of using both opaque and translucent colour, and achieved relief effects using moulding and 'casing' – building up a piece using successive coatings of different coloured glass. Sometimes he used acid to striate or pit a vessel's surface, or embedded metal leaf, gold dust or enamel within it. The use of enamel in combination with glass gave Gallé the opportunity to create the deepest colours. Other firms making Art Nouveau glass in Nancy, such as Daum and Muller Frères, employed technicians who had been trained by Gallé.

There was also a strong tradition of glass-making in Germany and Austria-Hungary, where Jugendstil designers produced pictures that pushed glass technology to its limits to create decorative iridescent effects and curvilinear shapes. It tends to be more delicate, and rarer, than French work.

In the USA, decorative glass-making was dominated by the work of Louis Comfort Tiffany. The Tiffany Glass and Decoration Company, founded in 1879, rapidly became a very successful enterprise. With the opening of a new glassworks at Corona, Tiffany began producing handmade pieces in Favrile, an iridescent, rainbow-hued glass, whose different surface textures and sheen were created using chemical soaks or vapours.

ART NOUVEAU

These three vases, standing on a marquetry table by Gallé, were made by glass-makers of the Nancy School. The one on the left with a seascape is by Muller Frères, and the central vase with toadstools on a streaked ground was made by Daum. The cameo vase, with an Oriental flavour, is by Gallé, who derived much of his inspiration from the simple shapes of Japanese ceramics and glass.

STYLE GUIDE

THE FIRM OF DAUM BEGAN TO produce art glass only in 1887. Their pieces have a mottled or streaked appearance created by adding powdered glass during smelting. Colours range from deep blue and green to orange – ideal for lamps, where the light shining through brought out their full potential. They are also noted for many-layered cameo glass, with successive layers cut away to show another of etched, engraved or enamelled glass beneath.

The two brothers who set up the company of Muller Frères in 1895 both trained with Gallé. Their glass could have as many as seven layers, each cut away to reveal different colours beneath. They also employed a special technique, known as fluorogravure, in which glass painted with highly coloured or iridescent enamel was etched away with hydrochloric acid.

ART NOUVEAU

Most of these vases come from Daum's workshops. Clockwise from right: Tall yellow and mauve streaked vase with painted yellow flowers; curved bowl painted in enamel with apple blossom; squat rectangular vase with an idyllic river scene – the reflections are extremely skilfully executed; vase with white and gold overlay of mistletoe and an unusual gold rim; Japanese inspired oblong vase with enamel-painted fuchsias; blue vase, dating from the turn of the 20th century with cameo decoration of peacock feathers; Muller Frères vase with purple and yellow crocuses on a typical mottled amber background; acid-etched dog roses in pink and green on a vase in the shape of an inverted bell; large, round Muller Frères vase with a blue rim, cameo cut and painted with a mountain scene to create a remarkable pictorial effect.

STYLE GUIDE

METALWORK

384

WORK IN THE TRADITIONAL precious metals, particularly silver, had sunk to a low level in the mid-19th century. To revive the skill of metalworking, Art Nouveau craftsmen worked across the complete range of metals, mixing them with enamel, ivory and wood, among other materials.

Oriental influence was paramount. The English designer Christopher Dresser, one of the few artist-craftsmen of the period to visit Japan, made household wares such as tea sets that are distinguished by their purity of line and elegance. There were other strongly influential trends. The metalworker Alexander Knox, whose work straddles the divide between Arts and Crafts and Art Nouveau, created a range of silverware, called Cymric, and later pewterware, called Tudric based on Celtic styling, for Arthur Lasenby Liberty's store in London. His tea sets and biscuit boxes are exquisite.

Collectors should beware when buying Art Nouveau metalwork, since there was a revival of interest in the style in the 1930s and again in the 1960s. Original moulds were sometimes used, and much of what is available is reproduction – of high quality, but not of real interest to the true collector.

▶ *The manufacturer WMF was noted for splendid pewterware in the extravagantly curvilinear style that characterized Jugendstil in Germany.*

▼ *Both of these photograph frames are silver, but the one on the right was made recently, while that on the left is an original. It is easy to check the date of a silver piece made in Britain because, by law, silver must be hallmarked with the date, place of registration, and maker's name.*

ART NOUVEAU

STYLE GUIDE

I N SCANDINAVIA, AND IN DENMARK in particular, there was an upsurge of interest in metalwork in the late 19th and early 20th centuries. The most important designer of silverware was the Dane Georg Jensen, who established his workshops in Copenhagen in 1904. Elements of Arts and Crafts design, as well as of Art Nouveau, or Jugendstil, appeared in his early work, and later he incorporated some of the features of Art Deco also. In addition, Jensen made silver to the designs of other artists, notably Johan Rhode, and his brother-in-law Harald Nielsen.

386

Jensen's interpretation of Art Nouveau motifs was very restrained. His purity of line and emphasis on the close relationship of an object's intended use with its appearance derives largely from the English Arts and Crafts Movement and William Morris's dictum that any ornament should be in proportion to the purpose it was meant to serve.

ART NOUVEAU

STYLE GUIDE

▸ *One of 12, made in 1900, this English brass fingerplate and doorknob were decorated in classic Art Nouveau style. The copper and brass kettle and muffin dish on a stand was made by Benson in the 1880s, and he used the same metals for the rather more ornate candlestick dating from c.1905.*

388

THE INFLUENCE OF ART NOUVEAU on metalworkers who used brass and copper was, in many ways, subordinate to that of the Arts and Crafts Movement. These metals appealed to those designers who felt that beautiful objects should be available cheaply for all, and they used brass, and especially copper, to make everyday domestic objects, such as kettles, lamps and candlesticks. Most important among them was the Englishman W.A.S. Benson, who set out to mass-produce beautiful forms by machinery rather than making art objects by hand. His influence was considerable in the early 1900s, and many fine decorative pieces from that period can be found.

▸ *The seven-branched brass candelabrum, which has holes for electric wires in the cups, was mass-produced by Benson c.1900, as was the copper and brass electric table lamp in the shape of an Aladdin's lamp, made in 1906. Gold-plated pewter was used to make the Austrian table lamp c.1900. The shade is a modern copy of the original one.*

ART NOUVEAU

STYLE GUIDE

Clockwise from top right: An easel mirror in polished pewter, adorned with peacocks, made in Germany c.1900; silver spoon made in 1901 for Liberty's Cymric range to commemorate Edward VII's coronation; pewter tureen with a helmet-shaped cover, made by

Archibald Knox for Liberty; pewter sweet dish by WMF c.1900; candlestick on three stems by Archibald Knox for Liberty; ornately decorated biscuit barrel with peacock handles in pewter and green glass, by WMF c.1900; pewter wall clock with enamel 'stones'

inset – part of Liberty's Tudric range; elegant, tall glass and pewter claret jug with a hinged lid, made by WMF; the cross on the silver-plated jug, made by Elkington in 1892, indicates that it might have been intended for use in a church.

L IKE BRASS AND COPPER, the use of pewter and silver plate enjoyed a revival in the late 19th and early 20th centuries, and for much the same reason – the desire to make beautiful objects available to the majority of the population who could not afford to buy silver. The wide range of designs covered by the term Art Nouveau is clearly shown in the pieces produced. In Germany, the major manufacturer, WMF, was turning out heavily ornamented objects, covered in curlicues and maidens with trailing garments and hair that flowed into plant forms, while designers such as Georg Jensen, Charles Rennie Mackintosh and Archibald Knox, with his Tudric ware for Liberty's, veered towards simpler, more austere, almost geometric lines closely related to the designs of the Arts and Crafts Movement.

▸ *Art Nouveau pewter ware displayed in a typical ornate cabinet of the period.*

ART NOUVEAU

STYLE GUIDE

JEWELLERY

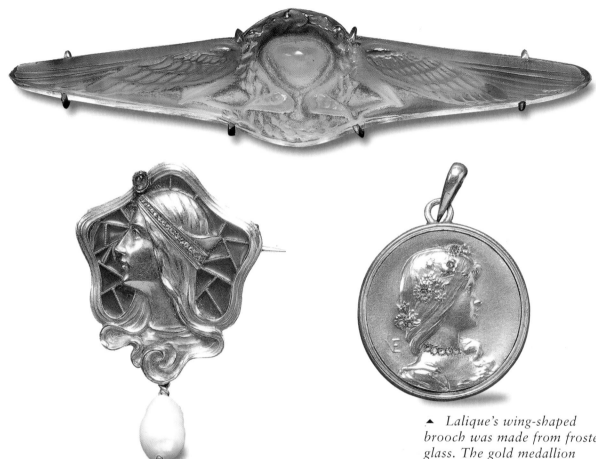

392

T HE GREAT INNOVATOR IN THE FIELD of Art Nouveau
jewellery was the Frenchman René Lalique, whose work
rejected social conventions and broke all the traditional
rules of design. He was willing to use any material, including
semiprecious stones for the sake of the colour, base as well as
precious metals, onyx, crystal, enamel, glass and mother–of–
pearl. He used a repertory of classic Art Nouveau forms,
including butterflies, dragonflies, peacocks and orchids.

Lalique's work not only set the fashion for jewellery in the
rest of Europe, but also exerted a strong influence in America.
Louis Tiffany of Tiffany and Co, which was already producing
Art Nouveau silver, glass and ceramics, set up what was to
become one of the most famous jewellery departments in the
world under the supervision of the designer Julia Munson.

Even in England, where the principles of Arts and Crafts
design still held sway in jewellery, Charles Robert Ashbee was
seduced by the highly ornamental possibilities of Art Nouveau
style. The use of decorative open wirework and a flowing, Celtic
line is characteristic of Ashbee's work.

▲ *Lalique's wing-shaped
brooch was made from frosted-
glass. The gold medallion
pendant shows the typical Art
Nouveau head of a girl with
flowers in her hair. The more
sophisticated brooch has a
background of champlevé
enamel and incorporates small
diamonds, an amethyst and a
pearl drop.*

▶ *It was in his jewellery that
Georg Jensen came closest to
true Art Nouveau design. Most
of his pieces are based on
insects or flowers – here that
favourite of Art Nouveau
artists, the orchid, is seen on
the cigarette case. In addition,
he set such semiprecious stones
as opal, moonstone, coral,
amber and agate into the silver
to complement its soft sheen.*

STYLE GUIDE
ART DECO

ALTHOUGH ART DECO IS USUALLY thought of as a movement of the 1920s and '30s, its origins lie in the last years of the 19th century, when Art Nouveau dominated design. It was then that the iconography of primitive and ancient art began to influence the art world. Western artists, designers and craftsmen seeking 'new' motifs and patterns looked for inspiration to African tribal art, Aztec and Mayan architecture, Greek and Roman sculpture and Egyptian hieroglyphs. And the discovery of the tomb of Tutankhamun in 1922, with its magnificent artefacts, created a craze for Egyptian stylings.

New trends in painting – such as Fauvism, Futurism and Cubism – in the early years of the 20th century were another major influence on the designers of the 1920s and '30s. And the continuing development of new technology and materials – particularly plastics – also contributed to the creation of a global design style characterized by exotic, if highly

ART DECO

stylized, decoration, a love of geometric
form, simple clean lines and smooth and
shiny surfaces.

This style was expressed in architecture,
jewellery, furniture, textiles, ceramics – in fact, in
virtually every area of design. Furniture was no
longer ornate and dark colours were banished. The
clutter of 19th-century rooms gave way to
large open areas, furniture was simpler,
often machine made, and pale woods
were used. Wall and fabric colours were lighter, clothes
and jewellery relied on simplicity for their effect, and
the overall feeling was streamlined, and
uncompromisingly modern.

The diversity of sources of inspiration for Art Deco
designers means that it is rare to find two
pieces exactly alike, and its air of
playful experimentation makes a
great deal of the commercial work of
the period collectable today. Signed
pieces by named designers – bronze
or chryselephantine figures, perhaps –
can be expensive and very valuable.

STYLE GUIDE
CERAMICS

ART DECO'S LOVE AFFAIR WITH geometry had a powerful effect on ceramics between the two World Wars, as is obvious in the potting and decoration of French and English wares.

396

Art Deco's influence on pottery was first felt in France, where the two most outstanding ceramicists of the 1920s were Emile Decoeur (1876-1953) and Emile Lenoble (1876-1953). Decoeur's faience, stoneware and porcelain vessels featured floral or geometric decoration, and their pale underglazes were often tinged with spots of dark overglaze. On the whole, though, his wares had traditional shapes, and Lenoble was perhaps the more adventurous craftsman. His wares were also decorated with floral and abstract designs, but were covered with brightly coloured craquelure glazes similar to those on Korean pottery. Highly stylized motifs were moulded in subtle bas-relief or cut into an applied 'slip' of clay.

In England, the name of the potter Clarice Cliff (1899–1972) is synonymous with the style. Cliff was strongly influenced by the new wares coming out of France, shown at the Paris Exposition of 1925. In 1928, at Wilkinson's Newport pottery, she produced her first line of Art Deco table ceramics, which she labelled Bizarre. This line, and others such as Fantasque, Bonjour and Crocus, contained both traditional wares and some radically new shapes. They were decorated with stylized and geometric designs in bold, usually warm colours. Cliff's wares were a great success throughout the 1930s and have enjoyed much renewed interest recently, becoming very expensive.

▼ *The angular shape and cubist-style decoration on this coffee pot are reminiscent of the modernity and functionalism of German Bauhaus design.*

ART DECO

397

▲ *Although the shapes and geometric decoration of this English coffee set, made by Crown Devon, are recognizably Art Deco, the colouring is more subdued, and there is a pearly lustre glaze inside the cups.*

◀ *The angular shape of the handle and spout on this jug, and its bold yellow, orange and black colouring, proclaim it as one of Clarice Cliff's pieces. She usually decorated her ceramics with simple landscapes, and floral or geometric designs.*

STYLE GUIDE

SUSIE COOPER IS the other name closely associated with Art Deco ceramics in England. Her stoneware was less angular in shape than Cliff's and generally more subdued in colour. Decoration, while remaining stylized, was more curvilinear and featured more elaborate designs, such as interwoven leaves, circles within circles, and animal and floral motifs. Later, in the 1930s, rather than freehand painting, she began to use lithographic prints, surrounded with hand-painted bands of muted colour.

There was also a considerable variety of Art Deco ceramics produced in the USA, although they tended to be less innovative than European wares. The larger potteries had both eyes on the commercial market. The Cowan Pottery of Ohio, for example, mass-produced ceramic figures of fairly high quality. One of its most gifted craftsmen, Vienna-born Victor Schreckengost, made a series of black-and-green porcelain wares carved with motifs evoking the skyscraper silhouettes and neon lights of American cities at night.

▼ *Subtle leaf patterns are used to decorate this hors d'oeuvres dish.*

▲ *A large serving dish with a ship design dating from the 1930s with a teapot in green and pink in the Kestrel shape.*

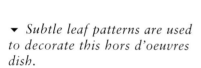

▶ *Clockwise from top right: Muted colours were used for this delicate banded design; the unusual abstract leaf pattern was painted by hand on this small vase a lidded vegetable dish from the 'Kestrel' range with the banding painted by hand (the lid when inverted forms a second dish; pottery coffee set made to match a dinner service; a teapot in the 'Kestrel' shape, designed in the 1930s but made for another 20 years or so.*

ART DECO

STYLE GUIDE

▸ A sugar basin and milk jug dating from c.1930 and made by Shelley. The shape of the handle gave the design its name – 'Butterfly'.

400

◂ The Carlton ware biscuit barrel was, unusually, part of a coffee set.

▴ These special small coffee spoons in electroplated nickel silver had fashionable bakelite handles in the form of coffee beans.

▸ Designed by Clarice Cliff, this small milk jug was part of a set in her 'Sunshine' pattern.

ART DECO

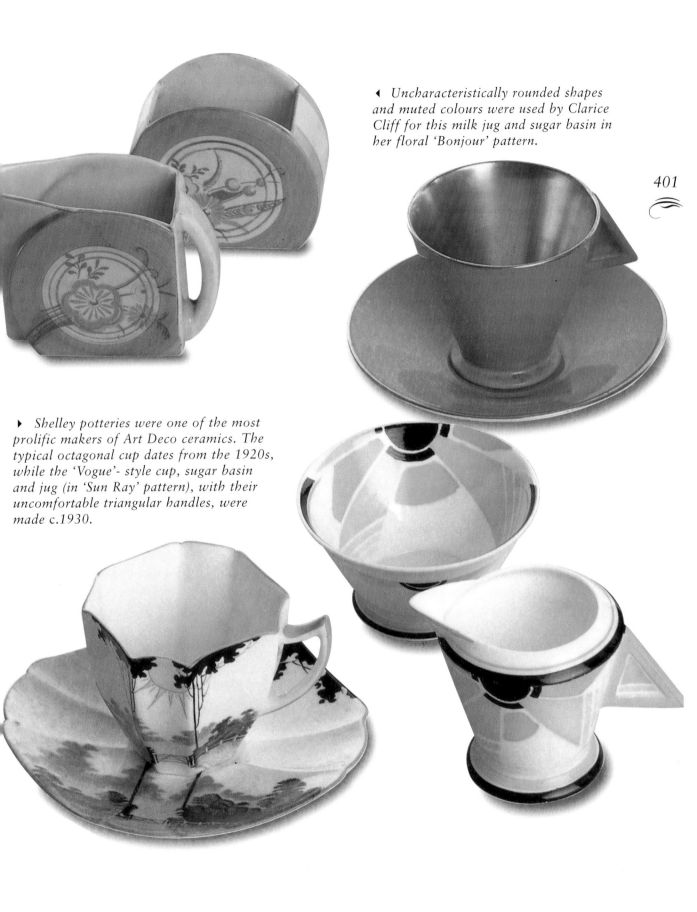

◄ *Uncharacteristically rounded shapes and muted colours were used by Clarice Cliff for this milk jug and sugar basin in her floral 'Bonjour' pattern.*

401

▶ *Shelley potteries were one of the most prolific makers of Art Deco ceramics. The typical octagonal cup dates from the 1920s, while the 'Vogue'- style cup, sugar basin and jug (in 'Sun Ray' pattern), with their uncomfortable triangular handles, were made c.1930.*

FIGURINES & MASKS

CHINA ORNAMENTS WERE one of the most popular decorative objects of the Art Deco age. Almost every home had a figurine or two standing on the mantelpiece or displayed in a glass-fronted cabinet. Often, as in those made by Royal Doulton, which turned out dozens of well-documented designs, they were figures of charming and pretty girls in crinolines or costumes that harked back to earlier times, but others – also of charming and pretty girls – showed them as modern, up-to-date misses. Portraying these young women in active poses, with bare legs and short skirts – or even daringly nude or lightly draped – presented the sculptor with problems because a china figure needs a broad base for stability, so most of them stand on a plinth or sit on a stool or bench. English figures tend to reflect the fashions of the time, and are often accompanied by the accessories deemed necessary, such as Scottie dogs. Figures made on the Continent are more recognizably Art Deco in style and subject, especially those by Goldcheider in Vienna and Dux in Czechoslovakia. These pieces are marked, but there are also scores of cheaper, more mediocre figures that are unidentifiable except for the country of their origin. Nonetheless, these little figures convey the vitality and charm of the period and are very collectable.

Another ubiquitous Art Deco artefact is the wall mask – usually the head of a young woman – hung up as decoration. Some of these masks were very glamorous – indeed in the 1930s stars of the screen were often taken as models.

402

ART DECO

403

▲ *Masks were made mainly in ceramics, but glass and metal were also used. It is more usual to find masks where the hands are not shown.*

▲ *Sophistication is the keynote of many wall masks – this one was made in plaster, using a young starlet of the 1930s as a model. Eyes were often shown closed, or even simply as holes, and in most masks the skin is pale, but here the golden brown colour gives the effect of suntan.*

▶ *These two masks are miniatures – generally they were more or less life-sized. The one on the left was made by the English firm of Beswick, the other by Goebbels in Austria. Typically, they show short hair and hats.*

STYLE GUIDE
WALL VASES & PLAQUES

404

LIKE WALL MASKS, wall vases, or pockets, and plaques are the trademark of the Art Deco period. They are not as striking as the wall masks but were probably even more popular, and wall vases, in particular, were often hung on either side of the fireplace. Today they still serve their original purpose and can be used to hold fresh flowers or the dried arrangements popular with decorators.

Wall plaques gave potters the opportunity to create imaginative designs that could be mass-produced and sold quite cheaply, giving everyone the opportunity to share in the vogue for Art Deco. Some of the designs – notably those by Clarice Cliff – are today expensive, but there is a wide range of other attractive subjects that afford the collector plenty of scope. Most of the designs ceased to be produced at the end of the 1930s, but others, such as the flying ducks, continued to be made into the 1970s.

▲ *Two hat-shaped wall vases by Beswick. The black one was also made in cream.*

ART DECO

▸ One of the most popular and long-lived designs, flights of ducks were produced by many makers.

405

▲ It is unusual to find a plaque showing ducks in flight – they were most often made individually. This was produced by Dux in the 1930s.

◂ Clarice Cliff made this circular wall vase in 1936 in the pattern of stylized flowers called 'Rhodanthe'.

◂ Goebbels, the Austrian potter noted for his unusual pieces, produced this wall vase in the form of a galloping huntsman.

▲ Three separate flower stems could be shown in this wall vase in the form of a gladiolus.

▲ Surprisingly, this crinolined lady is also by Clarice Cliff – it is a far cry from her usual style and colours.

◂ Flowers were inserted into a hole in the top of the fan-tailed pigeon's body in this unusual wall vase.

STYLE GUIDE
FURNITURE

Aᴿᴛ Dᴇᴄᴏ ꜰᴜʀɴɪᴛᴜʀᴇ ᴅᴇᴠᴇʟᴏᴘᴇᴅ out of Art Nouveau pieces. The Art Deco style was embraced by both designers creating one-off pieces to commission and by manufacturers of commercial furniture. In general, furniture shapes changed substantially, particularly as a result of Oriental influences. The seats of chairs and sofas were lowered and backs were raised, and low coffee tables were introduced.

Lacquerwork, and all kinds of exotic wood and veneers came into favour, ranging from the very light fruitwoods through bird's-eye maple to teak and mahogany. Ivory or shagreen (sharkskin, both real and imitation) were used for trimmings and mouldings, and materials such as chrome, bent

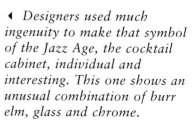

◀ *Designers used much ingenuity to make that symbol of the Jazz Age, the cocktail cabinet, individual and interesting. This one shows an unusual combination of burr elm, glass and chrome.*

ART DECO

plywood and glass were readily employed in one-off and popular pieces. Art Deco furniture usually had smooth, sleek surfaces, and was often designed to be built into the walls and alcoves of apartments, rather than be free-standing.

On the whole, the top-flight Art Deco furniture-makers such as Emil-Jacques Ruhlmann (1879–1933) were essentially conservative in outlook, although some, such as Pierre Legrain and Marcel Coard, who made stools and chairs inspired by African art, were more adventurous.

Commercial Art Deco furniture-makers raided a host of different sources, such as Cubism and African tribal art, which might be combined in the same piece. The stepped shapes of the pyramids of the Aztecs were recycled, for example, in case furniture, including entirely new pieces such as cocktail cabinets and radio sets.

407

▼ *Pedestal supports on Art Deco dining tables were often made in a U-shaped curve, as here, although curved supports at each end were also common. Veneers of exotic woods gave a light, lustrous finish.*

STYLE GUIDE

▼ *This small, geometric-style 'Grandmother' clock was made in walnut with a black ebonized surround to the face, and ivory hands and hour markers.*

408

▲ *Many cocktail cabinets, such as this one with a fluted front, were curved, creating the illusion of a bar in a small café. Inside, as here, there might be an interior light, a mirror glass back, steel fittings to store bottles and glasses, and a pull-out shelf to hold glasses while drinks were poured.*

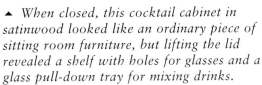

▲ *When closed, this cocktail cabinet in satinwood looked like an ordinary piece of sitting room furniture, but lifting the lid revealed a shelf with holes for glasses and a glass pull-down tray for mixing drinks.*

◄ *Art Deco design extended even to electric fires – this one in enamel and chrome has legs that echo the curved shapes of armchairs and cabinets.*

STYLE GUIDE

410

▲ *This fine desk has the serpentine tambour top typical of 19th-century desks, but the choice of oak and mahogany, the clean lines and simple wooden handles all proclaim it as a 1930s piece.*

▸ *The 1920s and '30s saw the building of dozens of small suburban houses around big cities. Small houses created the need for practical small furniture, and this walnut table with two shelf units that fit underneath it is an elegant solution to the problem.*

ART DECO

▶ *This stylish and compact 1930s sideboard in veneered wood, with plastic handles and a slightly stepped back, would have been useful where space was restricted.*

▼ *The curved doors at the sides of this large, sycamore cabinet, with a glass top and ivory handles, are typical of Art Deco furniture.*

STYLE GUIDE

▼ *Although made in three sections – a fashionable trend – and in pale wood, this English 1930s dressing table remains quite classical in appearance. The cabriole legs and curved top to the mirror hark back to the Queen Anne Revival in the late 19th-century.*

412

▲ *Many cocktail cabinets had to do double duty, and the lower part of this one, made from walnut veneer and peach-coloured plate glass, might have been used for storing books or china.*

ART DECO

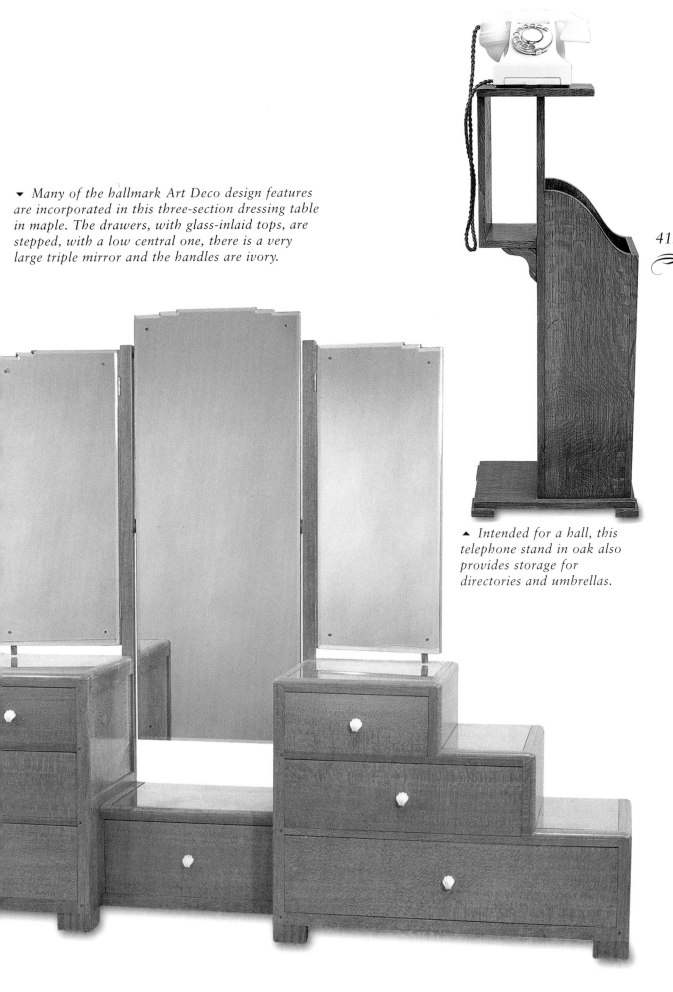

▼ *Many of the hallmark Art Deco design features are incorporated in this three-section dressing table in maple. The drawers, with glass-inlaid tops, are stepped, with a low central one, there is a very large triple mirror and the handles are ivory.*

413

▲ *Intended for a hall, this telephone stand in oak also provides storage for directories and umbrellas.*

STYLE GUIDE

MIRRORS

414

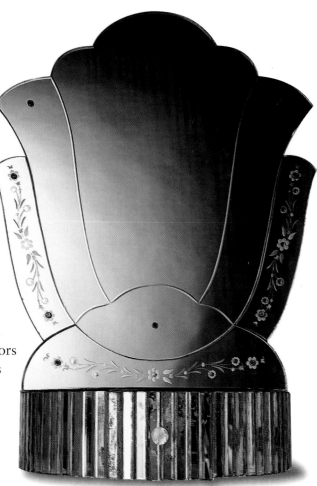

IRROR GLASS was one of the favourite decorative materials of the 1930s. Its appeal lay in the effect it gave of light and spaciousness. Entire walls were covered in it, and in the 1920s glass such as vitroflex and vitrolite had been produced that could be moulded to fit architectural details and incorporated into furniture such as cocktail cabinets.

Mirrors themselves were given shapes that reflected the architecture of the time and old techniques were revived for decorating glass by colouring, etching and engraving. Many mirrors were simply attached to the wall, and the hunt was on for new materials for framing freestanding mirrors – wrought iron, cork, shagreen (sharkskin), plastics and lacquered wood were all employed. Most mirror glass was produced on the Continent, notably in France and Belgium, and then mounted and finished elsewhere.

The variety of styles of mirror available – some functional, some purely decorative – is clearly shown by this selection from the 1920s and '30s.

ART DECO

◀ *The tulip-shaped console mirror, with engraved panels, was made in sections and then screwed to a wooden backing. It is attached to a slatted glass drawer.*

▶ *Strips of vitrolite with curved ends in shades of cream have been used to make a frame for a typical 1930s wall mirror.*

▼ *Fashionable Art Deco geometric shapes and pale creamy colour are combined in this bathroom mirror.*

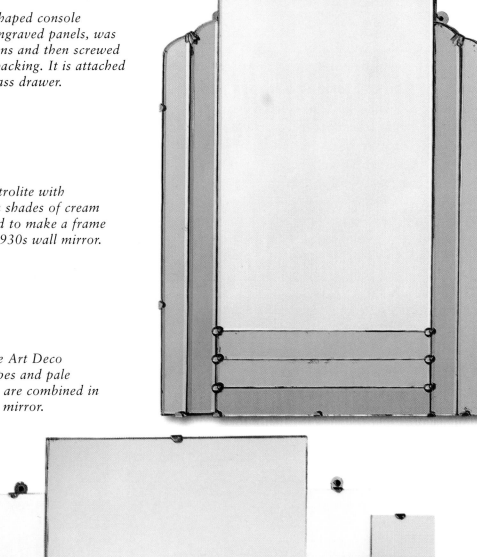

STYLE GUIDE

DRINKING GLASSES

416

ENGLISH GLASSWARE IN the Art Deco period continued to be made by old established firms, such as Thomas Webb and Sons and Stuart and Sons, who 'went modern' to some degree by hiring well-known contemporary artists, among them Paul Nash and Graham Sutherland, to design their glassware – not always very successfully. In continental Europe, however, glass-makers were keen to adopt the new ideas epitomised by Art Deco design, and the French, in particular, created a range of fresh styles and colours, using both old and new techniques. These were applied to both one-off art objects and mass-produced items, foremost among which were table glass and cocktail glasses.

Cocktails, introduced from America, were all the rage among people of the upper- and middle-classes, and along with the new drinks came smart new glasses and special shakers. Most glasses had a flat, conical bowl that flared out from a short stem and wide base. They were generally decorated with bands of enamel – red, black and white were popular colours – but coloured and frosted glass were also common. Shakers normally formed a set with the glasses.

◀ Some early cocktail glasses resembled heavy-bottomed tumblers. Here, the frosted diamond pattern etched into the glass is outlined with black lines and silver squares. The matching pourer is chromium plated and has an inbuilt strainer in the lid.

ART DECO

▲ Clockwise from the top: Swizzle sticks used for stirring; cut-crystal glasses; frosted decanter and glasses trimmed with silver; yellow glass set; glasses silvered inside, with black decoration; decanter with a moulded cockerel's head stopper.

◄ The cocktail glass on the left was designed by the French glass-maker René Lalique in the 1920s; the other is a modern version of the cocktail glass.

Style Guide

▸ *Inset: novelty decanter in red glass, made in the USA.*

418

Clockwise from top right: liqueur set with a heart-shaped decanter and glasses; water set in tinted glass with bands of gold; conical frosted glass water or lemonade set; water set with green bases and bands of colour; sherry set with an engraved pattern; wine decanter and glasses with areas of pale pink etching and delicate etched lines.

ART DECO

STYLE GUIDE
SCULPTURES

420

A CONSIDERABLE AMOUNT OF sculpture was produced in the Art Deco style. The most characteristic – and most widely imitated – were small, decorative figures in chryselephantine, a combination of carved ivory (used for the exposed flesh of the figures) and cold-painted bronze, perhaps, in the best pieces, studied with semiprecious stones. While they were never mass-produced, pieces were produced in Germany in editions of several hundred or even thousands – they were usually made until the bronze moulds failed or the makers had no orders. The factory owned by the prominent sculptor Ferdinand Preiss, for example, produced naturalistic statuettes, often of dancing girls dressed in elaborate, flowing costumes, in hand-carved ivory and cast bronze on marble or onyx bases.

These decorative pieces, much admired in their day, are sought after by collectors now, as are those of his contemporary Bruno Zach. Where Preiss's statuettes were perfectly innocent, Zach is best-known for topless 'dominatrix' figures, fashioned expressly to serve the always lively private market in erotica.

◀ *The dancing girl in silvered bronze, on a polished marble base, dates from 1930. It is signed by the Austrian designer Josef Lorenzl.*

ART DECO

▲ *Animal sculptures were also popular. This forceful, almost abstract, bronze of a black panther is very impressive.*

▶ *A more romantic style is evident in this silver and bronze statuette by Alexander Kelety, entitled 'Antelope'.*

◀ *The abstract, formal style of this bronze by Genevieve Granger (see detail left) is reminiscent of Egyptian forms, which influenced artists at the time.*

STYLE GUIDE

422

▸ Entitled
'Balancing Act', this
bronze was signed
by Marcel Bouraine.
The limbs of female
dancing nudes were
often exaggeratedly
long.

▲ As this detail of the group below
shows, bronze was often embellished by
cold painting in metallic tints of blue,
green or, as here, grey, and silvering.
Where ivory was used, it might be
painted in bright colours.

▸ A romantic piece, 'The Dancing Couple'
was created in bronze by the French artist
Claire Colinet in the 1920s. The marble
base, with its bronze-coloured veining,
complements the material of the figures.

ART DECO

LAMPS

THE FIGURE LAMPS of the Art Deco period were the logical extension of the immensely popular bronze figures, and they were often a lot more affordable, since the materials used for them were inferior. Instead of bronze, spelter (a zinc alloy) was used for the casting, and it was then gilded, silvered or chromium plated. Alabaster, too, was used, often carved in Egyptian-style forms.

Designers encountered problems with incorporating female figures into reading lamps, since with a normal type of shade the stem of the lamp – the figure – was obscured, unless she was made very tall. The simpler solution was for the light bulb to be enclosed in a frosted or etched glass globe, which could, for instance, double as a beach ball being held by the girl; another common pose was a kneeling girl, holding the globe in her lap. Many other ingenious solutions were found that met Art Deco's criterion that the lamp should light the room with a soft, clear light.

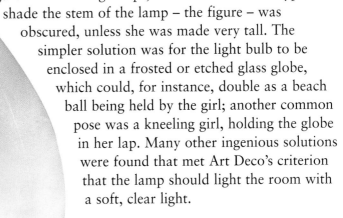

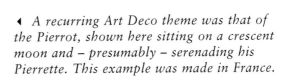

◄ *A recurring Art Deco theme was that of the Pierrot, shown here sitting on a crescent moon and – presumably – serenading his Pierrette. This example was made in France.*

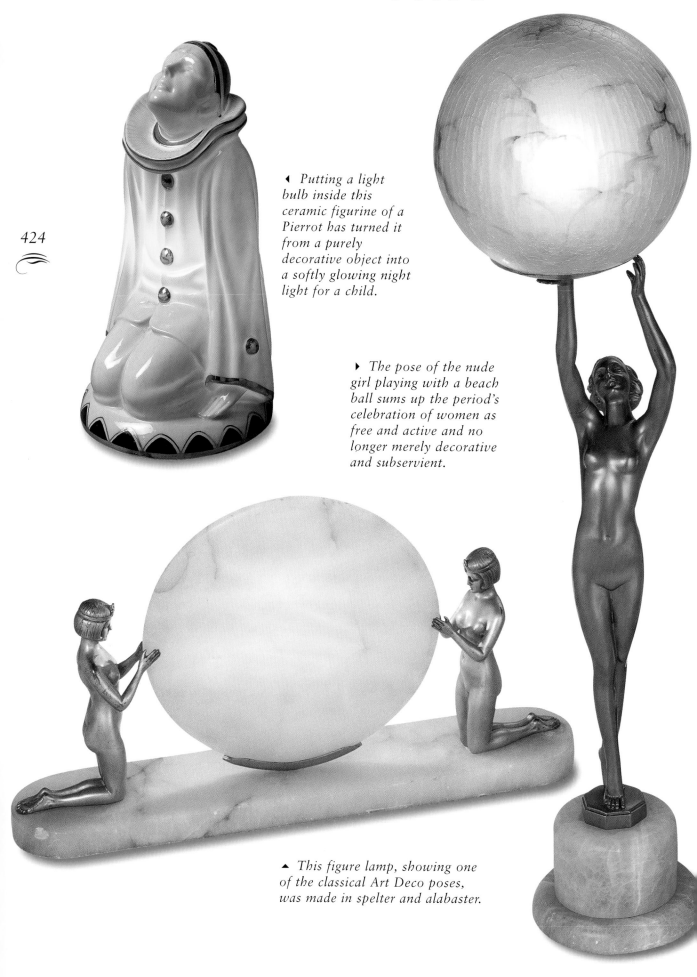

424

◄ *Putting a light bulb inside this ceramic figurine of a Pierrot has turned it from a purely decorative object into a softly glowing night light for a child.*

▶ *The pose of the nude girl playing with a beach ball sums up the period's celebration of women as free and active and no longer merely decorative and subservient.*

▲ *This figure lamp, showing one of the classical Art Deco poses, was made in spelter and alabaster.*

ART DECO

◀ *The glass in figure lamps was often coloured, and that forming the wings of the charming 'Butterfly Girl' is a deep amber, which is greatly enhanced when the light is on.*

▶ *Alabaster has been used for the lights in this lamp by the Frenchman Le Faguays. The figure of the dancing girl is bronze.*

STYLE GUIDE
JEWELLERY

426

IN THE ART DECO PERIOD jewellery was extremely varied. Some pieces were rigidly geometrical or abstract, others were influenced by Egyptian or Oriental art. Several French craftsmen continued to make small but floridly designed Art Nouveau-inspired works in platinum and gold, encrusting them with gem stones of many colours.

Most Art Deco jewellers, though, tended to favour simple, strong designs. While firms such as Van Cleef and Arpels, Cartier and Fouquet were at the forefront of such work, notable pieces were also made by individual designers. Jean Dunand, the famous lacquer-worker and metalsmith, also designed brooches, earrings and bracelets, usually made of hammered silver and decorated with black, red and gold lacquer, while his contemporary, Raymond Templier, made outstanding jewels by combining different metals and gems in striking settings.

Thousands of relatively cheap, anonymously designed pieces emerged in the Art Deco period, in styles developed from a number of sources and exploiting the new materials and technologies of the period to the full. Bracelets, brooches or clips made of bakelite, celluloid or other synthetics are highly prized by modern collectors. Many of them were manufactured in the USA, but firms in Czechoslovakia also made inexpensive, brightly coloured pins, necklaces and other jewellery.

This is the type of jewellery that the average collector today is likely to be able to find and afford. But care must be taken when buying – since the revival of interest in Art Deco, many poorly made modern copies are on the market.

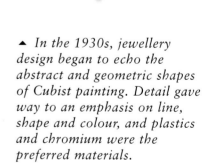

▲ In the 1930s, jewellery design began to echo the abstract and geometric shapes of Cubist painting. Detail gave way to an emphasis on line, shape and colour, and plastics and chromium were the preferred materials.

ART DECO

▲ *Clockwise from the top: bakelite bangles with minimum decoration to emphasise their shape; two pairs of pendant earrings, one in diamanté, the other in chrome and bakelite; silver ring with cornelian and marcasite; Egyptian-style necklace with an abstract design; yellow bakelite earrings; necklace made from carved and plain bakelite, paste and silver plate; matching brooch and bracelet in dark blue bakelite and chrome; segmented bracelet made from paste, which resembles diamonds but was quite inexpensive.*

▼ *Bakelite was also used for this buckle. The ends of the belt were secured to bars on the back of the roundels, which clipped together in the middle.*

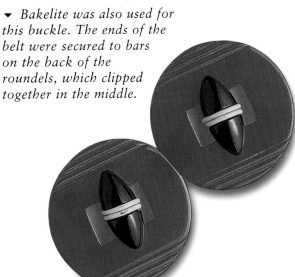

STYLE GUIDE

428

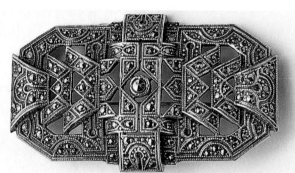

▲ *Designers enjoyed making clever pieces of jewellery, and in this diamanté and green bakelite link necklace the cleverly made clasp is invisible when it is closed.*

▶ *Although more classical in style, typical Art Deco materials, enamel and diamanté, were used for this brooch, dating from the 1920s.*

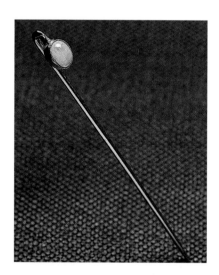

◀ *Men about town wore tie pins in the 1930s. A plain gold pin would probably be worn in the daytime, but in the evening pins set with jewels, such as this opal, were common. Tie pins are a good field for the collector.*

◀ *On the left is a fine pair of cuff links in silver and enamel, dating from the 1930s. The hallmark is clearly visible and the enamel is immaculate, without chips or discoloration. The links on the right are a modern copy, and it is easy to see that both materials and workmanship are inferior.*

ART DECO

Figurative design was also popular
for jewellery. Materials were an
eclectic mix, with silver, diamanté,
paste and coloured glass, bakelite,
enamel, lacquer, chrome and brass
all used separately and in
combination. Motifs ranged from
stylized floral objects and classical
shapes to African and Egyptian
heads, insects, animals and many
symbols of speed, such as the
arrow, motor car, greyhound,
racehorse and gazelle. Female
athletes and dancers also made
their appearance on brooches and
earrings. Such pieces were
produced in quantity and are fairly
easy to come by today.

429

◄ As the date inscribed
on these gold
monogrammed cuff
links shows, Art Deco
styles for gentlemen's
jewellery lasted beyond
the period. Cuff links in
the classic style should
have identical heads on
either side of the link.

LIBERTY AND FREEDOM

Collectables

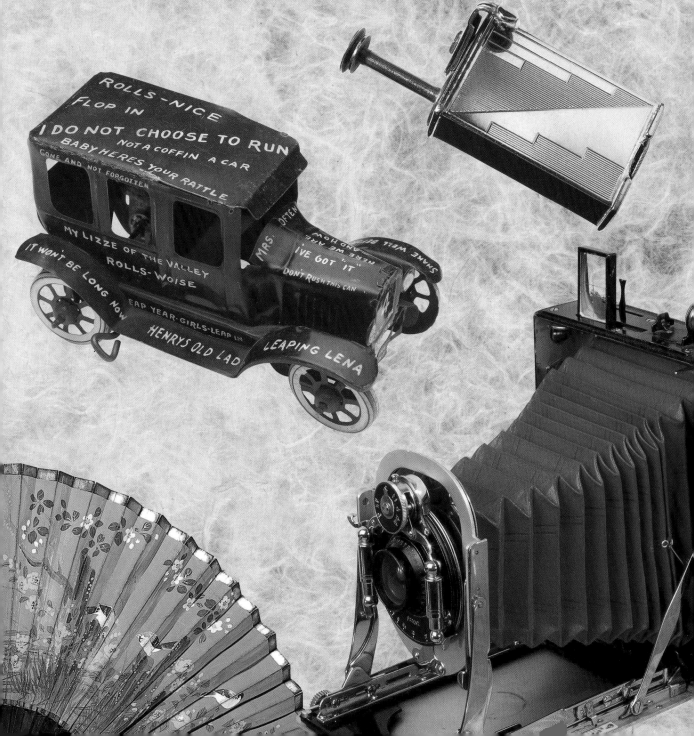

COLLECTABLES

WHAT IS A COLLECTABLE?

THE DIFFERENCE BETWEEN collectables and antiques is much debated. It was once generally accepted that items were 'antique' if they were more than 100 years old, and almost anything of more recent origin was a 'collectable' (provided, of course, that the object had acquired some value in the eyes of collectors themselves). While this still is still broadly true, it fails to take account of the vast array of 19th-century objects that are not considered valuable as 'antiques' per se, but might well become so if there is sufficient competition among collectors.

An astonishing range of objects can be regarded as collectable, everything from bus tickets to Art Deco figurines. Yet trends and fashions seem to have far more impact on collectables than on the antiques market. A signed antique Worcester vase, for example, will always command a good price, while the demand for 20th-century ceramics can rise and fall violently. (Poole pottery was fetching amazingly high prices at auction in the late 1980s, but some three years later the price had levelled out.) When this variation in fashion occurs, collectables dealers often store away the goods in the hope that the price will rise in future. This may explain why, at any one time, the source of a particular collectable dries up.

432

COLLECTABLES

The cut-off date for collectables moves ever onward. Collectables from the 1950s, '60s and even '70s are now much in demand, and can still be obtained for reasonable prices at car boot sales and jumble sales. Lava lamps from the 1950s, for instance, can be found at these markets for much better prices than in specialist lighting shops or at antiques and collectables fairs.

But what should you collect? This, of course, is largely a matter of personal preference. However, your instincts can be backed up by consulting the many excellent reference books now on the market and in libraries. These will give good guidance as far as availability, sources and potential appreciation in value of collectables are concerned.

It should be added that collectors often find the process of research – learning about a subject's background and history – as rewarding as acquiring the objects themselves.

COLLECTABLES
BRONZES

434

AN ALLOY OF COPPER AND TIN, bronze has been used for metal sculpture for more than 4000 years. The traditional technique of casting sculpture, 'lost-wax casting', was a painstaking, time-consuming process. Inevitably, this was reflected in the cost of the final product. But in the 19th century, electrotyping was developed. Using electrolysis, a thin layer of bronze could be deposited on the surface of the plaster mould. The result was that relatively cheap and attractive metalwork statues could be produced en masse to decorate middle-class homes.

Probably the most popular subject for mid-19th century decorative bronzes was animals. The French school of animal sculptors, the animaliers (Antoine-Louis Barye, Emmanuel Frémit, Auguste-Nicholas Cain, Georges Gardet and Pierre-Jules Mene) produced extremely lifelike sculptures of chamois, lions, dogs, deer with fawns and many types of birds.

The most common figure subjects, on the other hand, were reproductions of classical nudes and mythological figures such as gods, goddesses, nymphs and satyrs. Busts or statuettes of contemporary and historical characters – Napoleon, Florence Nightingale, Rousseau, Voltaire, Shakespeare, Milton and Mary, Queen of Scots – also had a solid market.

At this time, the arts were infatuated by all things 'exotic'. Bronze workers were no exception, producing scores of Arab figures, some mounted, others engaged in hunting or falconry. Influenced by bronzes from China and Southeast Asia, they also depicted what they regarded as typically 'Oriental' scenes – sages, fishermen and women of the court.

Decorative 19th-century bronzes were produced in considerable quantities and are readily available in antiques shops today. Exceptions are some of the finest pieces by Bayre and his followers, which are more likely to appear at specialist auctions.

BRONZES

◂ *Bronze figure of a Greek scholar – one of a pair dating from the last quarter of the 19th century. Classical scholars were popular subjects for Victorian figures.*

435

▴ *Cleopatra, her breasts exposed, riding on an elephant. The elephant has its right foreleg on the head of the Sphinx. This little fantasy-piece, made around 1870, was the work of Alfred Barye.*

◂ *Late-19th-century hollow-cast bronze of a woman in classical attire.*

▸ *There is an air of austere classicism about this mid-19th-century bust of a naked female.*

COLLECTABLES

436

▸ Jean Baptiste Carpeaux was one of the leading French sculptors of the 19th century. This *Chinoise* bust, made in the 1860s, is a marvellous example of his work. The face has a strikingly human quality and the folds in the garment have a real fluidity. The golden patina on the face and neck are particularly attractive.

▸ Seated female with lyre, in pensive mood. Mid 19th century.

▲ Satyrs and other mythological creatures were, perhaps somewhat incongruously, common ornaments in Victorian drawing rooms.

COMMEMORATIVE
COMMEMORATIVE POTTERY

COMMEMORATIVE POTTERY TENDS to be something of a British obsession. British potteries have produced far more ceramic souvenirs than those of any other country – and most pieces commemorated royal events.

It was the accession of Queen Victoria to the throne in 1837 that marked the beginnings of a royal souvenir industry. After that, every major occurrence in the life of the royal family was celebrated in ceramics. Individual plates and mugs are most common, although complete tea and dinner services can be found. China figurines and other ornaments were also highly popular. Royal marriages, births and anniversaries continue to be commemorated in ceramics, but plainly these are of less value than 19th- and early 20th-century pieces.

Less common, but of perhaps greater interest, were the pieces made to commemorate major political movements, personalities and events of the 19th century. Since the popularity of these ceramics fell after 1900 (though a few items relating to the suffragette movement and World War I were made), the older pieces have a certain rarity value. Napoleon, the Duke of Wellington and Gladstone were frequently depicted.

Since World War II, non-royal commemorative figurines have continue to be made, the focus being on such prominent political and military personalities as General Montgomery, Winston Churchill and Margaret Thatcher. These can be found at antiques fairs and even car boot sales, and are of small value in comparison with 19th-century pieces.

▼ *Pottery figurine commemorating D-Day. Churchill rests his left foot on a bust of Hitler, which has been toppled from its pedestal. A puppet-sized bust of General Eisenhower, Supreme Commander of the Western Allied Forces, brings up the rear.*

437

COLLECTABLES

438

Jug and beaker commemorating the hapless but popular Queen Caroline, who refused an annuity of £50,000 to renounce her title and live abroad. A few days before her death in 1821 she was turned away from the coronation of her husband, George IV, at the door of Westminster Abbey.

◄ British bulldog, wrapped in the Union Jack. Doulton, 1900. Two years later the firm of Doulton and Co received the royal mark.

▶ Napoleonic memorabilia have always been popular, due to the renown of their subject. The two figurines are Staffordshire ware. The matching pipe and cigar holder are in amber and meerschaum.

COMMEMORATIVE

COLLECTABLES

▸ *Coronations always occasion a flood of memorabilia. The coronation of Edward VII in 1901 was no exception.*

440

KING EDWARD VII

Edward VII and Queen Alexander. Matching pair of French figurines.

COMMEMORATIVE

▸ *Churchill, relaxing with cigar and lion.*

▾ *The lady's not for turning. Mrs Thatcher, handbag at the ready, clutching a copy of Adam Smith's* Wealth of Nations.

441

▸ *Field Marshal Montgomery captured the imagination of the British public after his victory over Rommel at the Battle of El Alamein in 1942.*

COLLECTABLES

▸ *Commemorative teapot celebrating the covenant of the League of Nations in 1919.*

442

▲ *Britain produces more royal memorabilia than any other other European country – a reflection of the monarchy's enduring importance in British life. The coronations of George III and IV were commemorated in a few items of pottery, but the royal souvenir industry really took off during the reign of*

Victoria. Following her accession to the throne in 1837, every major royal event was immortalised in ceramics of one kind or another. The artistic quality of these items varies widely. The best of them come from the well known Staffordshire factories such as Doulton, Burslem, Copeland, Spode and Minton.

COMMEMORATIVE
COMMEMORATIVE MUGS

L IKE COLLECTORS OF ALL kinds, collectors of commemorative wares often focus on a particular area of their chosen subject. Commemorative mugs, for instance, form just such a subcategory, and there is sufficient variety to keep the collector on the look out in antique shops for years.

Mugs were produced to commemorate such events as Queen Victoria's Golden Jubilee in 1887 and Diamond Jubilee in 1897. Some of these were 'clobbered' – enamel colours were applied to china to make it appear richer and therefore pricier. But the royal souvenir industry was not completely respectful of the wishes of Windsor: some appalling portraits of the queen appeared on mugs known, deservedly, as 'uglies'.

Of the major political events commemorated by mugs must be listed the Great Reform Bill, passed in 1832, the Armistice of 1918 and the Treaty of Versailles in 1819. More humourously, the cartoon character Old Bill was frequently made the subject of both mugs and character jugs.

▲ *A rather attractive example of the ceramic memorabilia occasioned by the coronation of Elizabeth II in 1953.*

▲ *Pair of beakers commemorating the victory of the allied forces in World War I, 1919.*

◄ *Two different faces of royal memorabilia: homage and lampoon. The beaker celebrates what at the time was seen as the fairytale union of Charles and Diana. The mug has the Queen encouraging Prince Philip to take a pot-shot at their other daughter-in-law, Sarah Ferguson, who is caricatured as a helicopter in reference to her children's book, Budgie the Little Helicopter.*

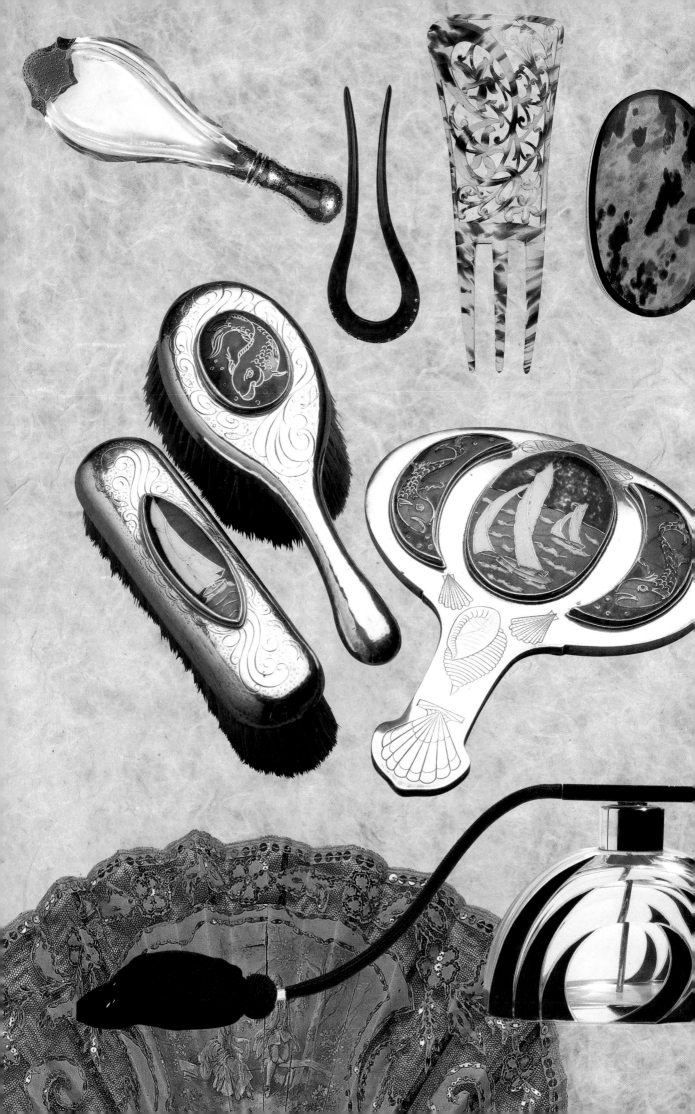

BEAUTY ACCESSORIES

COLLECTABLES

FANS

FANS ARE OF ORIENTAL ORIGIN and have been known for at least 2000 years. Their design and role has changed dramatically down the ages. Originally they had purely practical functions – to keep the user cool, to fan the flames of a fire or to ward off flies. But it was not long before they began to acquire ritual and social significance. Being fanned by a servant or slave proclaimed a person's status; and the open, flat fan became an indispensable accessory for the aristocracy and wealthy merchant class in China and Japan.

The folding fan, which probably originated in Japan, made a fan highly portable, since it could be folded away and slipped into a sleeve, pouch or bag. By the 17th century, folding fans had been imported into Europe in the baggage of pioneering merchants, and soon formed an important element of women's

446

▶ Top left: 1960s mock-oriental painted paper and plastic cockade (i.e. full-circle) fan. Top right: hand-painted Japanese fan, c.1900, with paper mount, wooden sticks, ivory guardstick inlaid with insects. Bottom right: French ivory brisé fan, c.1850. 'Brisé' indicates that the fan has no mount; instead, the blades carry the decoration. Bottom left: exquisitely detailed Chinese pierced ivory fan, 1840. Centre: embroidered net fans were made in great quantities in Spain during the 1960s and 1970s for the tourist market.

◀ Silk fan with sequinned decoration, c.1860. Fans had, of course, an ornamental aspect, but in the days before air conditioning they were often essential accessories. In the theatre or opera house, for example, the gas lighting would also generate a great deal of heat, and a fan was the only practical way of staying reasonably cool.

FANS

COLLECTABLES

dress. No fashionable lady would be seen in society without one. Especially in the duplicitous world of the court, they could be used as a cover for whispered asides, to conceal facial expressions or as signals to lovers.

Most folding fans have three parts. The blades are stuck or sewn to a mount. The stick at the end, usually of at least double thickness and often made of different, stronger material, is known as the guardstick.

Older fans can be dated by their size, the shape of their sticks, the proportion of the sticks to the mount, their spread (the extent to which the fan opens), and by the style and subject of the decoration. The principal methods for decorating mounts were painting, printing and embroidery, while sticks and guardsticks – usually made of bone, wood, ivory or horn – were carved, painted or lacquered and inlaid with mother-of-pearl, tortoiseshell, metal or semiprecious stones.

Hand-painted, bespoke fans from the 18th century tend to fetch the best prices, and often feature in auctions. But antique shops, sale rooms and junk shops are all good places to look for reasonably priced 19th- and early 20th-century fans. Decorative fans are easily damaged, and should be kept in a cool, dark, dry place.

448

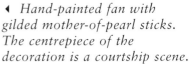

▲ *This colourful Japanese fan is decorated in a style known as* washi. *The technique requires several layers of lacquer.*

◀ *Hand-painted fan with gilded mother-of-pearl sticks. The centrepiece of the decoration is a courtship scene.*

FANS

◀ *A collection of colourful fans opened out makes an eye-catching display. Remember, though, that fans are delicate and may soon deteriorate if they are exposed to constant light, heat or damp.*

COLLECTABLES

PERFUME BOTTLES

450

UNTIL THE 20TH CENTURY, WOMEN bought perfume in plain bottles and decanted the contents into more elaborate containers on the dressing table at home. A packaging revolution in the early 1900s changed all this. It was sparked off by François Coty, a Corsican, who produced the first custom-made packaging for perfume in 1905. In 1907, he commissioned the glass-maker and designer René Lalique to design his perfume bottles. The success of the Coty-Lalique partnership encouraged other parfumiers to produce their own packaging for perfume.

Early bottles showed Art Nouveau influences, principally flower designs and arabesques. By the 1920s, when Art Deco was all the rage, bottles took on geometric shapes, the stoppers carrying much of the styling and even dwarfing the bottle. (At this time, fashion designers such as Coco Chanel, Jeanne Lanvin and Elsa Schiaparelli were bringing out their own perfumes and needed bottles to go with them.) In the 1930s and '40s, novelty and figure bottles for cheaper perfumes became popular, and featured such diverse subjects as birds, Dutch boys and Bonzo the dog – which was produced in clear glass with a small plastic top for Woolworth.

Such mass-produced bottles are much more affordable today than the perfume bottles made by master-craftsmen such as Lalique or Baccarat, which now command premium prices.

▶ *The blue glass of this French scent bottle has been cut to scintillating effect. The flamboyant stopper echoes the shape of the bottle itself.*

PERFUME BOTTLES

COLLECTABLES

From the collector's point of view, the bottle-maker and the brand is more important than the object's date. Perfume bottles are difficult to date, since classic designs often remained in production for more than 30 years. The bottles themselves varied in size from tiny, sample flacons to large 230ml–examples made for cologne, and scaled-up versions of the standard bottles for rarer perfumes made for counter display.

Perfume bottles by the top makers can be found at fine-art auctions and specialist dealers, while more ordinary bottles can be obtained at car boot sales and antiques fairs. In all instances, condition is very important. Any chips or cracks will devalue a piece, as will a missing stopper. Paper labels should be intact and show little sign of wear, rubbing or tearing.

452

▼ *Collection of 1930s scent bottles. The atomizer bottles in pink and blue glass are typically deco. The pumps have been covered with tasselled silk. The three-piece table set in blue glass with black enamel decoration is Bohemian; such sets invariably sell at premium prices. The glass powder box, front centre, has a moulded top by René Lalique. The pair of frosted glass bottles with golliwog stoppers are very much of their time.*

▶ *René Lalique and the Baccarat Crystal Factory were two of the leading glass manufacturers commissioned by parfumiers to produce scent bottles. The bottle on the far right is Baccarat, the rest are Lalique.*

PERFUME BOTTLES

COLLECTABLES

19th-century miniature perfume bottles in glass and silver. Anticlockwise from top left: French, c.1830; French, c.1870; French, c.1830 – the glass is opaque; Hungarian, c.1890 – glass with enamel decoration; French, c.1890; English, c.1870; double-ended ruby glass barrel with silver tops; double-ended amber glass bottle with white enamel teardrop decoration and garnet-encrusted tops; Dutch, c.1850; Napoleonic crystal scent bottle.

454

PERFUME BOTTLES

▲ *Double-ended ruby glass scent bottle with silver gilt tops, English, c.1880.*

Vinaigrettes.

The word is French, but the vinaigrette was an English invention – a small, pocketable box containing a sponge soaked in aromatic vinegar. Popular during the Georgian and Victorian eras, they would be brought out and sniffed whenever it was necessary to mask a particularly unpleasant stench.

COLLECTABLES

456

Silver scent bottles. From top down: French, silver gilt, c.1860 – made for a chatelaine; English, 1882 – the spiralled fluting is simple but attractive; English, late 19th century – a highly ornate design; English, c.1900 – the tapered shape is beautifully set off by the fluting.

▸ *Small glass bottles for perfumes, scented oils and essences have been made since ancient Egyptian times. From the 13th century, fine scent bottles in clear, opaque and patterned glass were made in Venice, and by the 17th century, scent bottles were being made almost everywhere in Europe. The extraordinary level of craftsmanship often lavished on these small containers reflected the high value of their precious contents.*

PERFUME BOTTLES

COLLECTABLES

In the design-conscious years of the early 20th century, a woman would choose her perfume as much for the bottle in which it was presented as for its fragrance – with good reason, to judge by these exquisite examples.

458

PERFUME BOTTLES

Perfume bottles have long been regarded as collectors' items. Although intact bottles of almost any period are worth buying, it is the style-conscious creations of the Art Deco period that attract the majority of collectors and the highest prices.

459

Collectables

Dressing-Table Sets

OR THE WELL-TO-DO WOMAN in the 19th century, the dressing table was a place of great importance. Here she prepared herself for social battle with a whole arsenal of cosmetics and trinkets. As yet, though, potions and powders were not packaged and pots and jars were needed to contain them. These were provided by attractive dressing-table or vanity sets, which first became common around the early 1800s. The more modest ones were made up of a few basic items such as a hairbrush and comb, a hand mirror and a few cut-glass bottles and pots with silver lids. But as the century progressed, larger luxury sets would have comprised varying numbers of silver-topped or silver-mounted cut-glass jars and bottles for rouge and face powder, lavender water and eau-de-cologne. Additional matching items might have included jewellery boxes, manicure equipment, pin trays, hair tidies, a pair of miniature candlesticks and an easel-support mirror.

Such 19th-century dressing-table sets tend to be fairly expensive, especially if they are complete. Cheaper and often no less attractive in their different way are the dressing-table sets and hairdressing equipment of the 1920s. Combs were made in great quantities in horn, tortoiseshell, ivory and synthetic materials. Such ornamental items, as well as tiaras, head bands and hair slides can be found in specialist shops, and at fairs and antique markets. Dressing-table sets of this period are worth more if boxed.

▶ *Dressing-table set with matching candlesticks. Also known as 'vanity sets' or 'tabletterie'.*

▲ *Part of an Edwardian silver dressing-table set decorated in Art Nouveau style.*

DRESSING-TABLE SETS

COLLECTABLES

462

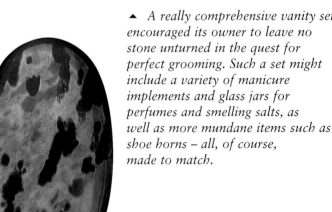

▲ A really comprehensive vanity set encouraged its owner to leave no stone unturned in the quest for perfect grooming. Such a set might include a variety of manicure implements and glass jars for perfumes and smelling salts, as well as more mundane items such as shoe horns – all, of course, made to match.

◄ Don't be deceived! At a casual glance, all three of these vanity items look like genuine tortoiseshell, but two of them – the combs – are actually plastic imitations. Real tortoiseshell is brittle and hard to the touch, while plastic feels lighter and bends more easily.

DRESSING-TABLE SETS

▼ A magnificent silver clothes brush dating from 1883, serpentine in shape and decorated with a pastoral tableau.

▼ Silver clothes brush, 1914.

463

▼ Edwardian trinket box.

◄ Silver-lidded rouge pot from 1889.

▲ Pair of perfume bottles on a stand. The bottle tops are silver, the stand silver plate.

◄ Silver perfume bottle, 1890.

◄ Ornately embellished Victorian die-stamped silver hand-mirror.

▲ Edwardian scent bottle.

▲ Silver-handled bonnet brush, c.1900.

COLLECTABLES

464

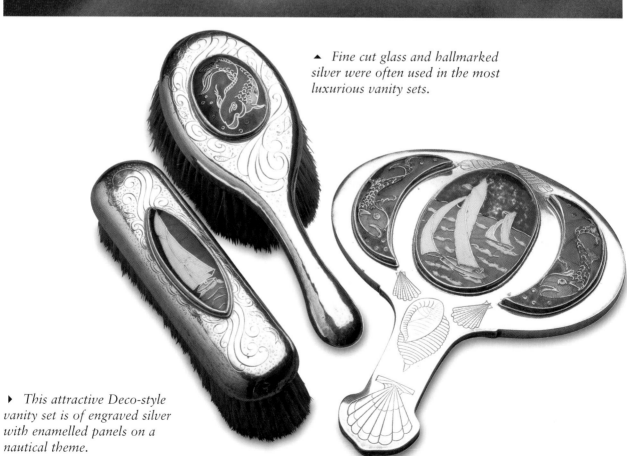

▲ *Fine cut glass and hallmarked silver were often used in the most luxurious vanity sets.*

▶ *This attractive Deco-style vanity set is of engraved silver with enamelled panels on a nautical theme.*

DRESSING-TABLE SETS

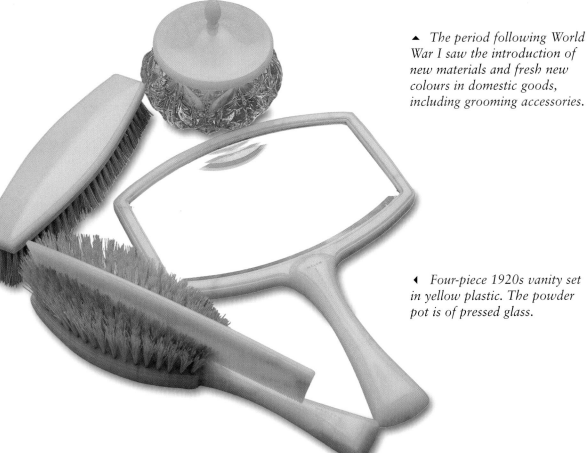

▲ The period following World War I saw the introduction of new materials and fresh new colours in domestic goods, including grooming accessories.

◄ Four-piece 1920s vanity set in yellow plastic. The powder pot is of pressed glass.

COLLECTABLES

MEN'S TOILET SETS

▸ *Wooden button box with mother-of-pearl inset.*

▸ *Ivory box for storing hairdressing or shaving lotions.*

▸ *Hog's bristle hair-brushes with tortoiseshell backs, 1820.*

▾ *Ivory and gold toothpick holder, 1790.*

▾ *Silver-handled shaving brush, 1858.*

▸ *Cutthroat razors with bone and tortoise-shell handles, 1830s.*

◂ *Toothbrush with silver holder and leather case, c.1792.*

▾ *Silver toothbrush holder, 1808.*

◂ *Shoe-horn of bone, 1830s.*

◂ *1830s bone-handled clothes brush.*

▸ *Silver and ivory tongue-scraper, 1800.*

ODAY THE MOST COLLECTABLE articles for men's toilet tend to date from the 1920s and '30s. At this time the emphasis on streamlined hairstyles and smooth cheeks gave new importance to men's grooming. The bathroom of the well-turned-out gentleman would, therefore, have contained a great array of lotions and equipment.

The most important item in any set of men's toiletries is the razor – cutthroat, safety or electric. Until the end of the 19th century, the cutthroat razor was in universal use. It was superseded in the early 20th century by the safety razor and – some 20 years later – by the electric shaver. All are collected by enthusiasts; they are more valuable if they come with their original cases.

The male bathroom cupboard would be also filled with other accessories such as shaving brushes, hairbrushes and manicure equipment in elegant chrome. Hairbrushes and combs were often made of bakelite or other plastics that imitated horn or ivory.

Grooming accessories from the 1920s and '30s can still be picked up fairly cheaply in such places as markets and junk shops. Items still in high demand are matching sets of articles such as shaving brushes and soap dishes, particularly if fashioned in distinctive, geometrical Art Deco style.

MEN'S TOILET SETS

▶ *Anyone who thinks that men have only recently started taking an interest in their appearance should take a look at Victorian and Edwardian men's grooming equipment which, in addition to a surprisingly large number of jars and bottles for pomade and oils, contained such items as hair brushes, manicure tools and curling tongs for facial hair.*

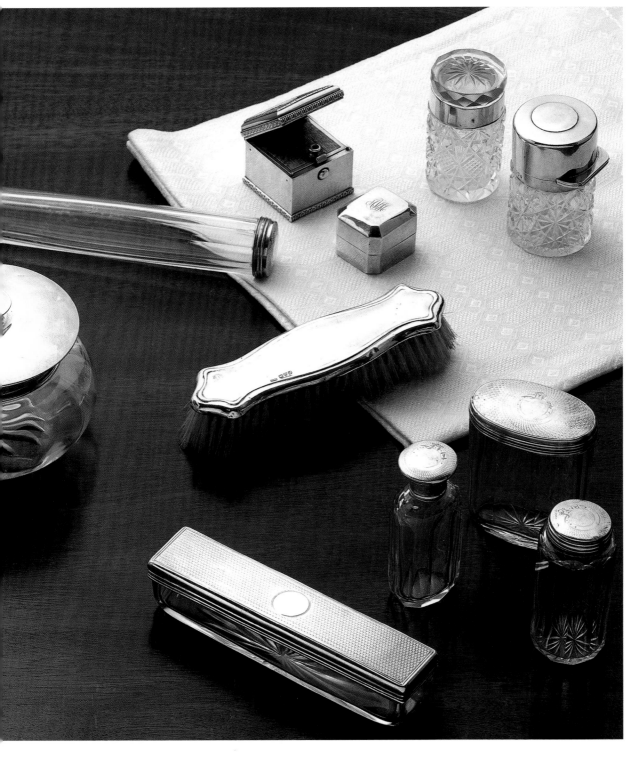

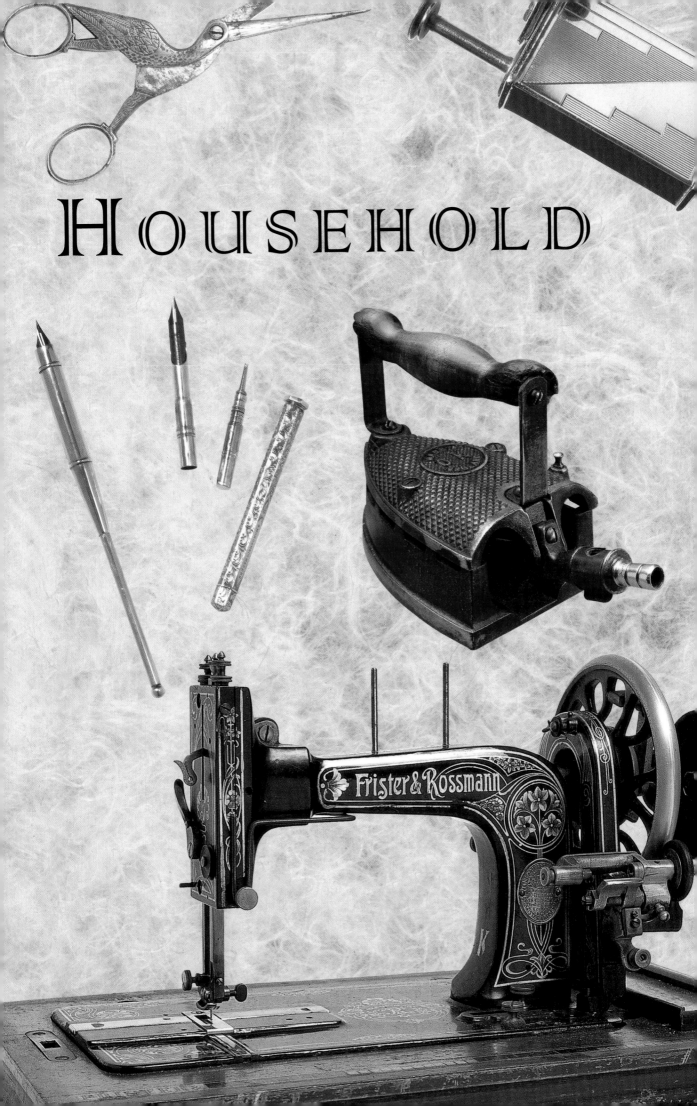

HOUSEHOLD

COLLECTABLES
SEWING ACCESSORIES

470

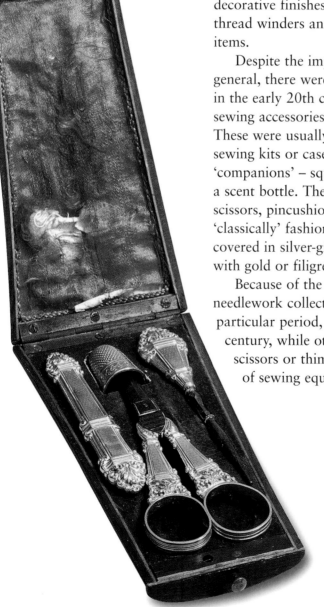

S EWING HAD ITS HEYDAY IN the 1800s, when the activities of embroidery, beading, knotting and tatting were part of everyday domestic life. But by the early 1900s, changing social patterns, combined with the growing popularity of the sewing machine, meant the decline of needlework in the home. Consequently, much 19th-century sewing equipment forms a collector's field in its own right. Thimbles and thimble guards are a prime example. Despite the fact that there is little variation in shape and size, they come in an amazing variety of materials and decorative finishes. Embroidery scissors, tape measures, cotton or thread winders and silver pincushions are also highly collectable items.

Despite the impact of the sewing machine on needlework in general, there were still many women who practised it as a hobby in the early 20th century. In this period, the more decorative sewing accessories from France gave way to simpler designs. These were usually presented in flat leather– or velvet–covered sewing kits or cases. Equipment also came in ladies' 'companions' – square or rectangular boxes which often included a scent bottle. The decoration of the tools inside – thimbles, scissors, pincushions and thread winders – though plain or 'classically' fashioned, was often of very high quality. Tools covered in silver-gilt, inset with coral or turquoise or decorated with gold or filigree work were all popular.

Because of the wide range of equipment available, most needlework collectors tend to specialize. Some concentrate on a particular period, such as the late 18th century or mid-19th century, while others restrict their buying to pincushions, scissors or thimbles. As with many collectables, the condition of sewing equipment is of great importance.

◀ *19th-century* etui *or pocket sewing case, containing scissors, thimble, needle-case and awl or stiletto used for making eyelets.*

▶ *Lockable burr yew workbox with wooden carrying handle, 1800.*

SEWING

COLLECTABLES

▸ *This workbox is of kingwood, with metal paw feet and handles. The box lid is inlaid with a floral panel.*

472

▲ *This workbox dates from 1718. Woods of different colour, marquetry borders and inlaid neo-classical mezzotint prints combine to create a rich effect. The ivory knob at the front opens a shallow drawer.*

▸ *Rosewood workbox with scrolled brass inlay. The compartment lids are covered with fabric, and the box lid itself is lined with ruched silk. Most of the sewing accessories inside are of ivory. The bottle tops, thimble and tape holder are silver.*

SEWING

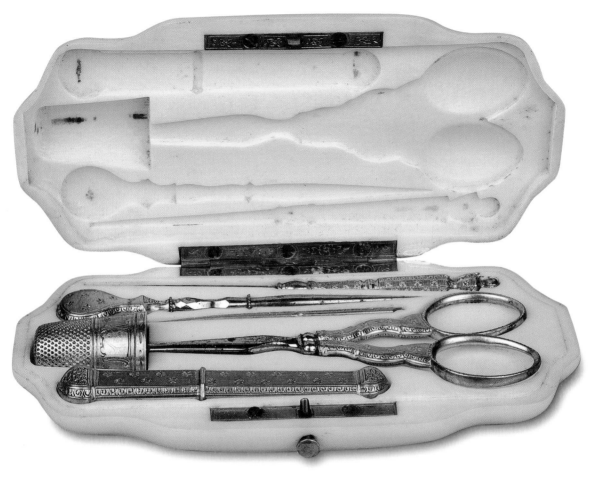

▲ *This fine ivory* etui *dates from 1850.*

▸ *Three 18th-century English enamel button boxes.*

COLLECTABLES

474

▲ The first true sewing machine appeared in 1846 – the patent of an American called Elias Howe. This machine was for professional use only, but within just a few years, Isaac Merrit Singer put his first domestic model on the market (1858). The new-fangled device took longer to establish itself in Britain than in the States, but by the early 20th century sewing machines were commonplace. This example, embellished with Art Nouveau motifs, was made in the 1880s by Frister & Rossmann.

◀ This kind of brass needlecase is known as an Avery.

▶ Enamel tape measure, c.1900. The clock face is purely decorative!

▼ An astonishing amount of care has gone into the design of these buttons. The materials are brass, glass, plastic, cut steel and mother of pearl.

▲ Brass 'nanny brooch' for needles.

SEWING

▶ *Thimbles come in an enormous variety of styles and materials, and form a fascinating collector's field in themselves. Over their long history they have been made in wood, ivory, silver, gold and even in glass and porcelain. Some are embellished with semi-precious stones like turquoise.*

475

Decorative enamelled needle-cases.

◀ *Edwardian pattern cutter. The twin steel wheels have pricks for pouncing.*

Steel needlework scissors, c.1900.

Darning mushrooms – the larger is for sock repairs, the smaller for gloves.

COLLECTABLES
KITCHEN UTENSILS

476

EARLY COOKWARE TENDS TO BE collected more for its historical interest than for any practical purpose. Cooking utensils were made to be used until they fell apart, and metal implements were thrown away or melted down, often by itinerant tinkers, to make new pots and pans. As a result, 18th- and early 19th-century pieces are rarer than might be expected. At any rate, old kitchenware provides the collector with fascinating insights into a time when the preparation of food was of great importance in any household.

Two basic types of cooking vessel were used for boiling or stewing. Round-bottomed, cast-metal cauldrons were hung over the fire, while flat-bottomed kettles made of sheet metal stood by the fire, often on three-legged stands called trivets. Frying was usually done in heavy iron skillets, which typically had three feet. Meat, fowl and fish were roasted over, or in front of, the fire on spits. These were turned by hand or by an ingenious device known as a bottle-jack.

Trivets are the easiest articles to find. Iron ones are older than brass, although not necessarily more valuable. Toasting forks, especially decorative brass ones, and heavy herb choppers are also relatively easy to come by. Unless a piece is rare, its condition is important. Damaged pieces can be difficult to repair, but rust spots and stains can be removed by gentle rubbing with a pan scourer or with steel wool.

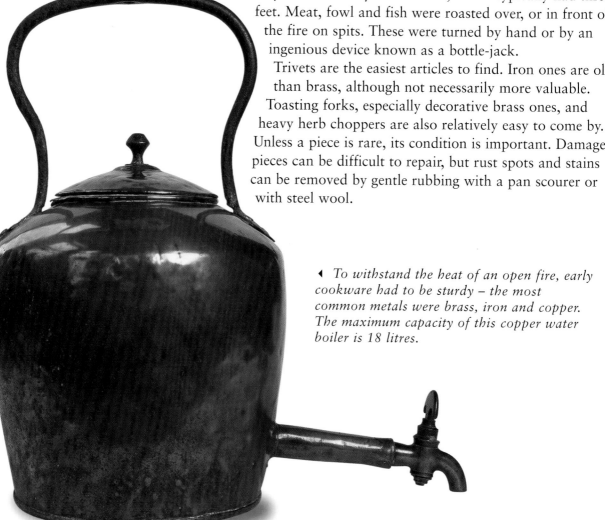

◀ *To withstand the heat of an open fire, early cookware had to be sturdy – the most common metals were brass, iron and copper. The maximum capacity of this copper water boiler is 18 litres.*

KITCHEN

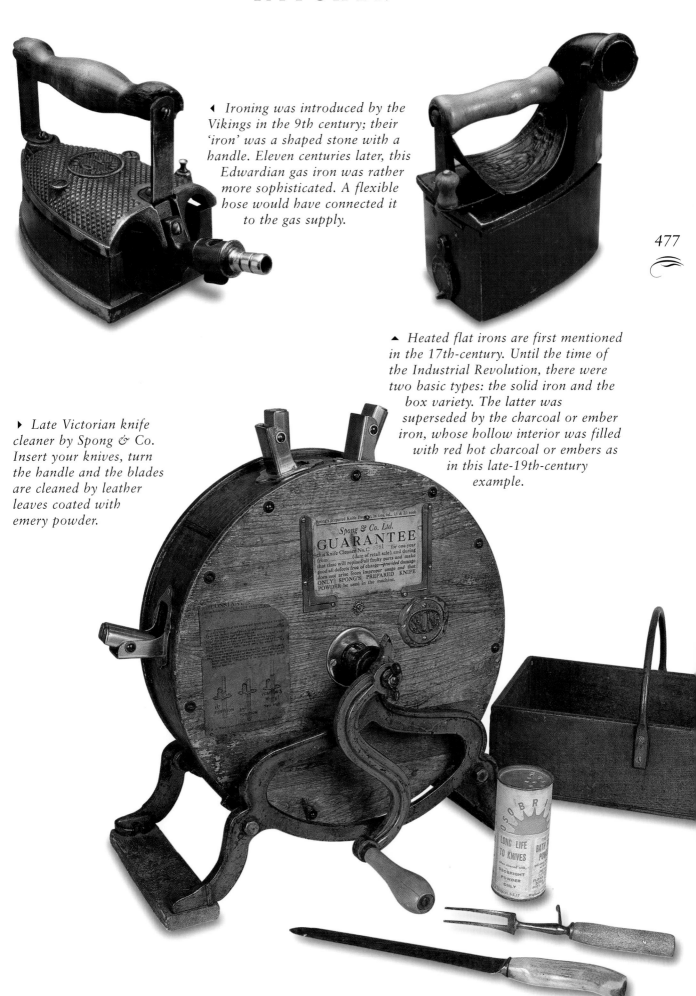

◀ *Ironing was introduced by the Vikings in the 9th century; their 'iron' was a shaped stone with a handle. Eleven centuries later, this Edwardian gas iron was rather more sophisticated. A flexible hose would have connected it to the gas supply.*

477

▲ *Heated flat irons are first mentioned in the 17th-century. Until the time of the Industrial Revolution, there were two basic types: the solid iron and the box variety. The latter was superseded by the charcoal or ember iron, whose hollow interior was filled with red hot charcoal or embers as in this late-19th-century example.*

▶ *Late Victorian knife cleaner by Spong & Co. Insert your knives, turn the handle and the blades are cleaned by leather leaves coated with emery powder.*

COLLECTABLES

BOTTLES

478

THE ANCIENT EGYPTIANS WERE the first to use blown glass bottles for transporting liquids, and their use was spread by the Romans as their empire expanded across Europe. The first bottles were globe-shaped and had a stopper of oiled hemp; cylindrical bottles were introduced when corks began to be used and it was necessary to lay bottles on their sides to keep the seal. Then in 1823 a Bristol maker, Henry Rickets, produced a mould for glass bottles, which meant that more bottles of the same size could be made more cheaply and, in addition, they could be embossed – a feature that has persisted.

When fizzy drinks became popular in the late 1800s, corks were found inadequate to keep the fizz, but an Englishman, Hiram Codd, came up with a solution – he patented a stopper consisting of a glass marble and rubber washer inside the bottle, which were kept in place by the pressure of gas and released by a wooden cap with a small dowel that pushed the marble down. This ingenious idea, which persisted until the 1940s, was the

◄ *Glass soda syphon in wire mesh casing.*
The curvaceous 'baluster' shape is unusual.

BOTTLES

forerunner of screw caps, the hinged wire china stopper and the crown cork still in use today. Codd bottles are among the most desirable and expensive for the collector, but be careful – many copies are on the market.

Instead of bottles for fizzy drinks, beer and cider, some collectors specialize in old medicine bottles and those that have contained foodstuffs such as mustard, and the best places to find these is old refuse dumps or domestic rubbish pits. If you cannot face this rather unsavoury way of satisfying your collector's instinct, bottles can often be bought from stalls at antique and flea markets. As well as glass bottles, there is a fairly large market for stoneware bottles and storage jars, which were usually a plain stone colour, sometimes with a tan top. The most common are those for ginger beer, but similar salt-glazed bottles were used for vinegar, whisky and various other liquids. Several of these together can make an effective decorative group.

◀ *Glass water dispenser by Ricard.*

479

▼ *Dr Nelson's Improved Inhaler, a Boots own-brand remedy. Jesse Boot's decision in 1885 that his company should start manufacturing its own drugs was an important factor in its early expansion.*

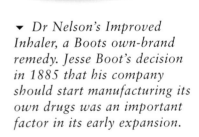

▲ *Staffordshire earthenware nursing bottle. The bottle was filled through the large central hole then corked with a boxwood stopper. The baby would drink straight from the tapered end. The bucolic decoration is suggestive of the peace and tranquillity which would, it was hoped, ensue!*

◀ *A variety of glass and stoneware bottles containing alcoholic and non-alcoholic beverages. The durability of stoneware made it perfect for transportation and storage. Each bottle was hand-thrown and, therefore, unique.*

COLLECTABLES

TREEN

▼ *Only in the past 20 years or so has treen has been regarded as collectable in its own right. For once, condition is not that important to the collector: signs of wear and tear can add to the character of the piece.*

S MALL ARTICLES MADE FROM CARVED or turned wood in everyday domestic or farm use are generally described as treen. The term can cover cruets, carved love spoons from Wales and Scandinavia, and basic turned bowls, platters, paperweights, spoons, toys, pen boxes, snuff and smoking aids, lap desks or tools, but not furniture or purely decorative art objects.

It is only in the last 20 years that treen has been seen as collectable in its own right, and the great majority of objects available today are 19th- or 20th-century work. That said, there is enough of it available to make it a fairly straightforward

TREEN

matter to build up a collection. Treen can be found in antique shops and is increasingly sold at auction, often as part of a furniture sale. The main determinants of price are age and the quality of craftsmanship, although unusual hardwoods such as lignum vitae also attract much interest. Unless a piece is actually broken, condition is not of the first importance. Even the most battered pieces can have a homely quality, and dents and nicks may make them all the more desirable, since they are a sign of age and use.

▶ *Two examples of Mauchline ware, named after the small Scottish town that was its primary centre of production. It was characteristically made of smooth, fine-grained sycamore and decorated with hand-drawn or hand-painted illustrations, although from the mid-19th century, various transfer techniques were introduced. Top: a simple wooden paperknife, decorated with 'A Welsh Tea Party'; above right, this axe is a memento of the – probably apocryphal – story of George Washington cutting down his father's cherry tree.*

▼ *The Edwardian housewife used elaborately carved confectioners' moulds to shape and decorate slabs of sugar and marzipan.*

COLLECTABLES

482

▸ *Pair of novelty tobacco stoppers, or 'tampers', in the guise of miniature bellows.*

▲ *Magnifying glass and case, late 18th century. The handle is of walnut, the case is of fruitwood.*

▸ *A nutmeg grater, c.1800, in the shape of an acorn. It is fashioned in coquilla, the nut of the piassava palm, much used by button makers and turners.*

TREEN

▸ *Elaborate carved wood Victorian pipe rack designed for wall-mounting.*

Tunbridge Ware

Small wooden objects decorated with a mass-production technique that imitated the effects of marquetry and parquetry are known as Tunbridge ware. It is named after the southern English town of Tunbridge Wells, where the technique was developed in the late 17th century. But in the 19th century it became so popular that it grew into a veritable industry.

Tunbridge ware manufacturers made a huge range of articles, such as stamp boxes, cigar boxes, trays, needle cases, cotton reels and measuring tapes. The most popular articles were those intended as souvenirs. In terms of decoration, floral motifs were common, as were butterflies, shells, dogs, cats and fish.

Pieces of Tunbridge ware are becoming increasingly hard to find, and prices have gone up accordingly. Generally speaking, the more unusual the article and design, the more expensive it will be.

Collectables

GARDENING

▼ *Late-19th-century galvanized metal watering can with brass rose. Galvanization stopped rusting; prior to its development, watering cans were either japanned or painted to prevent corrosion.*

THE CATEGORY OF GARDEN COLLECTABLES comprises a wide range of articles such as statues, furniture and tools. The fashion for garden statues was revived in the 18th and 19th centuries for the landscaped gardens of the well-to-do, but these statues can look equally good in today's gardens. Statues made before the 20th century generally fall into three categories: human, mythological and allegorical figures; real and imaginary animals; and objects. The only departure from the classical tradition was the growing popularity of more naturalistic statues,

GARDENING

▶ *20th-century Italian composition figures: two Chinese boy musicians.*

such as children holding baskets of flowers and fruit, and animals. Auction rooms are good places to buy authentic garden statues, as are architectural salvage yards. Reproductions are usually cheaper. They can be aged by the application of natural yoghurt, which encourages the growth of lichens, algae and moss.

Nineteenth-century iron garden furniture, with its delicate filigree lines, is much in demand today because it provides a perfect contrast to the simple lines of a modern conservatory. Mid-19th century designs are the most ornate; by the end of the century, leaf forms and twisted stems were still a common motif but were more controlled and ordered – rather like the early Art Nouveau style. By contrast, the original designs from Coalbrookdale, England, are far more 'rustic' in appearance.

Collecting old garden tools is a specialized field that appeals to only a limited number of enthusiasts. Prices are still relatively low for items such as trowels, forks, galvanized watering cans and garden shears. Rust and woodworm are the main enemies of all tools, so condition is all-important in determining price. Although old garden tools can be found in antique and bric-a-brac shops, perhaps the best bargains are to be found at house clearance sales and local auctions.

▶ *This cherub bearing a lion mask is a 20th-century Italian composition model of an original piece of fountain statuary. Composition is an aggregate of sand, cement and crushed or pulverized stone or marble. Artificial stones of this sort were used from the 18th century onwards to reduce production costs.*

485

COLLECTABLES

486

Left; matching set comprising
hand fork, shears and trowel;
right: pruning shears, scissors
and secateurs.

▼ This handsome garden table with scalloped
marble top, cast-iron base and lyre-shaped
supports would make an attractive addition to
any conservatory.

GARDENING

◄ *There is a simple, flowing elegance to this wrought-iron garden chair.*

487

▲ *The Coalbrookdale Foundry (near Telford, Shropshire) was renowned for its cast-iron work. This garden chair in fern and blackberry design is typical.*

◄ *Cast-iron garden bench with 'honeycomb' seat and back support.*

COLLECTABLES
WRITING

THE 19TH-CENTURY WRITING DESK was the centre of communication and household management in every bourgeois household. Although the quill had long been abandoned, dip pens and inkstands were still essential features. These were made of various materials – polished wood, bakelite, glass, ceramic, marble, silver or brass. Ceramic inkwells are much sought after today, especially those made by Royal Doulton, Wedgwood, Royal Copenhagen, Limoges and Delft.

Letter openers were also much used and can make an extremely attractive collection. For the most part, they were narrow and dagger-like in shape, and made of metal, wood, bone or ivory, or silver.

The first reliable and leakproof fountain pens revolutionized handwriting. The material of which the pen is made is the most significant factor as far as the collector is concerned. In general, the most sought-after pens tend to be those from the turn of the 20th century, since this was the heyday of Parker and Waterman, the two most important names in fountain pen manufacture.

Since the late 1980s, there has been an upsurge of interest in vintage fountain pens, with a consequent steep rise in price. Pens are now an established specialist field, and auction houses sometimes devote sales exclusively to them.

▸ *This late-19th-century Mabie, Todd and Bard pen was designed specifically for ladies – hence the hooks in place of a pocket clip, enabling the wearer to hang it from a chatelaine.*

▲ *Silver- and gold-plated pen and pencil sets were the mark of a successful businessman; the office worker's pen was steel.*

WRITING

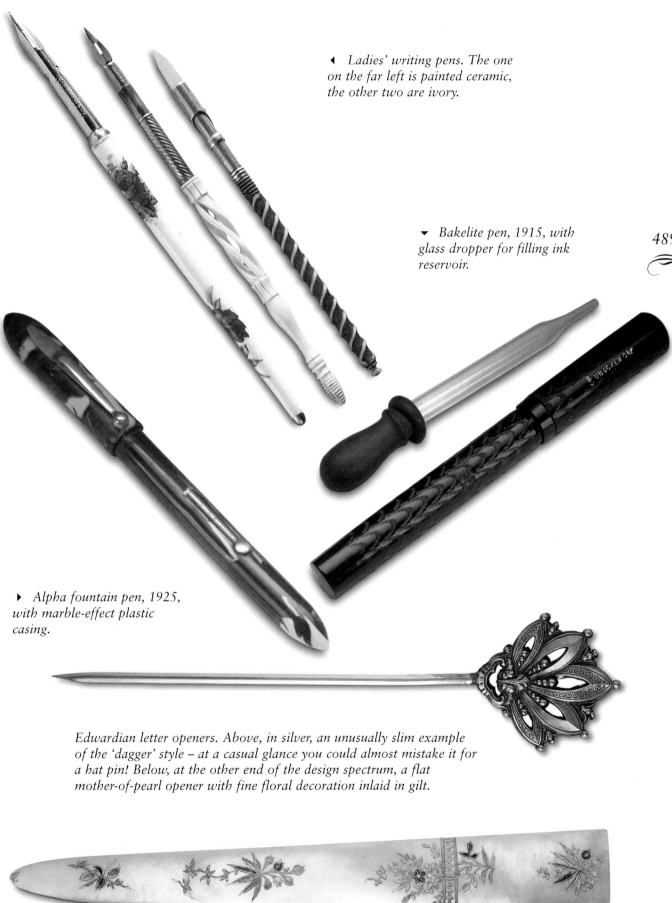

◀ *Ladies' writing pens. The one on the far left is painted ceramic, the other two are ivory.*

▼ *Bakelite pen, 1915, with glass dropper for filling ink reservoir.*

489

▶ *Alpha fountain pen, 1925, with marble-effect plastic casing.*

Edwardian letter openers. Above, in silver, an unusually slim example of the 'dagger' style – at a casual glance you could almost mistake it for a hat pin! Below, at the other end of the design spectrum, a flat mother-of-pearl opener with fine floral decoration inlaid in gilt.

COLLECTABLES

490

▸ *An elegant cut-glass ink bottle with a silver top, probably part of a desk set.*

▾ *This double brass inkwell with pen tray and stands is embellished in Art Nouveau style.*

WRITING

▲ White china transfer-printed double inkwell with exquisitely coloured floral patterning.

Seals

Personal envelope seals – 'desk' seals as opposed to ring seals – were used to impress a blob of hot wax applied to the 'tongue' of the envelope. Such seals were made of ivory, silver or gilded steel and tipped with a disc of semiprecious stone, glass, basalt or jasper. The disc might be incised in reverse with a monogram, family crest or personal symbol.

Seals are highly collectable, but prices vary considerably. Ivory seals bearing the crest of notables may have historical as well as material value. On the other hand, ordinary steel seals can be picked up at antique shops fairly cheaply.

Personal envelope seals: left, in gilt steel; right, in carved ivory. The seal patterns are, respectively, a monogram and a small bird.

COLLECTABLES
SMOKING

CIGARETTE SMOKING IN the 1920s and '30s was an inseparable part of the fashionable life, and an array of attractive accessories was produced to accentuate the 'civilized' impression of the habit. Cigarette boxes, cigarette cases, ashtrays and lighters – many of them beautifully fashioned – are all considered collectable today, and can readily be found in antique shops and at auctions.

The cigarette box had pride of place in most bourgeois homes, placed for easy access on the sideboard or the coffee table. Cigarette boxes made by famous design houses, such as Tiffany and Cartier, are available at higher prices. More modestly priced, but well worth looking for, are the inlaid wooden boxes

Art Deco cigarette lighter.

▲ *Tennis ball ashtray in pink and black.*

Three table lighters by Dunhill. From left, eight-day clock in silver, 'golf ball' in silver, and Giant Unique Lighter in silver plate.

SMOKING

▸ *Clockwise from left: brown bakelite swivel-action smoker's companion; Far Eastern wooden cigarette dispenser; red bakelite cigarette box with matching ashtray; bakelite cigarette holders – Scottie and bird designs.*

and cigarette dispensers produced by Dunhill of St James's, London.

Outside the home, no gentleman worth his salt would be seen without his cigarette case and lighter. Cigarette cases were made in a variety of materials, from traditional silver to mirror glass or the new plastics; the designs also ranged from traditional to the sharpest Art Deco stylings. Heavy chrome-plated lighters tended to be the most widely used, but novelty lighters, often made in the shape of aeroplanes or rockets, were also popular.

Small oval ashtrays from the 1920s might be set with a graceful, seated woman dressed in a modest bathing suit, while novelty ashtrays – many of them made in Japan and Germany – were adorned with amusing animals, such as spotted cats or dogs, and included holders in which to store unlit cigarettes ready for use. Prices for ashtrays rise according to their attractiveness and rarity.

493

A selection of ashtrays. Above: mirror-glass ashtray with ribbed edges; far right: bakelite 'Scottie' dog ashtray; right: naked woman in chrome; left: black and white phenolic resin ashtray.

COLLECTABLES

494

SMOKING

◀ *Selection of Art Deco cigarette cases: miniature works of art in gold and silver, enamel and lacquer; some restrained, some colourful, some with inlay, others with engraved or engine-turned decoration – all exceeding their basic functional requirements in the most exuberant fashion.*

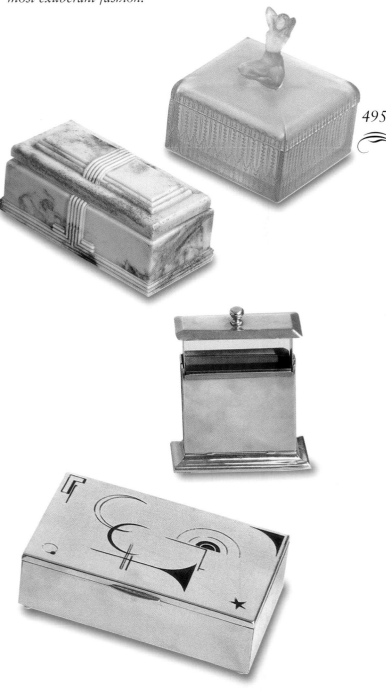

495
⁓

▲ *Cigarette boxes. From top left, clockwise: translucent, marbled plastic cigarette box – an early use of plastics; Lalique cigarette box in opalescent glass, in a design known as 'Sultane'; electro-plated nickel-silver cigarette dispenser, 1931; Deco cigarette box in chrome with black enamel designs.*

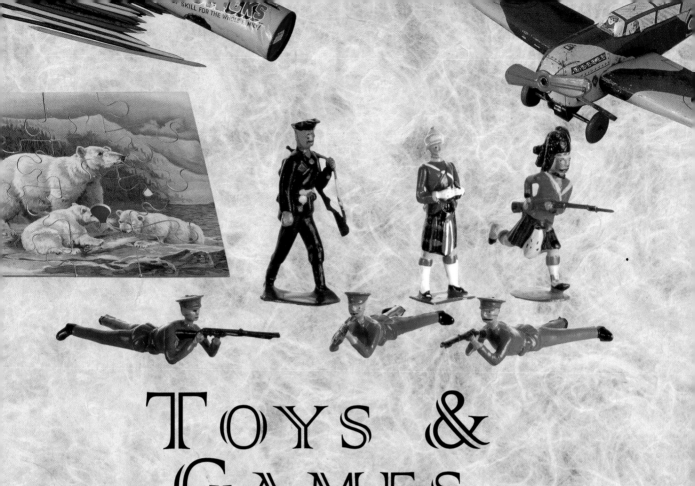

TOYS & GAMES

Collectables

WITH THE OCCASIONAL EXCEPTION, it is only in the second half of the 20th century that people have begun to collect toys, games and other bygones associated with leisure and childhood. Many pieces that would be worth a good deal of money today must have been thrown away or stowed away in a forgotten corner of a loft in the 1950s and 1960s.

Many collectors are intent on collecting or reassembling their own childhood. Some continue a consuming childhood interest – in model trains, for example – into an adult passion. Because of this, toys can go from current to collectable very quickly. Collectors of toys and games from before World War II tend not to have this personal involvement. Their interest is largely in historical detail or the fine craftsmanship that went into making some pieces. The quality and attention to detail of a Bassett-Lowke tinplate locomotive, a Jumeau doll or a Chinese ivory chess-set attract many collectors today.

In the 19th century, toys were increasingly mass-produced. Ceramic heads began to be used on dolls in the middle of the century, while soldiers were made of lead and toy vehicles of brass – in the more upmarket versions – or colourful tinplate.

By the turn of the 20th century, the toy market was dominated by the mechanical tinplate vehicles, figures and novelties made by German manufacturers such as Bing, Lehmann and Märklin. This period also saw the introduction of what has proved to be a perennial favourite, the teddy bear. Once again, a German firm, Steiff, spearheaded the change.

Germany's dominance of the toy market began to fade after World War I, as British and American firms took over. Self-assembly model kits and construction systems such as Meccano were popular between the World Wars, when sturdier die-cast

TOYS & GAMES

metal models began to take over from tinplate toys.

Although popular toys were often made in huge numbers, they can be surprisingly rare. Many failed to survive the attentions of an enthusiastic child, while others were simply thrown away when their owners outgrew them. Collectors tend to make things harder for themselves by searching for pieces in as near mint condition as possible. The original box, packaging and any advertising ephemera associated with the toy when first sold always adds value, particularly to tinplate or die-cast models.

COLLECTABLES

EARLY TOYS

▼ *Painted or transfer-printed wooden toys such as these are typical of the first part of the 19th century. The doll's crib on the right is joined much like a full-size piece of furniture. The simple wooden donkey may have been part of a Noah's Ark or farmyard set, while the wooden building blocks have letters of the alphabet and pictures of animals and birds. The pull-along wagon contains a lion-tamer and his charge.*

MOST COLLECTABLE EARLY TOYS are made of wood, often painstakingly carved and painted. Building blocks, armies of soldiers, dolls, animals – sometimes two by two in a wooden Noah's Ark – and simple pull-along toys survive, as do perennial favourites such as hoops, spinning tops, hobby horses, marbles and kites. Although tinplate toys were first made in the early 19th century, survivors from this period are seldom found. Toy animals and figures were also made in ceramic and plaster, but their fragility makes them rare survivals.

Toy theatres were another popular plaything of the early and mid-19th century. The actors – characters in appropriate poses – were cut from a printed sheet and pasted on board, then moved on and off stage using a wire slide. About 300 popular dramas of the day were issued in toy theatre form, with printed sheets containing the characters and backdrops and a condensed script from which the children could read.

TOYS & GAMES

◄ *The hinged and jointed acrobat, swinging on and around a bar or string, has been made in various styles and materials for a couple of centuries. It would have been a typical fairground toy, sold by itinerant hawkers. This painted example is from late in the 19th century.*

▸ *While most tops were made of wood, the use of metal permitted the creation of the humming top. Sound is produced as the air passes over the holes. Many of these metal tops were made in Germany.*

501

▾ *The humble wooden top could develop some sophisticated forms. The parachute top, produced by the firm of Jacques, was made of turned and polished beech with a brass spindle and came in a wooden presentation box.*

COLLECTABLES

TOY HORSES

502

ROCKING HORSES ORIGINATED in the 17th century but remained expensive toys for the wealthy few until the 19th century, when they became more readily available. The first rocking horses were two semicircular pieces of wood with a seat fixed between them, a solid wood horse's head at the front and a counterbalance at the back. A more recognizable form soon appeared, with a realistic horse standing on a platform mounted on a bow, as with a rocking chair. In the late 18th century, the horses tended to take on a galloping, racy profile, and the legs were attached directly to the end of the bows as the platform was done away with.

The only problem was that these mounts could sometimes throw an over-enthusiastic junior equestrian, and from the 1880s the safer trestle rocker, in which the horse rocks on hinges on a fixed trestle base, gradually took over, although the traditional style was still made.

Some rocking horses were painted – usually some variety of dapple – and some were left in the natural colour of the wood, although most had manes of real horse hair. Occasionally, rocking horses were covered with pony hide for a realistic effect. The harness and saddle were usually made of leather and were scaled-down versions of real tack.

▼ *The quality of this late 19th-century horse can be seen in its ornately designed red leather saddle and bridle.*

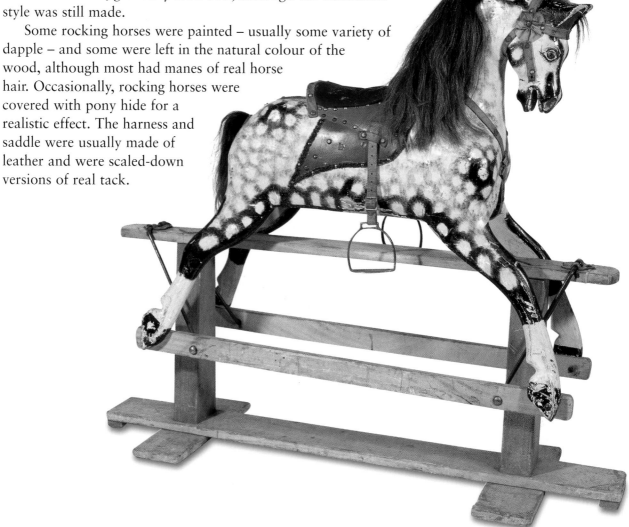

TOYS & GAMES

▸ *This charming hybrid from about 1870 has a finely-crafted wooden horse in typical galloping pose mounted on a tricycle frame for extra mobility.*

503

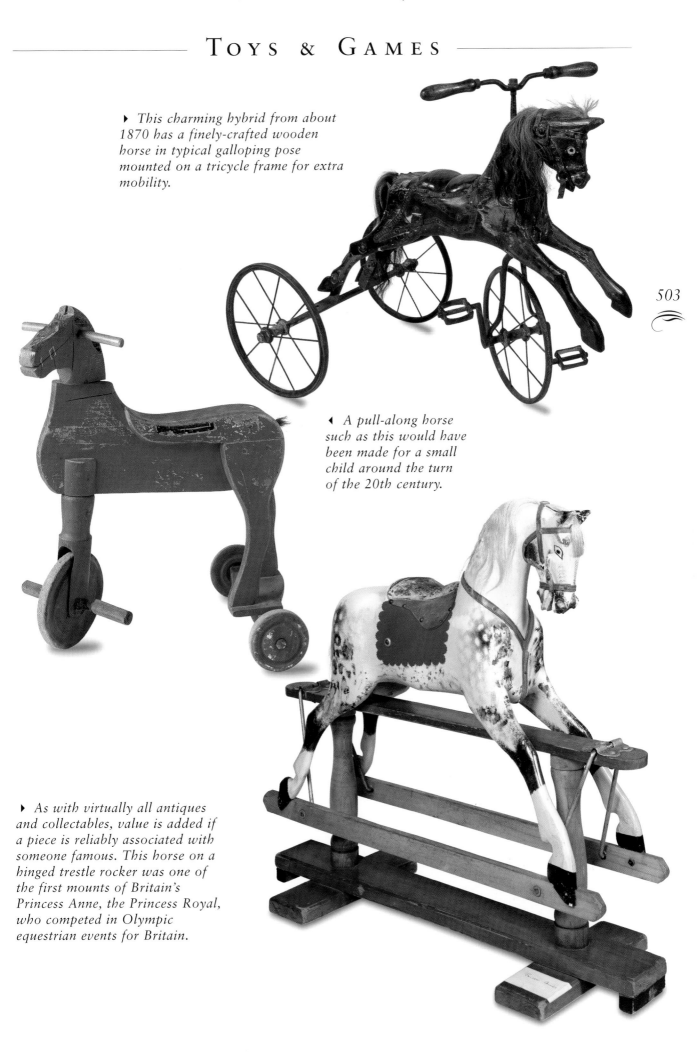

◂ *A pull-along horse such as this would have been made for a small child around the turn of the 20th century.*

▸ *As with virtually all antiques and collectables, value is added if a piece is reliably associated with someone famous. This horse on a hinged trestle rocker was one of the first mounts of Britain's Princess Anne, the Princess Royal, who competed in Olympic equestrian events for Britain.*

MONEY BOXES

504

THE FIRST CUSTOM-MADE boxes for saving money – ceramic pigs with slots in their backs – appeared in Europe in the 17th century. Pigs tended to be associated with saving owing to the custom of keeping a pig to be fattened up for Christmas and other festivals. In the 18th and 19th centuries, other pottery designs were introduced – castles and cottages were popular subjects in Europe, and banks in the USA – but different materials were increasingly used, including wood and, in the USA in particular, cast iron. Printed tinplate was used in Europe from the end of the 19th century.

American cast-iron banks were the first to be made specifically for children. While European money boxes were 'still boxes' – basically containers with a coin slot – many of these cast-iron boxes, whose heyday was 1870 to the early 1900s, were mechanical; coins were placed somewhere on the bank, then swallowed, shot or thrown into the slot by a mechanism operated either by the weight of the coin itself or by a switch or lever. Companies such as Shephard Hardware and J & E Stevens of Connecticut put out wide ranges of very collectable money boxes which, being cast iron, have survived a little better than their tinplate equivalents.

Printed tinplate was the preferred material for money boxes in the 20th-century. Germany specialized in tinplate versions of mechanical banks, while French children preferred banks that yielded a piece of chocolate every time a coin was put in.

▲ *'Sambo' and his female equivalent 'Dinah' were common subjects for 19th-century American boxes. The weight of a coin on the figure's hand activated a mechanism that tossed it into his or her open mouth and made the eyeballs roll appreciatively. Reproductions may be passed off (having been subjected to suitable aging treatment) as originals.*

◀ *This British copy of a 'Sambo' money box is adapted to the still format, with a coin slot in the top of the figure's head.*

TOYS & GAMES

◀ *The mechanical version of Uncle Sam has a lever movement that lets him swallow any coin placed in his hand; the same applies to the monkey's dish.*

▶ *The figure of a monkey on a barrel organ was a popular motif for American boxes, along with acrobats, bucking broncos and obdurate, kicking mules.*

▼ *This selection of still boxes from around the turn of the 20th century illustrates the range of designs and materials – tinplate, cast iron and ceramics – employed. Still boxes are generally less expensive than mechanical ones, while tinplate, unless it is, unusually, in very good condition, usually fetches less than cast iron.*

505

COLLECTABLES

AUTOMOBILES

506

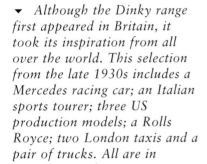

▼ *Although the Dinky range first appeared in Britain, it took its inspiration from all over the world. This selection from the late 1930s includes a Mercedes racing car; an Italian sports tourer; three US production models; a Rolls Royce; two London taxis and a pair of trucks. All are in excellent condition.*

THE MOTOR CAR IS PERHAPS the machine that defines the 20th century, and toy versions were made throughout. Early cars, racing models and roadsters alike, tended to have tinplate bodies. Most were made in Germany.

In 1932, the British Meccano company produced a series of 'modelled miniature' vehicles in die-cast metal – much more durable than tinplate – as accessories for their train sets. These sold so well that in 1934 Meccano introduced them formally as the Dinky range, which soon expanded to take in boats and aircraft. From this date on, toy cars were rarely made in anything other than die-cast metal until plastics and other modern synthetics were introduced in the 1960s.

Most early toy vehicles with working wheels were push-along models, although some were driven by clockwork. Tinplate models with wheels simply printed on the side have long been made alongside those with working axles.

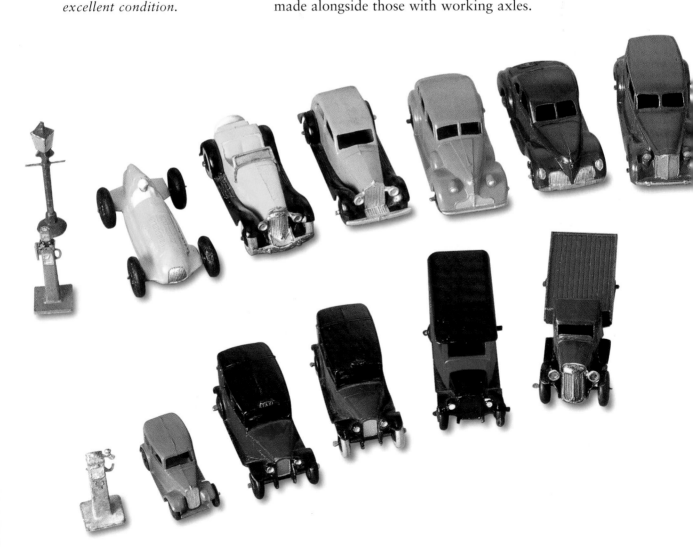

TOYS & GAMES

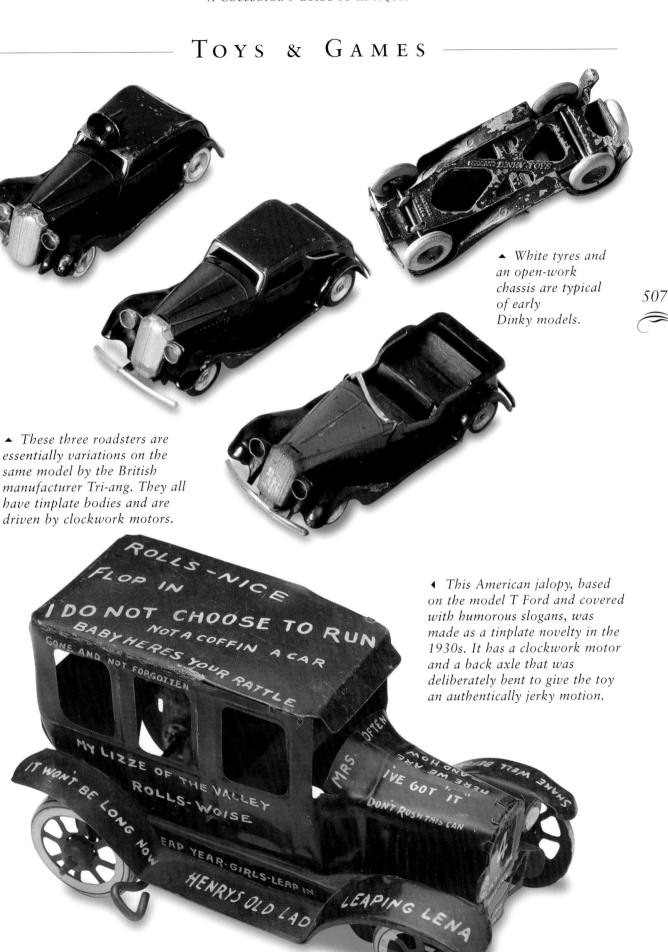

▲ White tyres and
an open-work
chassis are typical
of early
Dinky models.

507

▲ These three roadsters are
essentially variations on the
same model by the British
manufacturer Tri-ang. They all
have tinplate bodies and are
driven by clockwork motors.

◀ This American jalopy, based
on the model T Ford and covered
with humorous slogans, was
made as a tinplate novelty in the
1930s. It has a clockwork motor
and a back axle that was
deliberately bent to give the toy
an authentically jerky motion.

COLLECTABLES

TRAINS

T OY TRAINS IN WOOD OR TIN are almost as old as the railways themselves, appearing in Britain around 1830 and Germany and France soon after that It was not until the 1880s, however, that they were sold with flanged wheels and tracks to run on. Before then, they were simply pushed or pulled along the floor, although some of these 'floor-runners' had clockwork motors and others working miniature steam engines powered by a spirit lamp.

The first commercial train sets – locomotives, rolling stock and track – were produced by Märklin of Göppingen, Germany, who also sold beautifully made accessories such as lithographed tinplate stations. Both Märklin and their rivals Bing were famous for the extraordinary attention to detail in their engines. This same ethic was taken up by an Englishman, Wenman Bassett-Lowke, who used German methods to produce very fine steam and clockwork engines that are among the most highly prized today. Toy manufacturers soon developed two standard scales, or gauges, for their models; 0 (1:30) and 1 (1:43).

After World War I, the focus of the industry moved away from Germany to British mass manufacturers such as Hornby and American companies such as Lionel Lines and Ives of Bridgeport. Many German and British locomotives of the 1920s and 1930s were made to smaller gauges, H0 and 00. The locomotives and rolling stock for these smaller gauges tended to be die-cast rather than fashioned in tinplate, which sometimes led to a lack of sharpness in the detailing.

Although toy trains powered by mains electricity had been made as early as the 1890s, it was only after the introduction of transformers in the 1920s that they were seen as generally safe for children to use. In the following decades, they gradually took over from steam and clockwork-powered locomotives.

Most manufacturers primarily produced models of their own country's trains in their specific liveries, but there was sufficient interest for copies of famous engines or trains to be made around the world. The historically accurate painting, transfers and liveries of both the locomotives and the rolling stock are part of the appeal.

Above centre: there were more than 3,000 locomotives in the Lionel Lines range. Models of locomotives with 'cow-catchers' on the front were particularly popular; models with working steam engines, driven by spirit lamps, were often made to resemble the earliest steam locomotives; goods wagons add colour and variety to a layout; the same double-bogie chassis here accommodates a relatively modern die-cast petrol tanker with stickers and a lithographed

TOYS & GAMES

509

tinplate boxcar; the British clockwork set of 1937 is reduced in value by the rather battered condition of the tinplate carriages; bottom: the sleek, streamlined locomotives that pulled the famous transcontinental trains such as the Superchief across the USA in the 1920s and '30s – the epitome of Art Deco design applied to engineering – were enormously popular and inspired this Lionel Lines model.

▲ The smaller 00 gauges allowed for more complicated track layouts within a smaller space, and created a huge market for accessories. Buildings, trackside furniture, level crossings, bridges, people, plants and landscape features were supplied for the enthusiast.

COLLECTABLES

AEROPLANES

510

▼ *Meccano model-aircraft kits combined standard pieces from the construction kit with custom-made ones. The Westland Wapiti came into production in 1934, and the kit, with hinged rudder, ailerons and elevators, followed a couple of years later.*

THE FLIGHTS OF THE WRIGHT BROTHERS, Blériot, Alcock and Brown, Lindbergh and many other aviators whose fame did not long survive their often tragically early deaths, made flying one of the great adventure themes of the first three decades of the century. Children played with, and sometimes assembled, models of all the famous aircraft, as well as some whose designs owed more to imagination than aeronautics.

As is also the case with toy trains, there are two sections to the market; those interested in toys, and those with an interest in the history and manufacture of the original machine. The latter tend to force up the price of rare, finely detailed models.

Toys & Games

▲ This 1920s biplane has been assembled from a wooden kit and hand-painted, although detailing, such as the checkerboard on the wings and tail, were supplied with the kit in the form of transfers.

▲ The English Mettoy company made this stylized passenger aeroplane c.1930. A clockwork mechanism turns the propeller and front axle.

511

▼ This tinplate craft was never meant to take to the skies; it is, in fact, a complicated form of die, or teetotum, made by Lehmann. If the toy is pushed along the floor, the numbered wheel mounted on top spins; when the plane comes to a halt, the pointer mounted behind the propeller points to a certain number.

▶ Although this printed tinplate fighter bears the insignia of the British Royal Air Force, it was made in France in the late 1930s.

COLLECTABLES

MODEL BOATS

WHILE MANUFACTURERS SUCH as Märklin, Fleischmann and Carette in Germany included tinplate boats and ships alongside their model cars and railways, an extra dimension was added to the fun of a toy boat if it was a working model, for use indoors in the bath or kitchen sink or outdoors on ponds, paddling pools or any relatively still, shallow water.

512

As with real boats, the main materials for building toy boats were wood and metal. Wood, with its natural buoyancy, was used for bath toys and the hulls of model yachts, although ones with hulls and keels of tinplate appeared in the 1920s and 1930s.

Models powered by means other than sails tended to have metal hulls. Tinplate boats could be made water-tight. Clockwork mechanisms drove an outboard motor, propeller shaft or – occasionally – paddle-wheels. Every craft from rowboats and speedboats through to ocean liners and battleships were copied in clockwork, even submarines (a plug was screwed into the keyhole before they were launched). Sometimes the copies were crude – when the toy was aimed at young children – and sometimes they were extraordinarily precise. The most painstakingly detailed – and most expensive – working model boats had their own miniature steam engines driving a propeller shaft. This type is much sought-after today.

▼ *The skill in sailing a model yacht was in setting the sails and rudder to make best use of the breeze, and using a long stick to fend it off from the bank. This wooden model from the first decade of the 20th century is also fitted with winged stabilizers, which could be lowered to keep the boat steady in deeper water.*

TOYS & GAMES

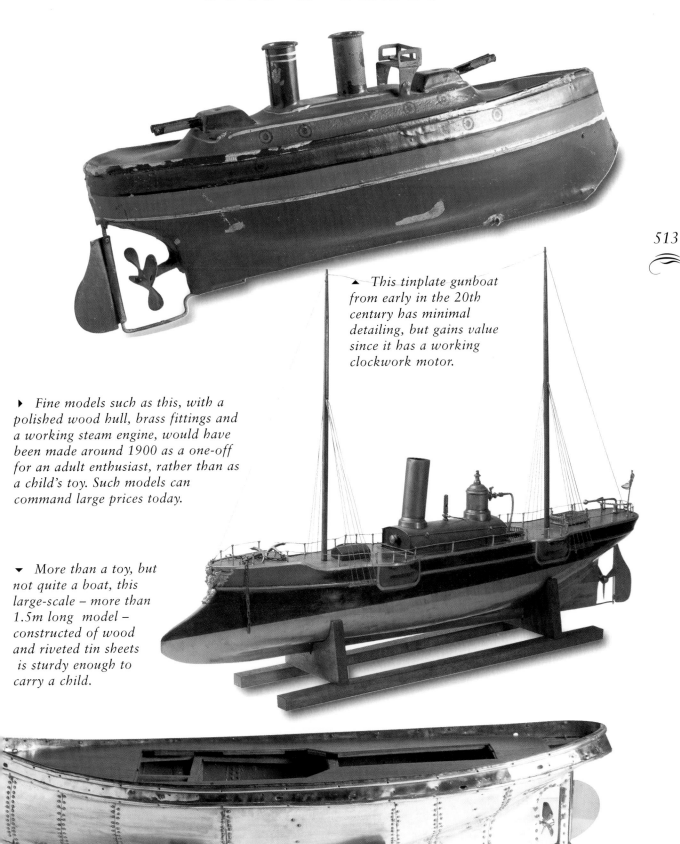

► *This tinplate gunboat from early in the 20th century has minimal detailing, but gains value since it has a working clockwork motor.*

► *Fine models such as this, with a polished wood hull, brass fittings and a working steam engine, would have been made around 1900 as a one-off for an adult enthusiast, rather than as a child's toy. Such models can command large prices today.*

▼ *More than a toy, but not quite a boat, this large-scale – more than 1.5m long model – constructed of wood and riveted tin sheets is sturdy enough to carry a child.*

COLLECTABLES

TOY SOLDIERS

514

ARLY TOY SOLDIERS WERE carved from wood. Often they were little more than painted skittles. Model soldiers cast in tin or lead exist from as early as the 16th century, but toy soldiers were produced in any numbers only after the introduction of soldiers in flat, moulded tinplate. The first nod towards realism came with the introduction of rather fragile, flat tinplate soldiers in about 1775. Later that century, various French and German companies began to make three-dimensional soldiers in solid metal, usually lead with a little tin and antimony. Some were of particularly high quality; all of them were relatively expensive.

In 1893 an English toy-making firm pioneered a new method: hollowcasting. Molten lead was poured into a mould as usual, but was then poured out again, leaving a thin shell of metal

▼ *The original packaging and a complete set greatly enhance the price of toy soldiers. The box will double the total price of the individual elements making up a set.*

TOYS & GAMES

▸ *Vehicles always add value. The motorcycle despatch rider was made in the 1930s, while the World War I foot soldier is a Britains' model of the same period.*

around the inside of the mould. The great savings earned on metal brought down the prices, and made toy soldiers a mass market for the first time. Several other firms began hollowcasting, although Britains' continued to dominate the world market, making painted figures in the battledress and parade uniforms of many armies. Hollowcast lead soldiers were sold until 1966.

The models were often marketed in boxed sets in order to persuade children to build up themed collections. Intact boxes with their contents complete and undamaged, fetch a high premium, as do early models with vehicles. Today, model soldiers of various kinds are collected by military enthusiasts and war-gamers, as well as those yearning after the simple pleasures of their own childhood.

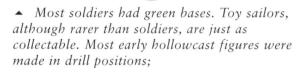

▲ *Most soldiers had green bases. Toy sailors, although rarer than soldiers, are just as collectable. Most early hollowcast figures were made in drill positions;*

the 1903 Britains' model of a Black Watch infantryman charging is an exception. Any soldiers with painted moustaches are likely to have been made before 1940.

◂ *Military bandsmen were as popular as fighting soldiers. The bugler is an early piece, part of a 21-piece Britains' set produced in 1910. The piper dates from 1936 and has moveable arms, a very rare feature before 1920. The mounted cavalryman was made by Britains' rivals, the John Hill Co. Similar models made by Britains' fetch three times as much.*

COLLECTABLES

MUSICAL BOXES

516

MUSICAL BOXES WERE DEVELOPED in the latter half of the 18th century in the Jura region of Switzerland, where they were made by watchmakers. The first mechanisms, in which raised pins, mounted on a rotating cylinder, plucked the fine teeth of a tempered steel 'comb' to produce the notes, were constructed as part of a clock or an automaton. But by the beginning of the 19th century they had become instruments in their own right, set in a wooden case or box and activated by lifting the lid. The outside of a music box could be plain – early examples often were – or masterpieces of inlay or enamelling. The inside of the lid, which showed when the box was in use, was generally also decorated.

Switzerland continued to be the main source of musical boxes, although makers in other nations – particularly the Bohemian firm of Řebíck – also gained a reputation for their

▲ *Many musical boxes had small automata built in, usually a Swiss singing bird, as in this Austrian example c.1845.*

TOYS & GAMES

boxes. The mechanisms became more complex in the 19th century, allowing for more and different tunes to be played, but musical boxes became very expensive owing to the precision work involved.

In the 1880s, however, Paul Lochmann of Leipzig introduced interchangeable metal discs in place of the cylinders, allowing for the mass production of boxes with a large potential repertoire. Germany became the main centre of production of musical boxes, and a German set up the Regina company in New Jersey, the most import US manufacturer. Disc boxes were generally larger than cylinder boxes; some were quite substantial pieces of furniture, made for the drawing room.

Cylinder boxes were still made, but the quality of both the mechanism and the cases declined, and musical boxes came to be seen less and less as a form of family entertainment and more as children's toys or as an elaborate form of trinket box; the spread of the phonograph in the 1920s and '30s hastened this change.

▲ *In the 19th century, mechanisms were sometimes disguised by mounting them in photograph albums or books. The successful miniaturization of the cylinder mechanism allowed other examples to be housed in tiny decorative boxes that could easily be slipped into a pocket.*

◄ *This selection of musical boxes dates from the late-19th and early 20th centuries. In the centre is a cylinder box of about 1870, with the list of tunes it plays printed on the inside of the lid. Clockwise from the top left: a Swiss disc-box from around the turn of the century; a well-engineered small cylinder box of roughly the same period, capable of playing six melodies; a 1905 Leipzig disc box, made for children and with a drawer for further discs below; a Swiss cylinder box from the 1850s; a Nicole Frères box of about the same period with a well-preserved piece of floral marquetry in the lid; a small mahogany box c. 1875.*

Collectables
Magic Lanterns

518

THE MAGIC LANTERN, an early form of slide projector, was widely used as a means of family entertainment and moral instruction in the 19th and early 20th centuries. It was used to project images on coloured glass slides on to living-room walls or large screens in public venues.

The first man to describe and illustrate a simple projector was a Dutchman, Christiaen Huygens, in 1649. By the end of the 17th century it was a popular novelty. The first lanterns used daylight, oil lamps or candles as a light source, with a concave lens to concentrate it. Later models used paraffin burners or, despite the dangers involved, limelight. By the end of the 19th century, electric lamps had become the main source of light.

Lanterns were particularly popular in the 19th century, when cheap tinplate models of limited optical quality were introduced. Top of the range models were fitted into elaborate cases of mahogany and walnut, with brass fittings, while enthusiasts could buy the lenses and create their own casing.

The slides, usually mounted in mahogany frames, came in one of two standard formats, 8cm x 8cm (most popular in Britain) and 8cm x 10cm (the

▲ *The Kromscop was a fascinating optical device introduced right at the end of the 19th century. It is not a projector, but a viewer, and one with a difference; three colour filters give an illusion of full colour to any monochrome slide put in it.*

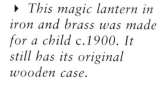

▶ *This magic lantern in iron and brass was made for a child c.1900. It still has its original wooden case.*

TOYS & GAMES

▼ *A French optical toy, the Praxinoscope explored the principles of cinema in the earliest years of its development. Strips of images line the inside of the drum; when it is spun, their reflections in the central rectangular mirrors appear to move, owing to the phenomenon of persistence of vision.*

519

standard in the USA and much of Europe). Before about 1850 they were generally hand-painted on glass, but after this date they were increasingly likely to be mass-produced lithographic transfers. They were sold singly or, more frequently, in boxed sets that told stories or illustrated religious and educational topics.

Various mechanical devices introduced in the second half of the 19th century allowed for the illusion of vertical, horizontal or rotary motion. Beale's Choreutoscope of 1866, for example, allowed several slightly different images (a dancing skeleton was the most popular) to be cranked past the small window in a lantern, giving an illusion of continuous movement – essentially the same principle as the cinema.

▲ *Lime-burning lanterns such as this example in tin and brass would have been used in both middle-class parlours and public halls during the 19th-century. It still has its original protective case.*

▶ *The rich colours and intriguing content of many 19th-century magic lantern slides makes them a fascinating subject for the collector.*

COLLECTABLES

INDOOR GAMES

INDOOR GAMES – SCALED-DOWN versions of outdoor activities, card and board games, jigsaw puzzles and other pastimes – have always had their aficionados, but they really came into their own late in the 19th century, when for the first time adults, as well as children, had leisure time to devote to them and the social strictures about frivolity melted away.

520

The genteel outdoor pastimes of tennis, bowls and croquet all had their indoor versions, played by adults and children alike when the weather forced them inside. Table tennis eventually evolved into a sport in its own right, while carpet bowls and table croquet faded away, but all three have left some interesting collectables, from the shaped and polished wood paddles used

▲ *Before table tennis was called table tennis, players might have used bats such as these, carved from beechwood.*

▶ *Table croquet was a parlour version of the game. The quality of the workmanship on this 19th-century set, with its turned stand in mahogany and decorative mallets, hoops and posts, is particularly fine.*

▶ *The game of quoits was another outdoor pursuit that came indoors in the 1800s.*

▼ *As the 19th century progressed, jigsaw puzzles became much cheaper. Most had only a few pieces and were made from lithographic prints that were glued to softwood before being cut out.*

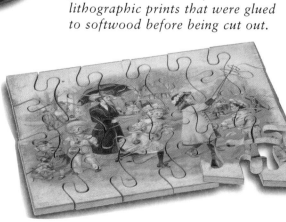

◀ *Bagatelle boards are the 'missing link' between the games of billiards, pool and snooker and the pintables of the 20th century.*

to play 'ping-pong' to gaily-decorated ceramic carpet bowls and the well-turned wood of a miniature croquet mallet.

Other popular indoor pursuits included playing cards and traditional games such as chess, draughts, backgammon and dominoes. Solitaire boards in polished wood with marbles for counters were popular, while the traditional Chinese game mahjong and the Indian parchesi (ludo) both enjoyed a vogue among adults in Europe at the end of the 19th century.

Games compendiums from the 19th century, containing the means of playing these and various other dice and counter games, are some of the most collectable items in this area. They were often presented in lavish boxes or cabinets decorated in lacquer, inlay, marquetry or parquetry, sometimes with metal mounts, and contained both boards that gave further scope for fine inlay and pieces and counters in carved ivory, ceramics, mother-of-pearl, fine metals and so on.

▲ *The game of solitaire has a long history. This 19th-century board is designed for German rules. Glass Nailsea marbles are used as the counters.*

521

▼ *Some games compendiums were extravagant* tours de force *of inlay, lacquer and other decorative work, but this plainer late 19th-century set shows its quality in its contents.*

▲ *The bone and bamboo tiles of this mah-jong set are housed in a handsome cabinet made of amboyna wood trimmed with brass.*

▶ *This little walnut box, possibly of German origin, contains a working miniature roulette wheel.*

◀ *Ceramic carpet bowls were usually brilliantly coloured and decorated.*

COLLECTABLES

522

▲ *Ludo developed out of the old Indian game of parchesi, the name by which it is still known in the USA. This 19th-century board is made of Welsh slate, stained and painted to give a wood finish, and marked out in blue paint.*

Boxed board games, where players move a counter along a numbered path at the throw of a dice, negotiating hazards and gaining rewards, are a creation of the 18th century. Early versions tended to have a moral or didactic purpose, and this continued to be true throughout much of the 19th century. Towards the end of the period, games like snakes and ladders began to get a little more lighthearted and were played solely for fun. Board games based on warfare began to be popular in the 1920s and '30s, but the impact of Monopoly, introduced in the USA during the Great Depression, outstripped them all.

The jigsaw puzzle was invented about 1760 by a cartographer, John Spilsbury. Early examples took the form of a lithographed print mounted on mahogany and sold in a

TOYS & GAMES

▸ *Boxed games and board games of any sort from the 1920s and '30s only give value if they are complete. As usual with toys, the presence of a box is important, although it is rare to find a box, as well as the contents, in mint condition.*

▾ *Games using magnetism to test children's dexterity were popular between the World Wars.*

▴ *In the 20th century, jigsaw puzzles were increasingly printed on card. The complexity of the illustrations increased greatly, as did the number of pieces in an average puzzle.*

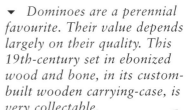

▾ *Dominoes are a perennial favourite. Their value depends largely on their quality. This 19th-century set in ebonized wood and bone, in its custom-built wooden carrying-case, is very collectable.*

▴ *Another indoor variation of the game of quoits requires hoops so small they cannot be accurately thrown, but have to be flicked up by striking down on one edge, as with tiddleywinks (above). As the box illustration suggests, such games were essentially sold as after-dinner pastimes for adults rather than as children's toys.*

mahogany box. These are the jigsaw puzzles most sought-after by collectors. The mahogany was soon replaced by whitewood (pine, deal or, in the 20th century, plywood), first for the box, then the puzzle itself. In the 20th century, jigsaw puzzles tend to be mounted on card or stiff board, allowing for a great increase in the number of pieces in the puzzle, but making them flimsier and much less valuable.

COLLECTABLES

CHESS

▲ *The typical 19th-century chess set was factory-made in stained wood. Although they were produced as playing sets, a good example such as this, in polished wood with its original baize-lined mahogany box, is very collectable.*

IT IS NOT KNOWN WHEN CHESS originated. Its direct ancestor spread from India to Persia at the beginning of the 7th century AD, and from there the game became popular throughout the Islamic world, then spread into medieval Europe.

The Europeans gave the pieces new shapes and new names; the elephant in the Persian version became an English bishop or a French fool, for example. In the 15th century, a change in the rules about the moves of the queen and bishop created the game that is still played today all over the world. In much of Europe, chess-playing was the preserve of the wealthy and leisured classes, and aficionados were willing and able to spend a great deal on their pastime. Boards were often made in fine inlaid woods or worked leather, while the pieces were moulded or carved according to national styles and current fashions. German and Austrian pieces, for example, had pierced, spiky crowns and double-headed knights.

Wood was the most common material, but ivory, stone, bone and horn were also carved into chess pieces. Among the finest of all chess pieces are Chinese, with kings and queens in Mandarin costume set on pedestals made up of up to seven delicately cut

TOYS & GAMES

▲ The seven pieces come from a ceramic set made early in the 19th century by England's Royal Worcester company. The figures, sculpted by John Flaxman, represent characters and locations in the Shakespeare play Macbeth.

▲ Naturally light and dark woods were used for the finely-carved Irish-made chess set c. 1800.

◀ Ivory pieces were usually produced in red and white, and sometimes in India in green and white, rather than the black and white favoured in Europe. This early 19th-century set is probably of Indian origin.

concentric spheres, cut from a single ball of ivory and all moving freely one inside the other.

Realistically carved ivory figures and other finely detailed or well-crafted pieces may well have been made for presentation rather than display. Although single pieces from such individually crafted sets can be appreciated as decorative objects in their own right, collectors are generally interested solely in complete sets of decorative or playing chessmen.

▲ This set was made in China in the 1820s for export. The lack of fanciful decoration, and the fact that the red pieces are colour-washed, rather than stained ivory, suggests that it was intended for the cheaper end of the European market.

COLLECTABLES

DOLLS

LTHOUGH DOLLS IN WOOD, terracotta, fabric and ivory
have survived from classical Greece and Rome, for most
collectors the history of dolls begins in the 18th-century
with the carved wooden dolls made in most of the countries of
Europe. Some of these were realistically made, with shaped
bodies. They were not playthings so much as miniature fashion
mannequins, and were sent by couturiers to European
courts and American salons to keep fashionable women
apprised of the latest styles. Later, the new, clinging
fashions of the Empire style required more
realistically modelled dolls, and German carvers
took to making jointed figures.

Wooden play dolls of the 18th and early
19th centuries were much less elaborate,
with bodies like skittles and stick
arms and legs with no movable
joints. The heads were either
carved wood or fashioned

*◄ In Germany and France, moulded
and painted papier-mâché was used
around 1800 to make the heads of
dolls such as this harlequin. This gave
a more realistic finish than wood, but
was softer and more liable to damage;
survivors in this condition are rare.*

526

TOYS & GAMES

▼ *Wooden dolls of the late 18th and early 19th centuries were usually dressed as adults, although neither of these dolls is wearing its original costume. The use of gesso and, after 1800 or so, wax, allowed some detail on the faces, but the eyes, mouth and hair were invariably painted on rather than modelled.*

527

from gesso, a type of plaster, and the hair and features were generally painted on.

There was a strong tradition of doll-making in Germany, and along with France it was to dominate the industry in the 19th century. These jointed German dolls were known as Grödnertals, form their area of origin.

The Germans also had a tradition of making dolls' heads in ceramic. By the 1850s, factories in Thuringia were mass-producing heads in bisque – fired but unglazed porcelain. These were fitted to fabric bodies stuffed with sawdust; the best were made in kid or linen, but most used rougher materials.

COLLECTABLES

BISQUE BECAME THE MATERIAL of choice for doll-makers in Germany and France. Delicate flesh tones were soon developed. Typically, the head and shoulders of dolls of the latter half of the 19th century were modelled in bisque, as were the lower arms and legs. The rest of the body was white cotton or pale pink or white leather stuffed with sawdust.

The French dollmakers' development of the 'composition' body – made of a malleable mix of glue, resin and whitening moulded over a wire frame and dried hard – was soon copied by their German counterparts. Wooden ball joints were fitted at the elbow, shoulder, thigh and knee, and the limbs joined together with elastic. The use of composition bodies made bisque shoulder plates redundant; by the 1880s the usual practice was to give the neck a ringed rim and set the head into a cup in the composition torso, which allowed it to turn.

In the 1860s and 1870s, French makers exploited the bisque technique to make dolls with more realistic expressions. Their innovations were quickly copied by the Germans for the mass market. Glass eyes, pierced ears and wigs of human hair or mohair all helped make dolls more lifelike. Facial expressions became selling points. Counterweight 'sleeping' eyes, which closed when the doll was put on its back, were introduced. Most dolls were made with their mouths slightly open showing painted or applied top teeth. Models with closed mouths were made in much smaller numbers, and as a result are more valuable today.

Generally speaking, French dolls were of higher quality than their German counterparts. They tended to be fashionably dressed, with plenty of hair; long, luxuriant locks are a general sign of quality, since both human hair and mohair were relatively expensive materials. By the end of the century, all the top dollmakers – Jumeau, Roullet et Decamps and Leon Casimir Bru in France, and firms such as Gebrüder Heubach, Simon & Halbig, Cuno & Otto Dressel and J D Kestner in Germany – were stamping their dolls (usually just below the hairline on the back of the neck) with mould numbers and factory marks. French heads of this period are stamped SFBJ for Societé Française de Fabrication des Bébés et Jouets.

528

▲ *From left to right: the doll by J D Kestner, mould number 192, has a partially closed mouth and sleeping eyes; Simon & Halbig doll with a partially closed mouth and sleeping eyes, dressed in white voile with pink ribbon;*

TOYS & GAMES

Kammer & Reinhardt small doll with a broderie anglaise bonnet and satin slippers; Simon & Halbig doll in lilac costume and matching hat has an open mouth with moulded teeth and sleeping eyes with real lashes; *large Simon & Halbig doll; small Kestner doll with a closed mouth dressed in a long pink frock and matching hat in the style at the turn of the 20th century.*

COLLECTABLES

ALTHOUGH DOLLS TENDED to be modelled as adult women for the first half of the 19th century, more child-like models were preferred by their customers, and these became the norm towards the end of the century. The beginning of the 20th century saw the ascendancy of the baby doll, which continued throughout the century until the introduction of dress-up character dolls, such as Barbie, after World War II.

530

In Germany, in the early 1900s, modellers who were tired of making the same sweet-faced, serene doll began to make heads with scowling, pouting or sad faces, eventually exploring the whole range of childish emotions. The first 'character' doll to be marketed was Kammer & Reinhardt's mould number 100, Baby, which also had a bent-limbed composition body.

The success of this doll inspired other firms to follow suit, while Kammer & Reinhardt expanded their range, giving each new doll a name. These are among the most collectable of German dolls. Other firms – including Gebrüder Heubach, who made a wider range of character dolls than any other firm – made non-European character dolls in black and brown bisque.

▲ *Most dolls tended to come dressed for bed in nightcap and gown, or wearing long cotton frocks, but this character doll, model 260 by J D Kestner, steps out in an orange top coat.*

▶ *From left to right: George Borgfeldt toddler, model 327, was made around 1920. The head was modelled by Armand Marseille, a Russian emigré who was the most prolific dollmaker of the late 19th and early 20th centuries; Kammer and Reinhardt mould 122 of c.1912 has a fully articulated composition body and sleeping eyes; Gebrüder Heubach model 7671 is very rare. Few were made, and fewer have survived – produced in 1910, this negro baby model is unusual in having moulded hair and intaglio eyes with painted highlights, rather than glass ones. The composition body has limbs bent into realistic positions and slightly closed hands for a more natural effect.*

TOYS & GAMES

COLLECTABLES

WHILE IT IS MOULD NUMBERS and appealing faces that usually catch the attention of the keen doll collector, original clothes are also important. French dolls tended to be fashionably dressed, but most turn-of-the-century dolls were sold in in pretty, simple cotton dresses or nightgowns, with perhaps a matching hat or nightcap.

Many collectors specialize in the children's or adult fashions of a particular time. Original costumes add value to a doll, but need more attention. They must, for example, be kept out of the sun lest the colours fade, the seams split and the fabric disintegrates. Silk and satin garments should never be washed. If a doll's costume is in a state of disrepair, it is acceptable to make a new outfits, although the remains of the original costume should be kept with the doll. Period fabrics and designs can be bought from specialist shops.

▼ Characterful expressions and colourful costumes make bisque dolls from around the beginning of the 20th century an enchanting subject for a collection, and a perennial reminder of earlier, perhaps more innocent times.

532

TOYS & GAMES

DOLLS' HOUSES

Dolls' houses often provide us with details of life and decorative styles in past times that would otherwise be lost. They were being built in Germany as early as the 16th century, although the oldest surviving example dates from 1611. These German – and later Dutch – houses were highly crafted, often made by cabinetmakers, and were made to commission for wealthy noblemen, complete with miniaturized pieces of furniture.

They were almost certainly never intended for child's play, although some may have been used to teach children about the workings of a great house; many of them were mounted on tables and stands out of a child's reach.

Only in the 18th and 19th centuries did dolls' houses come to be seen as playthings, although they remained the preserve of well-to-do families. A hinged front, carved, painted or (later) papered to resemble the frontage of a town house or country villa, opened to reveal a set of rooms in several stories, each decorated and supplied with the appropriate furniture.

This, along with the dolls and the majority of 19th-century houses, was likely to be made in Germany, but other countries produced their own.

It was only in the late-19th century that dolls' houses began to be mass-marketed. From the 1920s on, companies such as Tri-ang in Britain began to produce reproductions of 18th- and 19th-century dolls' houses, and these too have some value.

Many collectors, seeing genuine old dolls' houses priced out of their reach, go for these reproduction models and use them as a starting point for collecting old miniature furniture, ceramics, metalwork and other dolls' pieces.

A typical arrangement of rooms is shown in this reproduction of an early-19th-century dolls' town house. A central hall and stairs give on to a music room, bedroom, living room and kitchen, all decorated and furnished in the contemporary taste to make a perfect setting for a collection of well-made accessories.

Collectables
Teddy Bears

Among the most successful of all toys in the 20th century are teddy bears: nonexistent at its beginning, ubiquitous at its end. Today, high-quality bears from the early years of the century – which in practice means bears made in Germany – can fetch at auction prices normally associated with fine art, jewellery or silverware.

The invention of the teddy bear has long been disputed by claimants from Germany and the USA. It seems that the basically unlikely idea of making a cuddly toy out of a large, ferocious and carnivorous animal occurred to people in both countries at about the same time.

Morris Michtom, who founded the Ideal Toy company in America, made some bears about 1902, but none has survived, and most people now attribute this popular toy to the German toymaker Margarete Steiff. The first batch of a cuddly bear with moving limbs – based on drawings her nephew had made of bear cubs at Stuttgart zoo – was released in 1903. They were such a success that toymakers in Britain and the USA, as well as others in Germany, began copying them. One undisputed claim by Michtom is that he gave the new toy its name, from the US President, Theodore 'Teddy' Roosevelt who had famously declined to shoot a defenceless cub when bear-hunting in Mississippi. The fact that King Edward VII of England was an ursine man known as Teddy helped to establish the name.

Early bears are much more bear-like than the ones produced after World War I, with long muzzles, humps on their backs and sometimes a suggestion of claws on their hands and feet. They were usually made in mohair, with pads of leather, felt or plush and eyes of glass, or perhaps shoe-buttons. The limbs move at the hip and shoulder, and in early bears are sometimes jointed at the knee and

▲ *The relatively small size of this Steiff bear (generally, the best prices are fetched by bears more than 65cm tall) is offset, so far as its value is concerned, by its unusual multicoloured pelt. The fact that the paws have been repaired detracts a little from its value.*

◄ *A real-life skating bear, known as Alice Teddy, that was toured as a performer around the USA at the end of the 19th century, may have been the inspiration for this German-made mechanical bear on short skis or long skates.*

TOYS & GAMES

◄ *An attractive cinnamon-brown Steiff bear which is a relatively early model, made around 1904. It has a typical early Steiff nose, hand-stitched in brown thread.*

▶ *Made by Gebrüder Bing just before the outbreak of World War I, this clockwork mechanical bear can perform somersaults. Such models in working condition fetch high prices today.*

◄ *This German bear dates from 1915. It is already beginning to acquire the flatter facial profile typical of post-war bears.*

elbow. The stuffing material varied, but included wood shavings, sawdust, kapok, cork and straw. Most bears were golden, but some were brown, red or black. 'Growlers', which made a noise when the bear was tipped up, were introduced in 1908. Bears proved so popular that mechanical toymakers, such as Bing in Germany and Decamps in France, entered the market, producing bears that tumbled, played drums or rode bicycles. Bears from the 1920s and '30s are generally more affordable than earlier examples. They can be recognized by their flatter faces, short limbs and the lack of a hump. Rexine, an artificial leather, was increasingly used for the pads.

COLLECTABLES

STEIFF BEARS

536

THE STEIFF FACTORY began making animals in felt. Richard Steiff joined his aunt at the firm in 1897, and five years later he had designed a prototype teddy bear, the first of the firm's products to have movable limbs. The first Steiff bears were shown at the Leipzig toy fair in 1903 and were such a hit that the factory struggled at first to meet the demand; other firms filled the gap with their own bears. By 1907, at the peak of the craze for teddy bears in Europe and the USA, Steiff alone was turning out close to a million a year.

Early Steiff bears, particularly those in very good condition, are the great prizes in teddy bear collecting. They can be recognized by their general quality and, in particular, by their noses stitched in brown thread and long, articulated limbs: when they are put into a sitting position, their arms invariably reach the ground.

Early Steiff bears, such as this one, have a realistic profile, based on Richard Steiff's drawings of brown bear cubs at the Stuttgart zoo. They have a distinctly humped back and long muzzle. Even modern Steiff bears tend to have longer muzzles than most contemporary bears, which increasingly resemble furry baby dolls.

▲ *The Steiff button, in stamped metal, was registered as a trademark in 1905. Some buttons are impressed with the factory name; others are blank. Really early Steiff bears did not have these buttons, and many later ones lost them. The lack of a button in the ear does not mean a bear is not a Steiff.*

Compare these two more modern bears with the now conventional straight back and short muzzle. Left: Chad Valley bear c.1930; right: Dean's bear c. 1960.

TOYS & GAMES

A long muzzle ending in a hand-sewn nose is characteristic of all early Steiff bears.

The hump on early bears' backs, although anatomically correct, was fairly soon seen as detracting from the bear's appeal and was gradually dropped.

537

In another nod to realism, the paws of Steiff bears are supplied with long, ferocious-looking claws sewn with dark thread.

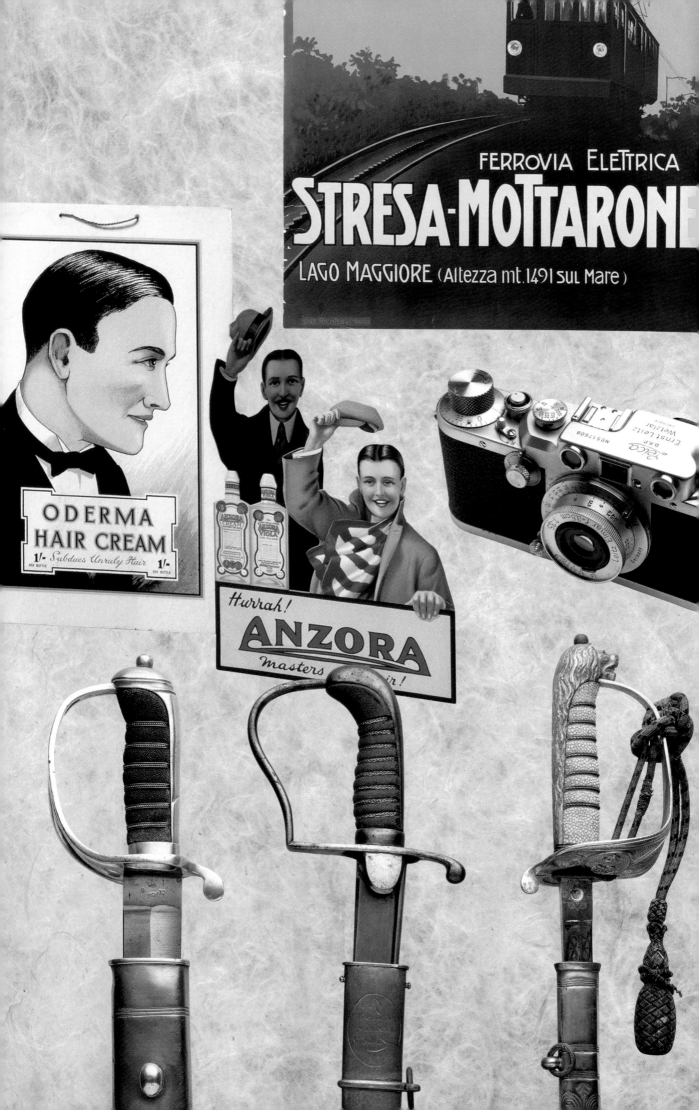

OTHER COLLECTIONS

COLLECTABLES

MILITARIA

540

THE HISTORY OF ARMS AND ARMOUR is much more than a series of technical improvements for killing, or protecting oneself from, the enemy. Another aspect of the armourer's craft was social, since he sought to make the most fashionable or impressive weapon or piece of armour for his wealthy or powerful client to exhibit. Indeed, purely decorative considerations were often more important than the lethal or protective function of the piece in question. Many kinds of armour or uniform were worn solely for parade or as a mark of rank, while court swords and small swords were rarely fighting weapons but a form of male adornment. Fine arms and armour can, therefore, be seen as works of art in their own right – and so highly collectable.

Laws governing the possession of the more modern kinds of firearms, particularly in the UK and parts of the Continent, can hamper the collector, while the finest arms and armour form a highly specialized international market. Still, there are still great opportunities for the more modest collector who is prepared to frequent the many arms fairs that now take place.

In theory, there is an enormous wealth of uniforms from the late 18th and 19th centuries, when it was finally borne in on generals that armour was useless against musketry and artillery, and armies began to be highly organized along regimental lines. In practice, however, old uniforms are harder to come by than weapons – being more difficult to preserve against moths and rot. Uniforms from 20th-century conflicts, are, however, relatively easy to find.

The basic clothing for 17th-century soldiers was a buff coat, made of cowhide. Soon various methods of discrimination, such as a coloured sash around the waist or a coloured plume, were introduced. Some regiments began to wear blue or scarlet coats, and by the end of the century the buff coat had the addition of coloured cloth across the chest, with matching cuffs. This led to identifying armies by colour. By the 18th century, most British

Opposite: early 19th-century English uniform with presentation sword. A fine example, with blade decoration and scabbard in good condition. The name and regiment of the owner are inscribed on the reverse side.

MILITARIA

COLLECTABLES

regiments had adopted scarlet with various colour facings, while the French wore predominantly blue and the Austrians white.

But armour did not die out immediately. A lieutenant of the Regiment de Cuirassiers in France in the early 19th century still wore a helmet and cuirass, which were of some value against edged cavalry weapons. French troops continued to wear this 'combination' uniform until 1914, as did troops in Russia, Prussia and Austria.

During World War I, almost all discrimination between regiments was abandoned on the field, and each army wore one identifiable colour – the British khaki, the French blue and the Germans grey.

542

Armour

Body armour was made not only of metal, but of linen, leather, silk, lacquer or bone. Padded, scale or mail armours were the most common in ancient times, and the jointed armour that makes up an entire 'suit' did not come into being until the late 14th and early 15th centuries.

But the era of the knight in full armour was to be comparatively short. Even by the mid-16th century, suits of overlapping plate armour were becoming less common and tended to be worn only for ceremony. Within another 100 years, it had become plain that no amount of body armour would shield the wearer from a well-aimed musket ball.

Some armour does survive from Renaissance times, but most of it is now in museums. In Britain, for example, the first truly collectable armour dates from the Civil War period (c.1640), and the odd pikeman's 'pot' helmet or breastplate can be found.

Headdress continued to be important and flamboyant well into the 19th and 20th centuries, and the most easily obtainable articles of armour tend to be helmets of all kinds. The English 3rd Dragoon Guards, for instance, wore helmets as early as the 17th century, and available helmets include the last pattern introduced in 1871, which has a red and black horsehair plume mounted on a finial, a regimental badge on the front of the helmet and a chain chinstrap.

Memorabilia of the German army are much sought after by collectors in Britain and America, and helmets are no exception. The helmets of the Prussian Garde du Corps, the elite heavy cavalry of the Kaiser, are particularly desirable. These were made of tombac (an alloy of zinc and copper) and, on full dress parade, the spiked finial was replaced by by a silver flying eagle. Such helmets can fetch considerable prices, with the not dissimilar infantryman's pickelhaube (spiked helmet) of World War I being perhaps more within the average collector's reach.

Real antique armour is impossibly expensive, but prints and engravings, such as this one of a 17th century German helmet, are easier to find.

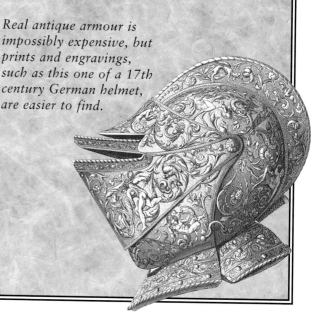

MILITARIA

FIREARMS

PRIMITIVE FIREARMS EXISTED as early as 1300, but it was not until the 17th century that firearms and artillery became the dominant weapons on the battlefield. The invention of the flintlock in France meant that firearms became increasingly reliable. All states then aspired to standardization of firearms for their armies, to rapidity of fire and to certainty of ammunition supply.

By the 15th century, the pistol had become not only a cavalry weapon but a favourite of the assassin and highwayman. Handguns such as the harquebus, caliver and musket became the mainstay of the infantry and helped to usher in the 'pike and shot' era from the mid-16th century. These weapons had matchlock and wheel-lock ignition systems.

The deadly effect of firearms fired from a good defensive position was a lesson that most European armies had learned by

▼ *.31 calibre Colt pocket percussion revolver, 1849 model, with underlever rammer, brass trigger-guard and wooden hand-grip. This example comes in its original box, complete with tools and cleaning instructions.*

A COLLECTOR'S GUIDE TO ANTIQUES

COLLECTABLES

the 18th century. Breech-loaders existed even in the 16th century, but were not particularly successful. The new industrial era of the late 18th and 19th centuries not only put the breech-loader back on the agenda but also made rifling of the bore more common, allowing bullets to be spun in flight for greater accuracy. Percussion ignition systems took over from flint and steel, and finally solid single-piece cartridges, rather than ball and powder, became the norm.

Another big area of development was multi-shot weapons. The earliest efforts concentrated on multiple barrels or superimposed loads in the same barrel. One of the first practical alternatives was the revolver, which lined up new charges successively behind the barrel. The great age of the revolver was the mid-19th century, when gunsmiths such as Elisha Collier, Samuel Colt and John and Robert Adams vied with each other to improve design.

Automatic and semi-automatic fire were the last major hurdles to be crossed. In the Gatling, a series of barrels was revolved in conjunction with a feed mechanism. But truly automatic fire came only with the Maxim gun in the 1880s.

Collectors' curios include the pepperbox pistol, an early form of revolver made from about 1850, which has several revolving barrels, allowing the hammer to strike afresh each time the trigger is squeezed. Another strange weapon is the blunderbuss, a favourite for self-defence from the 1670s to the 1840s, after which it was superseded by the more effective pistols and shotguns. The wide muzzle was designed for easy loading on a bucking coach or a pitching ship.

▲ *Pepperbox chambers –
the six notched chambers of
a pepperbox revolver.*

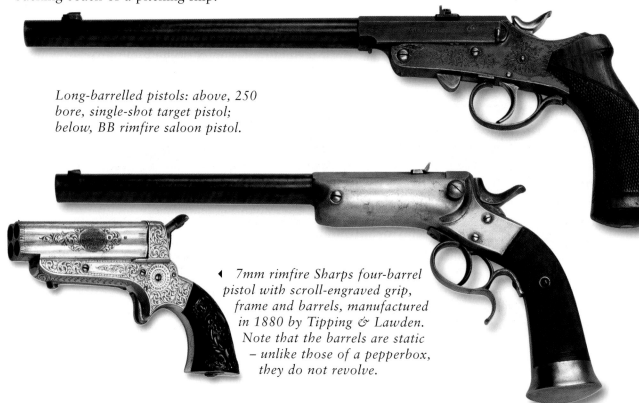

*Long-barrelled pistols: above, 250
bore, single-shot target pistol;
below, BB rimfire saloon pistol.*

◀ *7mm rimfire Sharps four-barrel
pistol with scroll-engraved grip,
frame and barrels, manufactured
in 1880 by Tipping & Lawden.
Note that the barrels are static
– unlike those of a pepperbox,
they do not revolve.*

MILITARIA

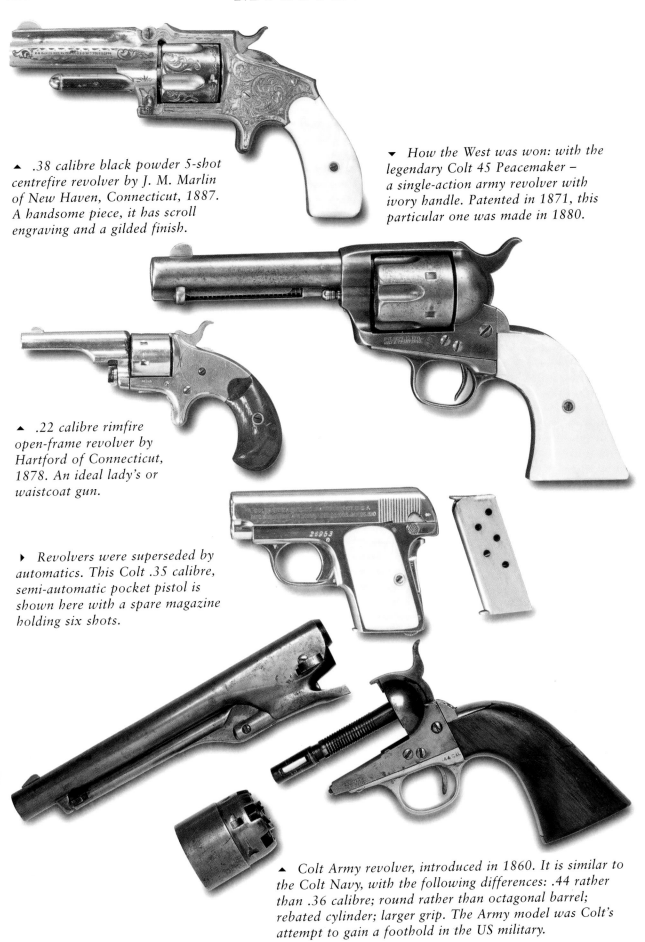

▲ .38 calibre black powder 5-shot centrefire revolver by J. M. Marlin of New Haven, Connecticut, 1887. A handsome piece, it has scroll engraving and a gilded finish.

▼ How the West was won: with the legendary Colt 45 Peacemaker – a single-action army revolver with ivory handle. Patented in 1871, this particular one was made in 1880.

545

▲ .22 calibre rimfire open-frame revolver by Hartford of Connecticut, 1878. An ideal lady's or waistcoat gun.

▸ Revolvers were superseded by automatics. This Colt .35 calibre, semi-automatic pocket pistol is shown here with a spare magazine holding six shots.

▲ Colt Army revolver, introduced in 1860. It is similar to the Colt Navy, with the following differences: .44 rather than .36 calibre; round rather than octagonal barrel; rebated cylinder; larger grip. The Army model was Colt's attempt to gain a foothold in the US military.

COLLECTABLES

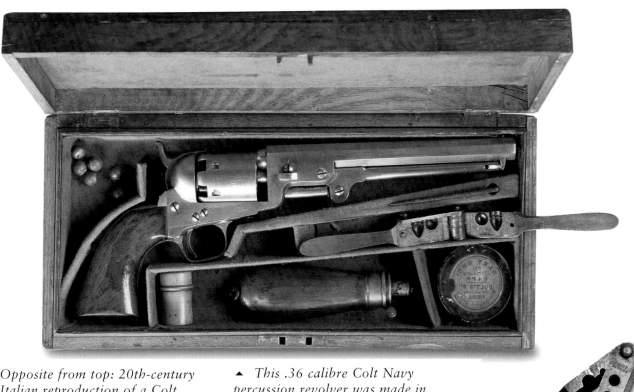

Opposite from top: 20th-century Italian reproduction of a Colt Navy revolver; 1878 Colt .45 Peacemaker Centre Fire model – also known as a Single-Action Army revolver manufactured in 1855; the Colt .36 Navy was one of Colt's best known guns; .31 calibre Colt Pocket revolver, 1849, similar in design to the Colt Navy.

▲ This .36 calibre Colt Navy percussion revolver was made in 1856. It is a single-action firearm – that is, it has to be cocked before each shot. The chambers hold five shots, which can be lead bullets or spherical lead shot. The 16cm barrel is octagonal. Also in the case are: underlever rammer for clearing chambers; bullet mould, for DIY bullets; tin of percussion caps; powder flask; and wooden box for spare striking pins.

▲ Colt-patented bullet mould.

▶ These flasks – shaped like bags – were used for storing gunpowder.

▲ Colt Army revolver.

◀ Tin of percussion caps – they explode when struck.

COLLECTABLES

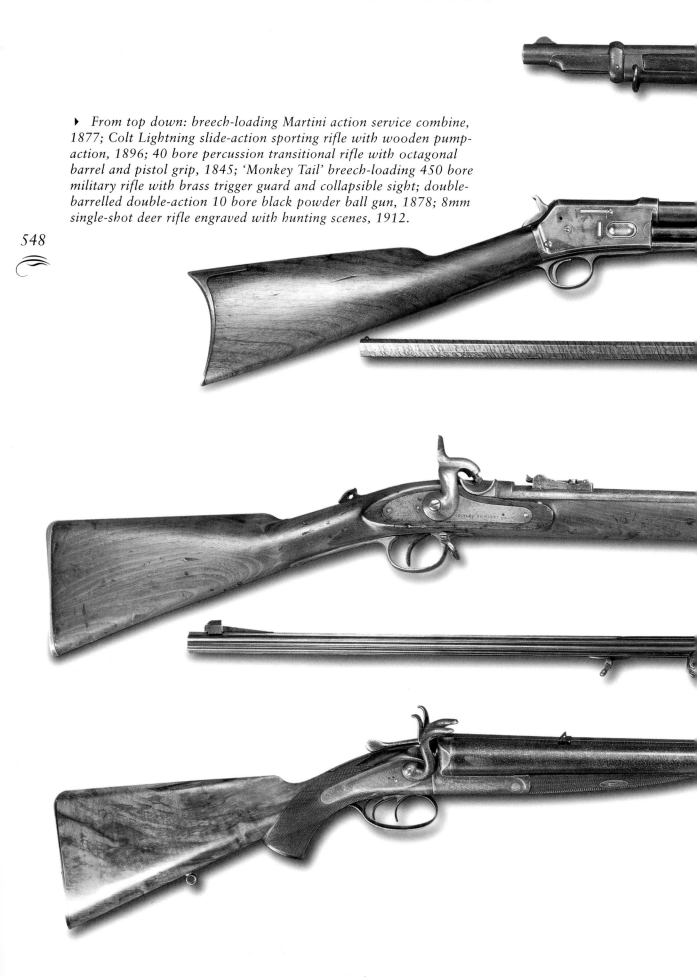

▶ *From top down: breech-loading Martini action service combine, 1877; Colt Lightning slide-action sporting rifle with wooden pump-action, 1896; 40 bore percussion transitional rifle with octagonal barrel and pistol grip, 1845; 'Monkey Tail' breech-loading 450 bore military rifle with brass trigger guard and collapsible sight; double-barrelled double-action 10 bore black powder ball gun, 1878; 8mm single-shot deer rifle engraved with hunting scenes, 1912.*

COLLECTABLES

◀ *Double-action hammers, set up to fire both pinfire and centrefire cartridges. The hammers are shaped like dolphins.*

550

▶ *A woodland scene featuring hinds and a fawn has been engraved on the action of this deer rifle.*

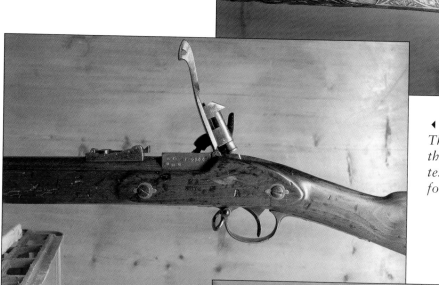

◀ *'Monkey-tail' lever. The proof marks show that the gun has been tested and declared safe for use.*

▶ *Carved stock on a German deer rifle, depicting a hunter in lederhosen and plumed hat.*

MILITARIA

BLADED WEAPONS

551

IN THE MIDDLE AGES, the sword acquired considerable symbolic power, which was reflected in offices of state as well as in art and literature. Considerable diversity existed. Knives and hangars were developed for the hunt, and curved swords from the East began to influence the mainstream of European design. Changes in fencing techniques in the 16th century also had considerable effect on the style of swords. The use of the point became more important than the edge, so swords became longer and narrower. By the middle of the 15th century, the addition of extra guards had become fashionable (the familiar long rapier is really a development of these hilts).

Great care and ingenuity went into the decoration of swords, especially since they were regarded by the aristocracy as items of costume jewellery. Hilts were chiselled and pierced, damascened in gold, made from precious metals and set with stone, and even at the time were expensive items. As with armour, some of the best artists produced designs for hilts. Those by artists working in the 'mannerist' style must have been extremely difficult to make in steel, and so were reserved for parade or state occasions. Distinctive patterns of sword came to be identified with different types of troop or the officers of different regiments. Styles of sword could distinguish a police officer from a courtier, or a general from a customs man.

The bayonet is arguably the most important post-medieval edged weapon, for both defence and attack. Arranged in squares, with bayonets pointing outwards, infantry could resist charging cavalry, while the bayonet charge could also be decisive at the climax of the 18th- and 19th-century battle.

In Britain before 1780 there was little standardization of military swords, since colonels of regiments were allowed to procure their own, to their own designs. But British patterns that date from 1788 can be collected, and the patterns for 1796, carried throughout the Napoleonic Wars, are much sought after. Officers were traditionally furnished with patterns to suit their mode of warfare – straight blades for the heavy cavalry, slightly curved for light infantry, slender, straight swords for the infantry. Officers' swords carry beautiful 'blued' and gilded designs on the blades – flowering tendrils and sometimes a standing or mounted

◄ *Pioneer's sword with serrated top edge. English and German soldiers used it to chop wood.*

COLLECTABLES

▲ *Royal cypher on English army sword – 'VR', denoting the reign of Victoria.*

military figure. These lavishly decorated weapons are very valuable today; infantry officers' swords with plain blades, on the other hand, can be found for more modest sums.

All Third Reich militaria is popular at arms fairs, and dress daggers are no exception. The more common army, navy and air force types can be bought for reasonable prices, depending on condition. Rarer examples, which include the daggers of the SS Honour, Railway Protection Force, Diplomatic Corps and Technical Emergency Corps, now command considerable sums.

Though many Europeans obtained swords during World War II from captured Japanese officers, these were usually mass produced and are relatively common. Much more valuable are Japanese swords from before 1867, when the Emperor banned the wearing of samurai swords in public. Because of the complex method of steel-making involved, Japanese swords had a reputation for quality that no other edged weapon can match. Though many Shinto blades can be found, any sword dating from before the 14th century fetches huge sums.

▼ *British military swords. Left: George V naval officer's sword with shark-skin handle and coppered-gilt guard; centre: '1796 Pattern' Light Cavalry sabre, 1830s. The P-shaped knuckle-bow is characteristic, the pipe-backed blade less so; right: heavy cavalry sword with brass hilt in triple-bar design and black fish-skin handle bound in gilt-wire wrap.*

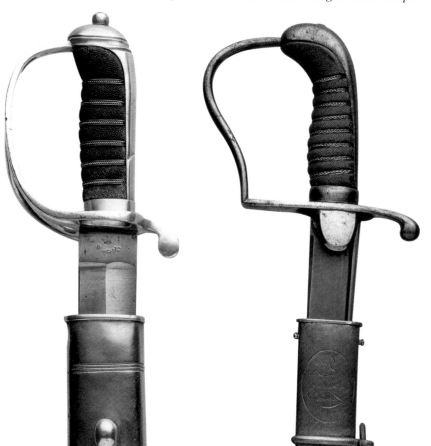

MILITARIA

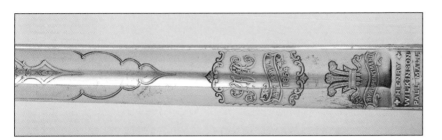

◀ *Wilkinson sword of 1854. The sword cutler's name is impressed on the blade.*

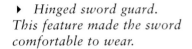

▶ *Hinged sword guard. This feature made the sword comfortable to wear.*

553

◀ *The script (see close-up detail) on this highly decorated Indian sword is a prayer to God.*

COLLECTABLES

554

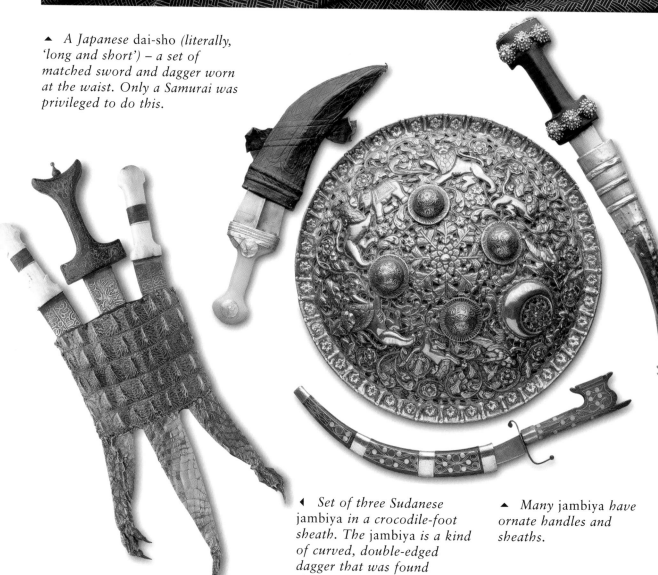

▲ *A Japanese* dai-sho *(literally, 'long and short') – a set of matched sword and dagger worn at the waist. Only a Samurai was privileged to do this.*

◄ *Set of three Sudanese* jambiya *in a crocodile-foot sheath. The* jambiya *is a kind of curved, double-edged dagger that was found throughout the Islamic world.*

▲ *Many* jambiya *have ornate handles and sheaths.*

MILITARIA
MEDALS

▲ *The Victoria Cross, one of the highest British awards for gallantry. This one is a reproduction.*

▼ *Victoria Cross poster, commemorating acts of bravery in battle.*

T HERE ARE THREE TYPES OF MEDAL: commemorative medals, celebrating a ruler or event; campaign medals, relating to a particular military operation; and medals for gallantry.
The modern history of medals begins in the Renaissance, when the artists Pisanello and Dürer, as well as the great goldsmith Benevenuto Cellini, all designed highly attractive pieces. But the 19th century saw the introduction of medals for purely military purposes. First, Napoleon commissioned his metalworkers to produce campaign medals for his veterans (which are now in great demand), and later, English artists such as William Gilbert, Sir Edward Poynter and William Wyon all turned their hand to military medal design.

Campaign medals awarded to any fighting man who took part in the two world wars are now obtainable for low prices, but gallantry medals command much higher sums. The first campaign medal to be awarded to all ranks in Britain was for the battle of Waterloo, issued in 1816. Throughout Queen Victoria's

555

▼ *Governments award medals for services to their country, whether it be for bravery in action, sporting achievements, or discoveries.*

COLLECTABLES

reign, medals were awarded for various wars in Africa, India and the Crimea – when the Victoria Cross was instituted to become the highest award for valour. The first Victoria Cross was awarded in June 1857, and to date 1351 have been awarded, including one with three bars. Until World War I, the metal for the medal came from a captured Russian cannon, thereafter from a Chinese gun.

In the 20th century, the equivalent medal for bravery in Germany was the Iron Cross, in France the Croix de Guerre and in America the Purple Heart.

556

▼ *Coast Life Saving Corps long service medal.*

▲ *Selection of Victorian campaign medals for campaigns in Burma, India and elsewhere.*

MILITARIA

TRENCH ART

MOST MEMORABILIA PRODUCED DURING World War I originated on the home front. Nonetheless, the soldiers in the trenches also filled in time between shelling and gas attacks to create poignant keepsakes from the chaos that surrounded them.

There was certainly no shortage of scrap metal to work with – pieces of shrapnel, spent bullets and brass shell casings. Broken rifle butts and pieces of duckboard also supplied wood carvers with plenty of raw material. But most examples of trench art found today tend to be metal pieces. Shell cases were made into pots and vases and ashtrays, while bullets were often turned into cigarette lighters. Models or pieces of sculpture were also fashioned from shrapnel splinters.

Trench art pieces still turn up periodically in sales rooms, specialist shops and even flea markets. It should be added that trench art is one of the few areas of collecting where condition is immaterial to price. Crude welding and the odd dent are often regarded as evidence that the piece is genuine.

557

▼ *Examples of trench art. Clockwise from top left: an old shell case transformed into a wine bottle holder and pourer; shell case vase – one of a pair – showing the defeated German eagle being trampled by the victorious French cockerel; a letter opener made from a cartridge case.*

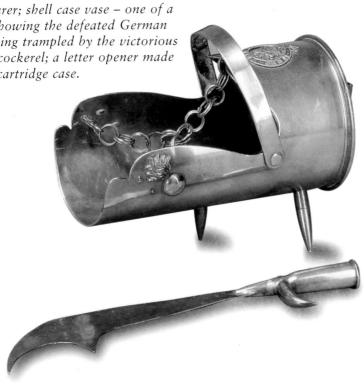

COLLECTABLES
SPORTING
EQUIPMENT

O VER RECENT YEARS, THERE has been a huge rise in interest in old sporting equipment, with articles for tennis, golf, snooker and fishing being the most sought after.

Tennis equipment worth looking for includes early wooden racquets dating from the 1920s and '30s. Those with racquet presses are likely to be more collectable than those without, and their 'cat gut' strings are also likely to be better preserved. As far as fishing equipment is concerned, it is undoubtedly in the field

558

▸ *Golf club with hand-made, mid-Victorian wooden head, hickory shaft and suede-wrapped handle. The head joint is of the older 'scared' (i.e. spliced) kind.*

▸ *A racing ordinary penny-farthing bicycle. These are usually thought to be museum pieces, but can sometimes be found in antique shops, usually in need of restoration.*

SPORTING EQUIPMENT

▸ *Golf balls are very collectable. Feathery balls are rare, and often damaged; gutta-percha ones are easier to come by.*

559

of trout and salmon fishing that collecting is most worthwhile. Reels, artificial flies, cane rods and other items such as nets and creels from the 19th and early 20th centuries can all be found in antiques shops and at auctions. Brass reels are at the most expensive end of the market, with reels made before the 1950s being the most collectable. Makers' names to watch out for are the British makers Hardy, Farlow and Ustonson. Rods are much less sought after than reels and usually sell for lower prices, although trimmings such as brass handles obviously enhance the value.

Golf equipment is also eagerly collected by enthusiasts. Although 19th-century golf clubs are expensive, those from the early 20th century are still reasonably priced, being mass-produced and factory forged. Golf balls of this period, usually made of gutta-percha, are also relatively easy to come by. Early balls tended to be smooth, until it was found that dimpled balls flew better. More rare are caddy bags, which were usually made of leather stretched over a wooden frame.

▸ *Early keep-fit equipment. Some early rowing machines had spring-loaded handgrips. Indian clubs were the predecessors of modern weights.*

COLLECTABLES

HUNTING & FISHING

Above from top: early 'wheel-lock' rifle, c.1630; double-barrelled flintlock rifle, c.1800. The flintlock mechanism was less cumbersome than the wheel-lock; Colt .38 calibre. Lightning, 1870; Colt 10 bore double-barrelled shotgun, 1870 – the kind used to protect the passengers on a stagecoach journey; Colt, .44 calibre Lightning Carbine – among the firearms given to the Irish Rangers by the Guinness family during the Boer War.

AMONG SHOOTING ACCESSORIES must be listed guns, binoculars and decoy ducks for duck shooting. Nineteenth-century sporting percussion guns and rifles are often overlooked in favour of more expensive 18th-century flintlock fowling pieces. Single-barrel shotguns were used mainly by farmers to shoot vermin and meat for the pot, and the lighter British sporting rifles are also quite rare because shotguns were usually used for small game. The best sporting, or Jager rifles, were made in Germany, notably by gun-makers in Suhl. An 8-mm single-shot deer rifle dating from 1912 and made by F.W. Kessler of Suhl, for example, has a beautiful engraved stock and a fluted steel barrel inlaid with silver. Such guns tend to be available at most reputable antique and specialist dealers, as well as at the occasional auction house.

The hunter would go out for the day taking a range of specialist accessories with him. Foremost among these would have been binoculars. Those dating from the 19th and early 20th century generally had brass barrels and, perhaps, a leather covering. A pair of antique binoculars will be more valuable if it comes complete with its original leather carrying case, which must itself be in good condition, with a working buckle.

Sporting Equipment

▼ *By the end of the 19th century, salmon reels were most commonly made of wood. The brass reel with ivory handle is earlier.*

▲ *Wet salmon flies – much prized by the fisherman, who would store them in a wallet or tin to prevent the dressings from being crushed. From humble beginnings in 1725, the salmon fly evolved into a highly decorative piece. Often, up to 30 different materials were used in the construction of a single fly.*

561

Decoys

Superbly lifelike wooden decoys dating from the 1800s and 1900s have recently soared in price. Indeed, simple working decoys from the 19th century are regarded as valuable folk art. The wooden shape was primed with water-resistant resin and then painted with ordinary household gloss paint thinned with petrol. It might have been allowed to dry outside in damp conditions to eradicate shine and make it look more realistic. North America was and is the source of most decoys, and it is here that their collection has become widespread.

It is still possible to find examples of decoys in Europe, but collecting early decoys can be expensive in a market lucrative enough to attract a significant number of counterfeits. On the other hand, great interest in decorative decoys has led many talented amateur carvers to take up the hobby. Buying a modern decoy might, therefore, be a good investment for the future.

◀ *Selection of decoy birds. Genuine 19th-century decoys can fetch a high price if they still have their original paint. All of the birds here were probably made for hunting. They are made from painted tin or wood, and include both floating and 'stick-up' models of ducks, pigeons, an ibis and other small shore birds.*

COLLECTABLES
TRAVEL

THE YEARS BETWEEN THE TWO world wars in the 20th century saw the beginning of international travel on a large scale. It was an age when the great cruise liners sailed the oceans, airline companies began to establish regular routes around the world, and luxury trains like the Orient Express rushed through the European countryside.

Foremost among collectables from this period are travel posters. Poster designs were often highly dramatic, even abstract, and drew on Art Deco's love of basic geometric shapes and acute viewpoints. A typical travel poster of the 1930s features a single large image, such as a looming cruise ship framed by solid blue ocean, or a steam engine thundering towards the spectator, and the appropriate slogan in a striking typeface. Some poster artists, such as Cassandre and Charles Dickson, are much in demand, while transport buffs tend to inflate the price of posters featuring steam engines or aeroplanes. This golden age of posters was ended by World War II and the widespread use of photographic images. Most old posters are sold mounted on linen, which may preserve them to some extent, but careful inspection is always needed before buying.

▼ *A well-stocked picnic hamper would include everything from crockery and cutlery to a teapot and burner.*

▼ *For the early motorist a spare can of petrol was a necessity, since garages were few and far between. This one is c.1920.*

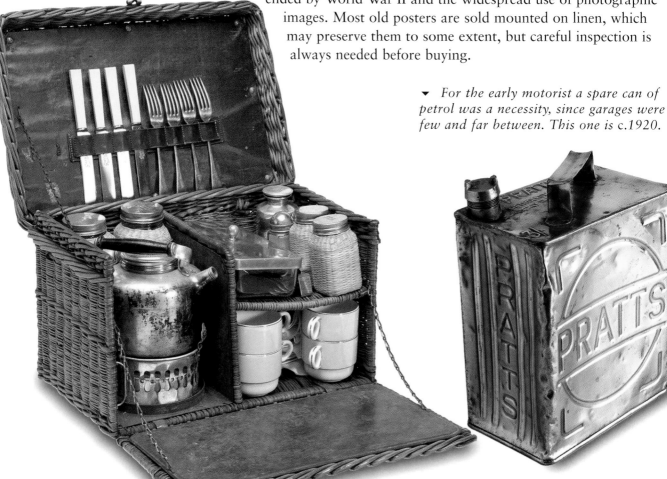

TRAVEL

While posters tend to be the most common target for collectors in the travel field, luggage also makes up a small but important subcategory. This was an era before the hurly-burly of mass travel: well-heeled cosmopolitan men and women travelled in style. This meant, in part, attention to luggage of a quality that would be near unthinkable today. Fine leather trunks and cases were ordered from one of the great luggage-makers of the time – Aspreys of London, Hermes of Paris or Oshkosh of Minnesota. Louis Vuitton, perhaps the greatest of luggage-maker of them all, had outlets in both Paris and London. Vuitton's pieces are now very expensive, but examples from less well known makers are much easier to find and are still relatively cheap.

563

▲ *Driving licence issued to one Dr John Robert Mitchell Collie by the County of London. Licences had to be renewed every 12 months.*

◄ *Horse's head motoring mascot.*

▶ *The most famous motoring mascot of all time, the Spirit of Ecstasy, introduced by Rolls Royce in 1910. This bronze example is unusual; most pre-1914 models were silver plated.*

▶ *The overlapping 'A's of the Automobile Association logo made their début around 1906. AA telephone boxes were marked with signs like the one on the left (1920s) – the glass balls acted as reflectors, for night-time visibility. The badge on the right (1914) was displayed on the car bonnet.*

COLLECTABLES

◀ Speed, power and the thrill of travel – all conveyed by the single image of a speeding train in this 1930s travel poster. The original poster has been cut down and mounted on linen.

564

▲ This poster for the Blue Funnel line evokes the dream holiday – a serene cruise through calm blue waters in exotic climes.

◀ A potent cocktail of technology and scenic beauty in this poster by Richter & Co of Naples. The subject is an electric railway in the Alps above Lake Maggiore.

TRAVEL

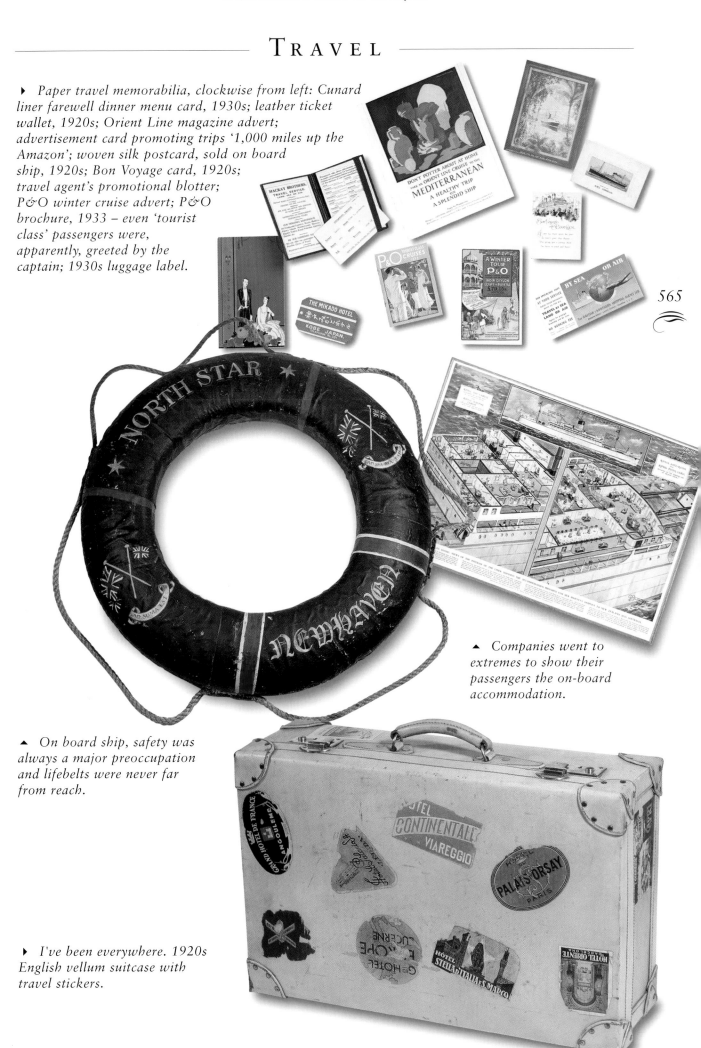

▶ *Paper travel memorabilia, clockwise from left: Cunard liner farewell dinner menu card, 1930s; leather ticket wallet, 1920s; Orient Line magazine advert; advertisement card promoting trips '1,000 miles up the Amazon'; woven silk postcard, sold on board ship, 1920s; Bon Voyage card, 1920s; travel agent's promotional blotter; P&O winter cruise advert; P&O brochure, 1933 – even 'tourist class' passengers were, apparently, greeted by the captain; 1930s luggage label.*

565

▲ *Companies went to extremes to show their passengers the on-board accommodation.*

▲ *On board ship, safety was always a major preoccupation and lifebelts were never far from reach.*

▶ *I've been everywhere. 1920s English vellum suitcase with travel stickers.*

COLLECTABLES

RADIOS

▲ *A remarkable technical breakthrough, this battery-operated Pye Model M78F, launched in 1948, was the first portable radio. The elegant black and cream case is in perspex.*

B EFORE THE ADVENT OF television, radio was the chief source of family entertainment. The cumbersome crystal set, which needed the help of earphones and a long aerial, was used at first, but this was gradually replaced in the 1920s by the more efficient valve set.

At first, valve radios resembled free-standing pieces of furniture, disguised in the fashion of the time by Jacobean- and Tudor-style cabinets. By the early 1930s, however, they were more likely to be contained in sleek, modernist-style tabletop

▶ *Ekco Radiogram, 1932 – a new development of the time housing radio and gramophone in the same cabinet.*

▼ *1930s 'Stand Up' radio by Murphy – designed as much as a piece of furniture as a radio.*

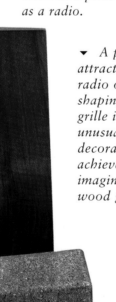

▼ *A particularly attractive Lisson radio of 1932. The shaping of the grille is most unusual, as is the decorative effect achieved by the imaginative use of wood graining.*

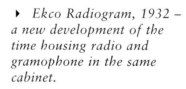

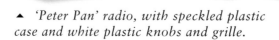

▲ *'Peter Pan' radio, with speckled plastic case and white plastic knobs and grille.*

RADIOS

cabinets made of mahogany, oak, walnut or plywood. The radio's speaker was protected from dust by a fabric cover, and this in turn was protected by a grille. The grille in particular gave leading designers ample opportunity to experiment with decoration. McMichael radios adopted the simple rayed sunrise motif that has proved popular even until recent times, while the grilles of other radios featured stylized trees, parallel lines and zigzags. The Ekco AD65 of Wells Coates, one of the first radios to feature the malleable properties of bakelite in its stylings, is just one of the classics of the period, and now fetches considerable sums.

567

▲ *Addison Model 2, 1940. Manufactured in Canada, it was available in a wide range of colour combinations.*

Many old, second-hand radios can still be picked up for reasonable prices on market stalls, at antiques fairs or from dealers specializing in the interwar period. Besides Ekco, other manufacturer's names to look out for are Lotus, Pye and Murphy. Before buying a second-hand radio, always check the veneer – scratches and cracks will reduce its future value.

▲ *Emerson Midget, 1937. Made in wood with an attractive maple veneer, this model featured green bakelite inlay and black knobs.*

◄ *'The Dalek' – the nickname given to this bright red Kloster-Brandes B.M. 20 model radio. Bright colours proved unpopular with the consumer.*

COLLECTABLES

JUKEBOXES

A LTHOUGH ASSOCIATED IN the public mind with the rock 'n' roll years of the 1950s, the true golden age of jukeboxes (coin-operated electric phonographs containing a stack of records) was in fact the Big Band and Swing era of the 1930s and '40s. The top manufacturers – Seeburg, AMI, Wurlitzer and Rock-Ola – were constantly on the lookout for new gimmicks to attract customers. While early 1930s boxes had simple wood-veneer cabinets, Wurlitzer's Model 24 introduced the use of back-lit moulded plastic; it proved enormously popular and soon every manufacturer used plastic and coloured lights on their cabinets. By contrast, the 1950's jukeboxes were sleek metal plastic designs that took their inspiration from the styling of contemporary motor cars. Along with some of the earlier machines, these rock 'n' roll boxes now command stiff prices. For the first-time collector, boxes from the 1960s may be both easier to find and easier on the pocket.

Most of the 'classics' offered for sale in Europe today have been imported fairly recently by specialist dealers. Second-hand jukeboxes tend to have been well used, and there is likely to be wear and tear on their cabinets. But this does not affect the price overmuch, since even missing pieces can be restored. Always insist on hearing a jukebox in action before buying.

◄ *Belgian manufacturer Van Den Eynde produced this Discophonette in the 1950s. Unusually, it has a radio mounted in the top of the cabinet, to provide an alternative to gramophone records.*

JUKEBOXES

◄ After World War II there was a brief boom in jukebox sales which stimulated the growth of new companies, many of which enjoyed a brief period of profitability before going out of business. One such was Filben, whose futuristic Maestro model, with its rippled glass front and visor-like speaker grille, is pictured here.

▲ It is relatively easy to find jukeboxes from the late 1950s and early 1960s, so these models tend to be less expensive than earlier ones.

▲ With its top-mounted speaker and a mechanism capable of playing both sides of ten records, the AMI Singing Towers of 1939 was an innovative design. The painted wood cabinet has a sleek, metallic look.

▸ Seeburg Symphonola from 1939, noted for its exceptional sound quality rather than for innovative cabinet design.

COLLECTABLES

CAMERAS

I N THE 19TH CENTURY, PHOTOGRAPHY was a largely mysterious process practised by professionals. With the invention of the relatively easy-to-use hand-held camera, however, it became a hobby enjoyed by millions of amateurs.

There is a huge range of collectables in the classic camera field, so collectors tend to specialize. Some concentrate on one marque, such as Leica or Nikon; others search for special items such as detective cameras or tiny spy cameras, known as subminiatures.

Whereas antique cameras were encased in wood and leather and had brass fittings, in the interwar period cameras with all-metal cases, sometimes trimmed with leather, were introduced by Eastman. This quickly became the norm, just as the norm of the modern camera tends to be a steel casing with leather and chrome fittings.

570

▼ *'Butcher's Little Nipper' - more formally known as the Hütting Aviso box camera, made around 1903.*

CAMERAS

▶ *This Ernemann camera, c1906, was known as 'The Bob'. It focused by means of bellows on brass tracks.*

Classic cameras are collected worldwide. Plate cameras from the 19th and early 20th centuries tend to be expensive and are rarely seen except at auction. But later examples, such as the Art Deco styled models of the 1930s and the high-quality 35mm cameras of the post-war period, can be picked up for reasonable prices and form the largest market. Classic cameras can be found at specialist dealers, auctions or antique shops, and in general worn or damaged bodies will affect price.

571

▾ *The Victory bellows camera employed a bulb shutter release to minimise camera shake.*

◀ *Klein Mentor, 1908 - a single lens reflex camera with the viewfinder on top.*

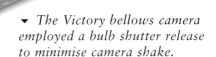

▲ *A roller blind shutter fitted over the front of the lens adapted an older camera to faster film.*

▶ *Once the invention of the gelatine dry-plate with its short exposure times had made hand-held cameras a practical reality, there was a brief vogue for so-called detective cameras – that is, for cameras that were disguised not to look like cameras. The point of this was that it enabled you to catch your subjects unawares. This example is encased in leather. Others were disguised in parcels, books, watches, hats or even pistols.*

COLLECTABLES

◄ Beau Brownie with two-tone deco
styling, early 1930s. The rose colour
is more sought after than blue,
green, black or tan.

572

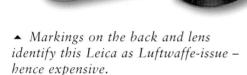

▲ Kodak folding plate camera, c1920.
Expensive in its day, it was more
advanced than the popular box models.

▲ Markings on the back and lens
identify this Leica as Luftwaffe-issue –
hence expensive.

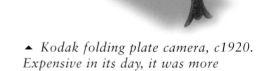

▲ The IIIc, a classic 1940s Leica. In
post-war specimens, the chrome is of
better quality, so they tend, like this one,
to remain in better condition.

◄ Nikon F, the first single lens reflex model
from Nikon – introduced in 1959. This
example was made in the mid-1960s.

CAMERAS

▸ Victorian and Edwardian amateur photographers often attained very high standards, as can be seen by leafing through photo albums of the period.

573

◂ When cameras could be made small enough to be portable, they started to be designed with collapsible parts to make them easier to carry. Camera cases were introduced around the same time.

▸ Miniature bellows camera, early 20th century. The original case increases its value.

◂ Mahogany plate holders with brass detailing. They are in three sizes: whole, half and quarter plate.

◂ Set of brass lenses by Taylor and Hobson, c.1900.

▸ Late 19th-century solid brass Watkins light meter.

COLLECTABLES
THEATRE & FILM MEMORABILIA

574

▼ *A selection of sheet music covers. In all cases but one ('Rock the Cradle, John'), the main focus is on the performer with whom the song was associated rather than the song itself.*

ILLUSTRATED SHEET-MUSIC COVERS and photographic postcards of old music hall and theatre stars offer the collector a fascinating insight into the bygone days of entertainment. On most of these postcards, the images were genuine photographic prints, with fine, crisp detail. Such portraits of the stars of the late 1800s and early 1900s are easy to find on stalls in antiques markets and at collectors' fairs, and are surprisingly inexpensive. Among the more sought-after performers are Sarah Bernhardt, Marie Lloyd, Musidora, Lily Langtry, Isadora Duncan, Josephine Baker and Mistinguett.

Collecting autographed letters and photographs – particularly those associated with the golden age of Hollywood in the 1920s and '30s – has become increasingly popular in recent years. Literally millions of signed photographs were sent to fans all over the world, and these form the basis of collections today. Bear in mind, though, that not all of them were signed by the stars themselves – film studios often employed skilled draughtsmen to copy their signatures. The value of showbiz autographs varies according to rarity, condition and fashion.

THEATRE & FILM

▲ *Selection of music covers and theatrical postcards summoning up some of the hit songs and hit performers of Victorian and Edwardian theatre and music hall. Such items are relatively inexpensive.*

Memorabilia from the golden days of Hollywood, such as these signed studio portraits, are highly collectable.

COLLECTABLES

THEATRE & FILM

Best Dishes Walt Disney

◄ An early, signed sketch of Mickey Mouse, drawn by his creator, Walt Disney, in 1934. Not surprisingly, this is a highly sought-after collector's item.

◄ Hollywood memorabilia ranges from sultry promotional portraits of the stars to cartoon character merchandise in a variety of materials – including wood, ceramic, tinplate and rubber.

▶ Plaster statue of Rita Heyworth in somewhat risqué pose, produced in the 1930s, at the start of her career. Hollywood executives spotted her as a dancer in a Mexican club; the rest is history.

Collectables

Advertising

▼ *Selection of food packaging, displayed in its natural setting on original grocers' shelves. The tea chest in the centre is hand painted.*

ADVERTISING POSTERS HAVE BEEN in existence since the 18th century. The first examples were hand-printed and simply provided the names and prices of products. By the start of the 19th century, however, improved printing methods meant that posters could be mass produced and they became increasingly sophisticated in content, although it was not until the 1890s that they included illustrations. When illustrations were introduced, they ranged from simple line drawings to full-colour images.

By the 1920s and '30s, advertising had become big business, and the public was bombarded with advertisements designed by the top illustrators of the day. Advertising experts stated baldly that if a poster that could not be absorbed in two seconds flat, it

Advertising

Adverting styles tend to be redolent of the period, as for example the Art Deco advertisement, bottom left, for an expensive brand of face powder.

COLLECTABLES

was not going to sell the product. Poster artists were therefore put on their mettle and used a wide range of techniques, ranging from humour to pathos, to get their message across.

Advertisements by famous illustrators obviously command the highest prices. Some of the finest work was done by Alphonse Mucha, who, although best known for his Art Nouveau-style theatrical posters, also did 'product work' for Job cigarette papers and for Néstle chocolate. The prolific John Hassall also designed some memorable posters for Andrew's Liver Salts, and Cassandre produced some superb advertisements for Dubonnet in 1937.

Another colourful form of advertising was through iIllustrated 'trade cards'. These first appeared in the 1870s and were given away with cigarettes, tea or some other product. Customers were encouraged to collect them – and thus to stay 'faithful' to the firm in question. The illustrations on the cards covered a wide range of popular subjects, including natural history, personalities, sport and transport. Complete sets of such cards are now fairly rare and, as a consequence, highly prized. More reasonably priced, and perhaps of greater general appeal, are postcards illustrating products or services. These give-aways were often cheaply produced on thin card and so were easily damaged, but often featured very attractive designs.

Selection of 1930s advertising material. Ephemera like these, designed as they were for instant communication, can capture the spirit of an era with great immediacy.

◂ *Brandy dispenser in ceramic, decorated with a coach and horses on white ground with gilt bands.*

ADVERTISING

▲ *Fry's catalogue from the 1930s.*

▶ *Spirits and wine were often served from spirit jars, kept on shelves behind the bar. These were made in pottery or, like this example, in engraved glass, and were fitted with a brass tap.*

◀ *1920s mahogany and glass cigar dispenser.*

▶ *The pub advertising mirror had a very practical origin. In the 1880s and 1890s there was a great boom in pub building and refitting, and mirrors were the perfect wall decoration for reflecting gaslight. They also allowed the publican to keep an eye out for trouble, even when his back was turned.*

COLLECTABLES

PRINTED EPHEMERA

582

OLD VALENTINE CARDS – TOKENS OF love from a bygone age – are popular collectables today. This custom of sending poetic messages of love on 14 February began at the the end of the 18th century, and the first valentines were simply bits of verse printed on sheets of paper. It was not until the mid-19th century, when printing techniques improved greatly and a variety of cards could be produced, that the sending of valentines became widespread.

Probably the most popular collectable cards are the traditional ornate mid-19th century examples. Such cards often featured verse laid out in elaborate patterns, sometimes taking the shape of bouquets of flowers or hearts and arrows. Since valentine cards experienced a slump at the turn of the 20th century, they have acquired a certain cachet among enthusiasts.

Nineteenth-century valentines can be found in antique shops and at specialist fairs. As the custom was thoroughly revived by the 1920s, modern valentines also make an interesting, and more affordable, field. Always check the condition of valentine cards before purchase – they should not be foxed (spoiled by small rust-coloured marks) or torn.

▸ *Flowers, frills and filigree: a collection of Edwardian Valentine cards. Between 1880 and the outbreak of World War I there was a significant drop in the number of cards sent, so Edwardian cards are relatively rare – and correspondingly more expensive.*

▾ *The origins of Valentine's Day are shrouded in legend. There are at least two different St Valentine stories, which may both relate to the same historical figure, or to none at all.*

PRINTED EPHEMERA

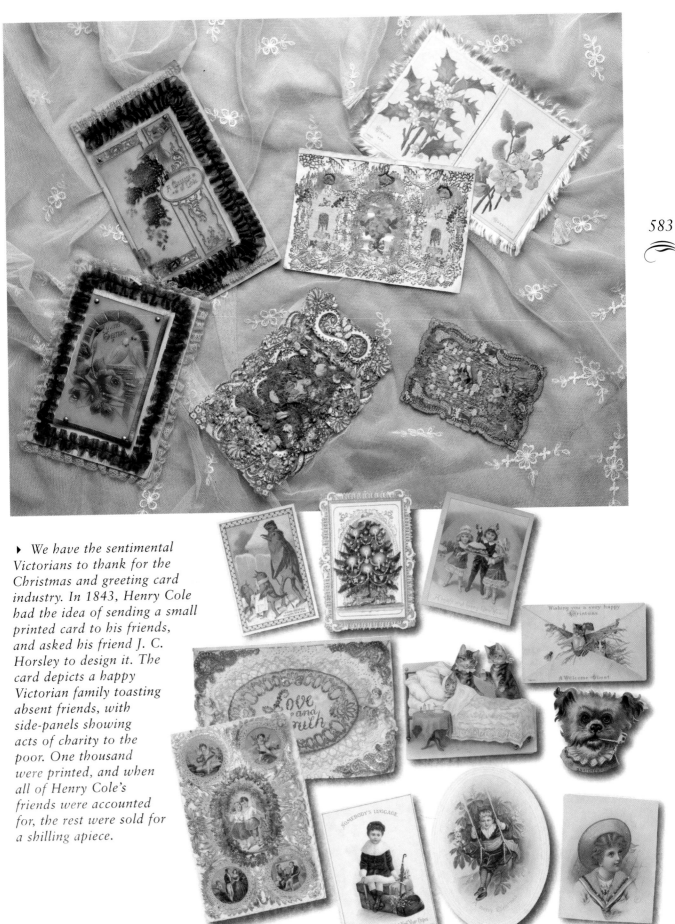

▶ We have the sentimental Victorians to thank for the Christmas and greeting card industry. In 1843, Henry Cole had the idea of sending a small printed card to his friends, and asked his friend J. C. Horsley to design it. The card depicts a happy Victorian family toasting absent friends, with side-panels showing acts of charity to the poor. One thousand were printed, and when all of Henry Cole's friends were accounted for, the rest were sold for a shilling apiece.

COLLECTABLES

Edwardian postcards. Postcards provide fascinating snapshots of their period, as well as of the private lives of the senders. They can also be of interest to collectors for their postal or other markings – a rare postmark will invariably add to the value of the card.

PRINTED EPHEMERA

▲ *Stocks, bonds and shares cover a remarkably wide range, since investors in London and other capitals were involved in major and minor ventures throughout the world. The bonds and share certificates shown here relate to dealings in the United States, pre-Revolutionary Russia, Britain, Egypt, Italy, the Ukraine and South Africa.*

When you think of war collections you probably think first of weapons, but weapon collecting is expensive and there are a lot of fakes about. Printed memorabilia offer a more straightforward route for the collector – there is a wealth of material in circulation, much of it easily affordable.

COLLECTABLES
BOOKS

586

THE FIELD OF BOOK COLLECTION is a vast one, and only a brief glimpse can be given here of some of its appeal to bibliomaniacs. Collectors themselves recognize the need to specialize, be that by subject – botany, natural history, crime and espionage, poetry, sport, children's literature, cookery, guide books, educational, reference or sport – or by edition (some first or limited editions can appreciate massively over the years). Some botanical and natural history books from the 1800s are among the most beautiful ever produced. Particularly delightful are the extremely detailed and accurate drawings. Any volumes with hand-coloured drawings are likely to be extremely valuable (many books have been stripped of their pictures for framing), as are those that concentrate on single plant or animal species. Not all natural history books were educational, however. Titles such as *Flowers and their Poetry* (1851) and *The Sentiment of Flowers* (1839) were more decorative and were aimed at a feminine readership.

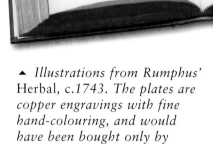

▲ *Illustrations from Rumphus'* Herbal, c.1743. *The plates are copper engravings with fine hand-colouring, and would have been bought only by wealthy subscribers.*

▲ The Genera of British Moths, *in a handsome cloth binding that would doubtless also appeal – though for different reasons – to the books' subjects.*

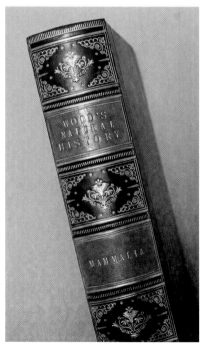

Left, gilt-tooled leather binding; above, marbling- the intricate patterning is achieved using a mixture of water and ink.

BOOKS

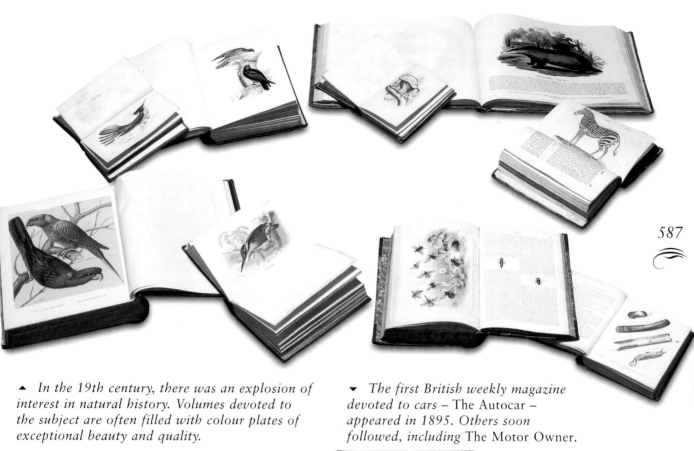

587

▲ In the 19th century, there was an explosion of interest in natural history. Volumes devoted to the subject are often filled with colour plates of exceptional beauty and quality.

▼ The first British weekly magazine devoted to cars – The Autocar – appeared in 1895. Others soon followed, including The Motor Owner.

COLLECTABLES

The art of children's publishing had its heyday in the 19th and early 20th centuries. Lavish volumes were produced that featured beautiful illustrations by fashionable artists. In fact, sometimes the illustrator (Arthur Rackham, Walter Crane, Kate Greenaway and John Tenniel are a few of the notable ones) is considered more collectable than the author. Nevertheless children's authors Beatrix Potter, C.S. Lewis, Robert Louis Stevenson, G.A. Henty, Jules Verne and A.A. Milne stand out.

Perhaps a more quirky object of collectors' interest are old cookery books. Many people read these purely for pleasure and make little attempt to follow any of the, often outdated, recipes. Early editions of works by Mrs Beeton or Mrs Marshall, the doyennes of 19th-century English 'domestic science', will command greater sums than books first published in the 1900s. An exception to this rule is made by first editions of such post-World War II classics as Elizabeth David's *French Country Cooking*.

The best place to look for old books is, of course, at a specialist dealer, although the occasional treasure can be found in second-hand bookshops. It is true of all books, no matter how rare, that they will fetch higher prices if they are in mint or good condition, and have their original dust-wrapper or cover unmarked and intact.

588

▼ *If you thought that pop-up books were a 20th-century phenomenon, you would be wrong; they were popular as long ago as the 1850s.*

▶ *Books illustrated by Kate Greenaway are very popular with collectors. Her idealized images of children were so successful that her designs were also used on a huge range of other products, from china to greetings cards.*

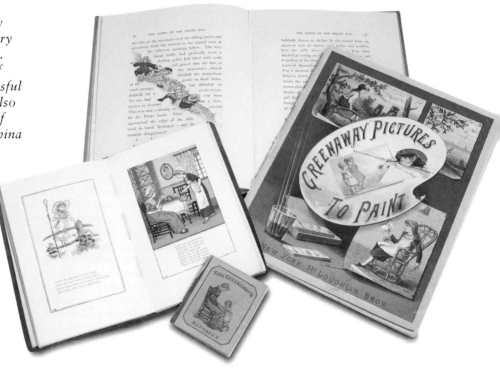

BOOKS

► The Story of Alfred the Great, *in the Picture Lives of Great Heroes series – a mixture of entertainment, history and moral example.*

▲ *It comes as no surprise to learn that nursery books are rarely found in pristine condition. This one of 1859 is in a fragile state.*

▲ *Randolph Caldecott was an enormously popular Victorian children's illustrator. His lively and appealing characters ensured excellent sales of his 16 books.*

GLOSSARY

The Glossary should be used in conjunction with the Index. SMALL CAPITALS refer to other Glossary entries.

A

acid etching The surface of glass or metal is coated with acid-resistant wax, gum or varnish and the design cut through it with a fine steel point. The item is then immersed in acid, to expose the design.

air beading Bubbles of air introduced into glass for decoration.

alabaster Easily carved, marble-like form of gypsum; translucent when cut thinly.

analine dyes Chemical dyes for fabrics and carpets introduced *c.*1870.

Animaliers, Les French 19th-C sculptors who made small lifelike models of animals, usually in BRONZE.

aneroid barometer BAROMETER operated by metal bellows instead of mercury.

anthemion Stylized flower motif derived from Classical Greek ornament; used on furniture and silver in the 18th and 19th C.

apostle spoons Set of 13 silver spoons topped with the figures of Christ and his 12 disciples; first made in the 15th C.

apron Lower front edge of a piece of furniture, e.g. below the top of a table. Also called the SKIRT.

arabesque Intricate intertwining leaf, flower, animal or geometric patterns familiar in Islamic and Hispano-Moresque designs.

arcading A series of rounded arches used as decoration on furniture backs and panels.

armorial Term used to describe a coat of arms on ceramics (armorial porcelain), silver etc.

Art Deco The name is derived from the Exposition des Arts Decoratif held in Paris in 1925. The style affected all areas of design in the 1920s and '30s.

Art Nouveau Decorative style influential from the 1880s to 1914 that employed sinuous, flowing lines, asymmetry and motifs drawn from nature.

Arts and Crafts Movement Begun in the late 19th C by a group of artist/craftsmen who rejected

machine-made objects in favour of hand-made ones.

astrolabe Early instrument used to measure the altitude of stars and planets and in navigation.

B

Baccarat Important French glassworks founded in 1764; noted for *millefiori* and sulphide paperweights.

back-plate Metal plate that holds the mechanism of a clock in place; often engraved with the maker's name.

bakelite Hardwearing, heat-resistant, opaque plastic patented by Leo Baekland in 1907.

balloon back chair Chair with an open 'O'-shaped back and a nipped-in waist.

baluster Turned column with a curved shape, used on table legs, chair legs and backs, glass stems.

banding A decorative inlaid or veneered strip of wood, or metal, used as a border on, e.g., a table top. **Cross-banding** is cut across the grain of the wood. See also STRINGING.

barometer Instrument that registers atmospheric pressure. See also ANEROID BAROMETER

Baroque style Heavy, ornate 17th-C Italian architectural style that influenced all European decorative arts.

beading In furniture, a narrow strip of material, usually wood, used for edging or ornament.

bentwood Lightweight or laminated timber made pliable by steaming or soaking and bent into curved shapes.

bergère Early 19th-C deep, tub-shaped upholstered armchair; revived in the 1920s and '30s.

Biedermeier Early 19th-C German restrained NEO-CLASSICAL STYLE.

birdcage mechanism Wooden hinged mechanism on the top of the pedestal on some 18th-C tripod tables that allows the top to tilt or swivel.

biscuit Fired but unglazed ceramics; used for busts and statuettes.

bisque Unglazed matt BISCUIT porcelain used for dolls' heads from mid-18th C to the 1960s.

body The mixture of raw materials from which POTTERY or PORCELAIN is made.

bombé French term for the bulging or swelling shape seen on commodes

and chests of drawers in Europe from the early 18th C.

boulle Marquetry technique using brass and tortoiseshell inlays; perfected by André Boulle (1642–1732), cabinetmaker to LOUIS XIV.

bow front Curving, convex front on a chest of drawers, cabinet etc.

bracket clock Portable spring-driven clock made to stand on a mantelpiece, table or a specially designed bracket.

bright-cut engraving Method of ENGRAVING silver, using a double-edged tool that removes metal and burnishes the cut at the same time.

bronze Alloy of copper and tin that develops a brown or green PATINA with age; used for statues, furniture mounts, ornaments etc.

bureau Chest of drawers with a desk above.

bureau plat French writing table with a FRIEZE drawer.

C

cabinet Furniture with both drawers and cupboard space for displaying small precious objects.

cabinet ware Porcelain made for display rather than use.

cabriole Furniture leg with an outward curve at the knee and an inward one just above the foot.

cachepot Ornamental plant-holder, normally without a drainage hole.

cameo glass Glassware made up of two or more layers in which the often opaque white outer layer is partly cut or etched away with acid. *See also* CASED GLASS.

canteen Set of cutlery in a fitted, usually wooden, case.

Hallmarks on silver identify the maker, date and place of origin.

GLOSSARY

Pewter has been used for drinking vessels, plates, spoons and forks since the early Middle Ages.

591

carcass The main structure of a piece of furniture, excluding doors, drawers etc.

cartouche Decorative tablet framing coats of arms or crests on silver and ceramics and ornamentation on clockfaces.

carver A dining chair with arms; an elbow chair.

cased glass Two or more layers of glass blown one inside the other, then reheated so that they fuse. The outer layer can be cut away to reveal the inner one.

case furniture Furniture made to contain something, for instance a chest of drawers.

casting Way of forming metal, glass or ceramic objects by pouring molten material into a mould and allowing it to cool.

celadon Pale greenish grey; the European term for Chinese stoneware glazed in this colour.

Celtic style Decorative style with patterns of interlacing curving lines and stylized animal and human motifs.

champlevé Process in which the GROUND is cut away and the hollows filled with ENAMEL paste.

chapter ring Circle on the face of a clock marked with divisions of time.

chasing Method of decorating silver by repositioning the metal. *See also* EMBOSSING, REPOUSSÉ.

cheval mirror or screen Tall piece standing on a four-legged base like a horse, or cheval in French.

china clay White clay free from impurities; an essential ingredient of porcelain; also called kaolin.

china stone Feldspathic rock; combined with CHINA CLAY and heated at high temperature, it makes hard-paste PORCELAIN strong and impermeable.

chinoiserie European imitations of Chinese decoration and motifs common in the 17th and 18th C.

chronometer Extremely accurate portable timepiece; originally developed for use at sea.

clobbering Overpainting an existing design on ceramics with coloured enamels or GILDING.

cloisonné Technique in which fine metal wire is fixed to the surface of an object and the spaces created (cloisons) filled with ENAMEL paste.

cold painting Painting on metal or ceramics in oil or lacquer-based pigments; fixed to the surface by varnishing, not FIRING.

cornice Decorative moulding or projection above the FRIEZE on furniture such as cabinets.

crackle Network of fine lines on ceramics caused by different expansion rates of BODY and GLAZE. Found in Oriental wares and revived by 19th-C art potters.

cresting Carved or moulded ornament on the top rail of a chair, mirror or cabinet.

crizzling Fine network of cracks in glass caused by excess alkali in the METAL.

cut-card work Decoration in which a pattern cut from a sheet of silver is soldered flush to a silver object.

cylinder fall Rigid or slatted curved lid that rolls or slides under the top surface of a desk or bureau when opened.

D

dentil moulding A row of evenly spaced, small square or rectangular blocks ornamenting furniture.

deutsche Blumen 'German flowers': painted flower designs based on botanical drawings. Used on porcelain from 1740.

die stamping Method of making a design on silver or other metal with a shaped block of metal by hammering or forming in a press.

drawn thread work Embroidery in which some threads are pulled out of the fabric to form patterns.

E

earthenware Clay product fired at low temperature that remains porous until glazed.

electroplating Electrochemical process by which a thin layer of silver is deposited on nickel to form EPNS (Electroplated Nickel Silver). It replaced the SHEFFIELD PLATE process.

Elkington Birmingham-based company whose owner George Elkington patented the first silver ELECTROPLATING process in 1840.

embossing Method of producing a design in relief on silver by hammering on the reverse side of the metal. See also REPOUSSÉ.

Empire style Heavy, stately style with much ORMOLU and brass inlay; popular in France *c.*1804–1830 and until later in the US.

enamel Decoration made from powdered glass and pigmented metallic oxides in an oily medium that are fused together, and to metal, glass or ceramics, by firing.

engine-turning Engraved decoration produced on a lathe.

engraving Method of decorating glass, silver etc. by cutting fine lines into it, using a diamond point or a rotating wheel with an abrasive disc.

epergne Elaborate glass or silver stand for the centre of a dining table, with removable dishes for fruit and sweetmeats supported on branching arms.

escutcheon On furniture, a metal plate, particularly a keyhole plate.

F

finial Carved, turned or metal ornament mounted on the top of a piece of furniture, such as a bookcase. *See also* KNOP.

firing The process of baking ceramics in a kiln. Temperatures vary for different types.

flashed glass Glassware dipped into molten glass to give it a thin outer layer, often of a different colour, which can then be cut or ground away to create a pattern. *See also* CASED GLASS.

flatware Silver tableware without a cutting edge made from a flat sheet. Today includes knives also.

foliated Term used to refer to leaf-shaped ornament.

fretwork Thin pieces of wood cut with a fine-bladed saw to form a pattern. In **blind fretwork**, the design is not cut right through the wood.

frieze Horizontal band beneath the CORNICE of a cabinet etc; the horizontal wooden rail beneath the top of a table or desk.

GLOSSARY

Since the mid-1800s, most ceramics have been decorated with transfer-printed designs.

592

G

gadrooning Carved or moulded border consisting of a series of raised curves; used on silver, ceramics and furniture.
garniture A matching set of three, five or seven ornaments for display.
gilding Gold coating on ceramics, silver, glass etc. Gold is normally mixed with water or oil for furniture and with acid or honey for ceramics. Poisonous mercury gilding was painted on the object then fired at low heat. In the 19th C, this was replaced by electrogilding: a thin coat of gold deposited by ELECTROPLATING.
glaze In ceramics, the glass-like finish that decorates and makes a piece waterproof.
gimbals Two or three pivoted rings at right angles to each other that provide free suspension for a compass etc.
Gothic style Characterized by soaring slender lines and pointed arches, it flourished from the 11th–15th C.
ground Background or base colour of an object.
guéridon Stand for holding a candelabrum, tray or basket. The term is now also used to describe a type of small occasional table.
guilloche Decorative pattern of interlacing circles on furniture.
gutta percha Rubber-like material made from the resin of an East Indian tree used for furniture decoration, dolls and golf balls.

H

hallmarks Official marks on silver, gold and platinum that guarantee the quality of the metal and identify the assay office, the date checked and the maker.
Hispano-Moresque ware *see* MAIOLICA
hood Removable part of a LONGCASE

CLOCK surrounding the dial and hiding the mechanism.

I

indianische Blumen 'Indian flowers' – painted floral designs based on Kakiemon designs and used at Meissen from the 1720s.
inlay Contrasting woods, ivory, mother-of-pearl or metal set into the surface of a piece.

J

japanning Technique whereby objects were coated in layers of shellac and varnish in imitation of Oriental lacquer. Often applied to PAPIER-MÂCHÉ.
japonaiserie European designs based on Japanese porcelain and lacquer; known as Japan patterns in the late 18th C.
jardinière Large ornamental container for a potted plant.

K, L

knop Ornamental knob or bulge on a teapot lid or stem of a wine glass.
latticino Threads of white or coloured glass embedded in clear glass in a pattern.
lead crystal Glass containing 25–30 per cent lead oxide, which gives it added brilliance; suitable for ENGRAVING and cutting.
lead glaze GLAZE with ground lead or lead oxide added. Used from c.1700 BC on EARTHENWARE, and later some PORCELAIN, to give translucency and depth of colour.
Limoges A major centre for ENAMEL work, painted on copper, mainly in blue, gold and white, from the 12th C, and ceramics from the late 18th C.
longcase clock Tall, narrow clock that stands on the floor; a 'grandfather clock'.
Louis XIV style Opulent BAROQUE STYLE noted for VENEERS, MARQUETRY and lavish use of exotic materials such as tortoiseshell and lacquer.
Louis XV style The height of the ROCOCO in France, typified by delicately painted PORCELAIN, tapestries and ORMOLU.
lustre An iridescent or metallic finish on POTTERY achieved by painting or

dusting a metallic oxide on the GLAZE and FIRING it.

M

maiolica TIN-GLAZED EARTHENWARE made in Italy from the 13th C. The term was first applied to Hispano-Moresque wares, which reached Italy via Majorca, hence the name.
majolica 19th-C LEAD-GLAZED EARTHENWARE that copied the relief work, GLAZES and colours of MAIOLICA.
marcasite Originally crystallized iron pyrites; later describes cut and polished steel or any white metal. Used in making jewellery.
marquetry Decorative VENEERS of different coloured woods or other materials laid on the surface of furniture in floral or swirling patterns.
mashrabiye Small pieces of turned wood fitted together to form a lattice pattern, which is filled with contrasting INLAY. Common in Islamic interiors.
meerschaum White porous mineral from Turkey, used for pipes etc.
metal The ingredients, either fused or molten, from which glass is made.
mihrab Motif based on the prayer niche in a mosque; a prominent part of the pattern in Islamic prayer rugs.

N

needlepoint Embroidery done on canvas entirely in the same stitch to resemble tapestry.
Neo-classical style Revival style inspired by art and architecture of ancient Rome and Greece. Popular in the mid-to late 18th C.

O

openwork Technique of cutting holes through the body of a piece of silver, ceramics or furniture to form a pattern.
ormolu Mercury-gilded BRONZE used for figures and mounts on clocks and furniture. The GILDING was later done by ELECTROPLATING.
ottoman A low upholstered seat without arms; the seat on a box ottoman lifts to provide storage space underneath.

GLOSSARY

overglaze Term used in ceramics to describe enamels or TRANSFER-PRINTS applied over the GLAZE to a piece that is then refired at a lower temperature.

overstuffing Upholstery in which the padding is taken over the edges of the chair frame.

P

papier-mâché A mixture of pulped paper, glue and chalk that is moulded, baked and decorated to make furniture, trays etc. The surface is ideal for JAPANNING.

Parian ware Marble-like white PORCELAIN developed by Minton in the 1840s and used for dolls' heads and SLIP-cast busts. Usually left uncoloured and unglazed.

parcel gilt Describes partially gilded silverware or furniture.

patina The build-up of polish and dirt that gives furniture a glowing appearance. Silver also develops a patina with much polishing.

pediment The triangular or curved gable above the front of a bookcase, cupboard or LONGCASE clock.

pewter An alloy of tin with a hardening agent such as lead or copper added. New pewter is silvery grey, but it darkens with age.

Poole pottery Pottery founded in 1921, in Dorset, England, producing hand-decorated EARTHENWARE and STONEWARE with a matt GLAZE.

porcelain True, or hard-paste, porcelain is made from CHINA CLAY (kaolin) and CHINA STONE (feldspar). It is white, strong, translucent, non-porous and heat resistant. Soft-paste, or imitation, porcelain is made from a mixture including white clay, flint, ground glass, bone, soapstone and CHINA STONE.

pottery Objects made from EARTHENWARE or STONEWARE.

pounce pot Small pot with a perforated cover that held a fine powder used to dry ink.

R

reeding Convex parallel ribs carved on wooden chair legs etc.

Regency style British furniture and decorative style popular c.1800–30. Named after the Prince Regent (later George IV).

regulator clock A pendulum-driven clock made for accuracy of timekeeping.

repoussé A form of CHASING silver in which parts of EMBOSSED designs are pushed back from the front to add detail.

Rococo style Highly decorative and elaborate style with asymmetrical motifs based on shell, rock, floral and leaf motifs; popular in 18th C.

S

sabre leg Chair leg shaped like a sabre blade.

salt-glazed stoneware STONEWARE with a slightly pitted surface, caused by throwing salt into the kiln during firing.

secrétaire-à-abattant French desk, introduced in mid-18th C, in which the top section drops down to reveal a writing surface.

serpentine Curving front seen on 18th-C chests of drawers, etc. Less extreme than BOMBÉ shapes.

Sèvres French national PORCELAIN factory, producing soft-paste from c.1740, hard-paste from 1768.

sextant Optical instrument employed in navigation; it uses mirror reflections to measure the sun's altitude.

shagreen Skin of sharks and stingrays, used to cover small items such as hip flasks; also coarse untanned leather.

Sheffield plate A thin layer of silver fused to copper sheet by heating and rolling; a cheaper alternative to solid silver.

silver gilt Silver-plated with a thin layer of gold.

skirt See APRON.

slip Liquid clay used for CASTING hollow items and for decorating POTTERY.

soapstone Form of magnesium silicate used for carvings, especially in China.

spelter An alloy of zinc, often containing lead, used as a substitute for BRONZE.

spindle Slender TURNED rod often seen on chairs.

splat Upright of a wooden chair back rising from the seat to the top rail.

sprigging Adding relief decoration to ceramics with SLIP before FIRING.

stoneware Objects made from clay fired to the point at which it becomes non-porous.

stretcher Horizontal strut or rail between the legs of furniture.

stringing Very fine BANDING on a piece of furniture.

swag Representation of an ornamental festoon of cloth, fruit or flowers on silver or furniture.

T

tambour A flexible shutter for a roll-top desk made from slats of wood glued to cloth.

tantalus Case for decanters with an overhead locking bar.

tea caddy Box with a hinged lid and lock for storing tea. Caddy comes from the Malay *kati*, a unit of weight for tea.

tea-dust glaze Greenish-brown GLAZE used on 18th-C Chinese PORCELAIN; achieved by blowing green glaze through fine mesh on to brown glaze before FIRING.

tin-glaze Opaque white-ground GLAZE with tin oxide added; used mainly on EARTHENWARE.

transfer printing Method of printing a design on ceramics or glass by taking a tissue print from a copperplate engraving and transferring it to the object. Invented in the mid-18th century in England, it made the mass production of designs possible.

turning Method of shaping wood, ivory or metal on a lathe.

twist Decoration of a drinking glass in which white or coloured glass rods or air are trapped in the molten METAL of the stem and twisted. *See also* LATTICINO.

U, V, W

underglaze Colours or designs applied or cut into clay before FIRING.

veneer Thin sheets of well-marked wood, such as walnut, rosewood or satinwood, applied to a surface for decorative effect.

Wellington chest Tall, narrow 19th-C chest of drawers with six to twelve shallow drawers secured by a lockable flap.

whitework White cut thread embroidery on a white ground.

593

INDEX

INDEX

595

INDEX

INDEX

INDEX

INDEX

ACKNOWLEDGEMENTS

All photographs in this book are reproduced with the kind permission of **Heritage Picture Collection** and **Marshall Cavendish Picture Archive** with the following exceptions:

p18 bottom, Bonhams, London, UK/Bridgeman Art Library (BAL)
p19 Christie's Images, London, UK/BAL
p22, Christie's Images, London, UK/BAL
p23 top, Private Collection/BAL
p28 top, Royal Pavilion Libraries & Museums, Brighton and Hove/BAL
p28 bottom, Victoria & Albert Museum, London, UK/BAL
p29 Fitzwilliam Museum, University of Cambridge, UK/BAL
p31 top, Bonhams, London, UK/BAL; p69 top and bottom, Private Collection/BAL
p33 Josiah Wedgwood & Sons Ltd, Stoke-on-Trent
p70 Partridge Fine Arts, London, UK/BAL
p71 bottom left, Private Collection/BAL
p71 centre right and bottom right, Antique Porcelain Company, London, UK/BAL